THE UNSPEAKABLE CRIMES OF DR. PETIOT

ALSO BY THOMAS MAEDER
Adverse Reactions
Children of Psychiatrists
Crime and Madness
Antonin Artaud (in French)

THE UNSPEAKABLE CRIMES OF

DR. PETIOT

Thomas Maeder

Ivan R. Dee   Chicago

www.ivanrdee.com

Library of Congress Cataloging-in-Publication Data:
Maeder, Thomas.
The unspeakable crimes of Dr. Petiot / Thomas Maeder.
    xiv, 302 p., [8] leaves of plates : ill. ; 22 cm.
  Bibliography: p. [301]-302.
  ISBN: 978-1-56663-797-8
  1. Petiot, Marcel. 2. Murders—France—Bibliography. I. Title.
HV6248.P43 M33
364.1'523'0924—dc19   80011164

To Morgan, Sara, and Max

CONTENTS

ACKNOWLEDGMENTS

Among the people who helped with this project, I should mention a few, and the many others must rest content with the knowledge that, whatever its merits or demerits, they were accomplices and must accept their due. My thanks to: the Procureur Général de la Cour d'Appel de Paris and the Director of the Archives du Département de la Seine et de la Ville de Paris for permitting me to consult the voluminous official court dossier on the Petiot case; the Director of the Musée de la Préfecture de Police, who showed me the Police Judiciaire files at his disposal; Drs. Christian Piédelièvre and Léon Dérobert for information on the coroner's report; Maître Paul Cousin, who showed me his copy of Maître Floriot's final plea and, together with Maître Eugène Ayache, supplied valuable information about the preparation of the defense; Avocat Général Elissalde for information on the State's preparation of the prosecution; Maître Bernard Massu for fascinating stories about his father and the investigation; Pierre Manière for a copy of his pamphlet, which provided much of my information about Petiot's political career; and Maître Jean-Marc Varaut for useful information and a delicious lunch.

Above all, I am indebted to Maître Pierre Véron, who gave me a wealth of information, a great deal of his time, and the pleasure of spending many enjoyable hours with him and his family. For assorted help, tolerance, and occasional enthusiasm, thanks to Francienne and Dr. Maurice Béjat, Marianne Lassner and Oliver Béjat, François Caradec, the late Florence Gilliam, Professor Henri Gouhier, Gilles and Paul Kujawski, and André Roumieux. Thanks also to Abigail Adams, John Coggeshall, and David Rashkis for their useful critical comments, and to Arnold Ehrlich for turning fancy into fact or vice versa.

PART ONE

1

THE BODIES IN THE RUE LE SUEUR

On March 6, 1944, thick, greasy, foul-smelling smoke began pouring from the chimney of an elegant private house at 21 rue Le Sueur in Paris. It was a three-story, nineteenth-century building with stables and courtyard located near the Etoile in the wealthy sixteenth arrondissement, and was the former residence of Princess Maria Colloredo de Mansfeld,* who had moved out in 1930 and allowed dust and dilapidation to take over. Since its purchase in 1941 by a Dr. Marcel Petiot, the building had remained uninhabited, though neighbors noticed several curious events. Almost every day, a man on a bicycle, dressed like a workman, arrived towing a wagon. Two trucks had come during the previous year — one removed forty-seven suitcases, and the other unloaded thirty or forty heavy sacks inside the double coach door. Otherwise no one entered or left the building. Neighbors would later tell police that a horse-drawn cart had

*A selected list of characters begins on page 289.

stopped in the street at 11:30 every night for the previous six months. They believed it had stopped at number 21, and some even reported hearing the doors open and close; but since it was wartime and the city was blacked out at that hour for fear of Allied bombings, nothing was actually seen, and the significance of this occurrence was never made clear.

The smoke increased in volume over the next few days, and on Saturday, March 11, a contrary breeze kept the suffocating stench in the rue Le Sueur hovering at the level of Madame Andrée Marçais's fifth-floor apartment across the street. When her husband returned from work that evening, she insisted that he do something about it. Jacques Marçais knocked at number 21 several times before noticing the worn paper fastened to the door: *Away for one month. Forward mail to 18 rue des Lombards in Auxerre.* At 6:25, Monsieur Marçais telephoned the police.

Two uniformed, bicycle-mounted policemen, Joseph Teyssier and Emile Fillion, tried the door and shuttered windows, then made inquiries at the neighboring houses. The concierge next door told them number 21 was owned by Dr. Marcel Petiot, who lived two miles across Paris at 66 rue Caumartin. She even had his telephone number: Pigalle 77.11. Teyssier ran to the Crocodile, a café on the corner, and phoned the doctor's home. A woman who identified herself as Madame Petiot answered and passed the receiver to her husband. "Have you entered the building?" he asked Teyssier after being told there was a fire. "Don't do anything. I will be there in fifteen minutes with the keys."

Half an hour later, no one had arrived. The smoke grew worse and the firemen were called. Fire Chief Avilla Boudringhin climbed to a second-floor window, pried open the shutters, smashed a windowpane, and entered with a few men. After searching the upper floors, they followed the stench to the basement. When they emerged from the coach door several minutes later, one of the young firemen leaned against the doorway and vomited, while a pale and shaken Boudringhin stepped up to the two policemen and said, "Gentlemen, I think you have some work ahead of you."

Teyssier, Fillion, and a civil-defense officer who chanced to be passing by were led down to the basement, where they found two coal-burning stoves. The one on the left was cold, but the smaller one, to the right, was going full blast, and a human hand, apparently female, dangled from the open door. From the light of the fire the three officers discerned a pile of coal and the bottom steps of a short staircase on which were littered a head, skulls, arms, two nearly complete skeletons, shattered rib cages, feet, hands, jawbones, large chunks of unrecognizable flesh, and a quantity of small bones. They left hurriedly and Teyssier again ran to the Crocodile, this time to call his superiors.

As Teyssier was returning, a hatless man in a gray overcoat rode up on a green bicycle and dismounted in front of number 21. He was in his early to mid-forties, with piercing eyes of such dark brown as to look black. He seemed surprised to find the doors to the building ajar, but with an air of confidence and authority approached Fillion and identified himself as the brother of the building's owner. Teyssier returned from the café, and the two agents led the man into the building; he began climbing the steps toward the main floor, but they quickly motioned him downstairs. Gazing calmly at the litter of human remains in the basement, the man said: "This is serious. My head may be at stake." The policemen were scarcely surprised. They accompanied the man back to the street to escape the smell of decayed and burning flesh. He turned to them and asked, "Are you Frenchmen?" Teyssier indignantly asked the reason for this strange and offensive question.

"The bodies you have seen are those of Germans and traitors to our country," he replied. "I assume you have already notified your superiors and that the Germans will soon learn of your discovery. I am the head of a Resistance group, and I have three hundred files at my home which must be destroyed before the enemy finds them."

By March 1944, Paris had already suffered nearly four years under the Occupation and German military rule. There were two Gestapo offices in the neighborhood of the rue Le Sueur, and a brothel reserved for German officers was just around the corner. The man spoke with conviction, and it seemed obvious to the French policemen that the carnage was the result of systematic executions by an organized group. Teyssier tipped his cap to a patriot and advised him to flee, promising not to mention the visit when his superiors arrived. And thus Dr. Marcel Petiot — for it was he himself — climbed back on his bicycle and rode off into the night.

Brigadier Henri Chanel soon arrived with three men from the local police station and, after briefly inspecting the still-burning stove, ordered the firemen back to their station and called the police commissaire for the *quartier* of Porte Dauphine and the appropriate judicial authorities. The commissaire arrived fifteen minutes later and promptly called back the firemen to extinguish the stove and remove some of the remains. He then examined the rest of the building.

Upon first entering the double front door of 21 rue Le Sueur, one came to a short vaulted passageway. Steps to the right off the passage led into the ground floor of the house, but if one continued straight along the corridor for thirty feet, one arrived in a flagstone-covered courtyard surrounded by the building on three sides and a four-story wall on the other; the yard was thus totally concealed from the neighbors' view. The house was large and had once been elegant, with six bedrooms, a spacious dining room and basement kitchen, half a dozen salons and other large rooms, and a library. It was presently in a state of filthy disrepair, and it was obvious no one had lived there for many years. A thick coat of dust covered everything, and most of the rooms were crammed with an incredible assortment of furniture, art objects, chandeliers, and gadgets stored in chaotic piles.

The outbuildings, located on the opposite side of the court from the main body of the house and connected on two floors by a narrow passage, had originally housed the stables and the servants' quarters. A second library was there now, as well as the only clean and orderly spot in the place: a doctor's consultation room. The commissaire found it odd that with dozens of large rooms in the house from which to choose, the owner had decided to repair a cramped, L-shaped passageway — little more than six feet wide and situated between a staircase, a storeroom, and the stable — and to neatly furnish it with a cabinet full of medical supplies and knickknacks, a tidy desk, a small round table, and two comfortable armchairs.

In the garage next to the consultation room, the commissaire discovered a pile of quicklime — fourteen feet long, eight feet wide, and three feet high at its peak. Interspersed throughout the pile were fragments of flesh and bone, among which he recognized a jawbone and a detached human scalp. In the adjacent stable he found a former manure pit; a block and tackle was rigged above it and a wooden ladder propped inside. Leaning over, the commissaire discovered it was half filled with several more cubic yards of lime and human remains. On a landing of the staircase leading from the courtyard down to the basement he found a canvas sack containing the headless left side of a human body, complete but for the foot and internal organs. At the bottom of the stairs, next to the mound of coal and corpses, was a hatchet covered with rust-colored stains and, a short distance away, a shovel.

Commissaire Georges Massu had just climbed into bed at 10:00 P.M. when headquarters called. Massu was a thirty-three-year police veteran with 3,257 arrests to his credit, and after recently solving a spectacular case he had been promoted to chief of the Criminal Brigade of the Police Judiciaire — a detective force that does for the Paris region what the Sûreté Nationale does for the rest of France. Massu had participated in most of the major criminal affairs of the past three decades, including the celebrated case of Eugen Weidmann, who murdered six people for profit and whose death on the guillotine in 1939 was the last public execution in France. Ten years earlier, Massu had befriended the young mystery writer Georges Simenon, who was then looking for realistic atmosphere to improve his novels, and the taciturn and methodical Massu was gradually transformed into the fictional commissaire Maigret. Massu himself claimed the pipe and habits of Maigret were more like Simenon, but details of some cases were so close to his own that Massu's own memoirs seemed redundant when they appeared. On this evening in 1944, Massu was awakened to investigate what he was later to call "the greatest criminal affair of the century."

Thirty minutes later, Massu arrived at the rue Le Sueur with his son Bernard, a seventeen-year-old law student who worked as a part-time inspector under his father whenever there was a case more interesting than his studies. Georges Massu stared at the piles of remains. He took off his overcoat and climbed into the pit; the bones crunched sickeningly under his shoes and his trousers became covered with lime. In the basement kitchen he noticed that the large double sink was just long enough for an outstretched body and that its sloping bottom was steep enough for blood to flow down without coagulating before reaching the drain.

Meanwhile, the other investigators had found, joined to the consultation room by a small corridor, a triangular chamber — six feet on the short side, eight feet on the longest, and completely empty except for eight heavy iron rings fixed in one wall and a naked light bulb attached to the ceiling. Opposite the entrance was a double wooden door, and beside it an electric doorbell. Given the layout of the building, the doors presumably led to a street in the rear, but when Massu forced them open he found that they were attached to a solid wall. The wires of the bell led nowhere. A zealous policeman began to remove the room's wallpaper and was rewarded by the discovery of the wide end of a spyglass such as those placed in apartment doors to identify visitors. The eyepiece was just over six feet off the ground in the stable on the other side of the wall, and next to it were two light switches: one for the stable itself, the other for the triangular room. As an experiment, Bernard Massu positioned himself between the eight iron rings in the room as though lashed to them. Through the viewer in the stable, the commissaire saw his son's enlarged face perfectly framed in the field of vision. On his way to the stable, Georges Massu noticed that the door to the triangular room had no knob on the inside.

As yet, there was no indication of who the victims might be nor why they had been killed, but the death scenes the house's arrangement conjured in Commissaire Massu's mind grew increasingly horrifying. Under some pretext, he imagined, the doctor instructed a patient to leave his consultation room by the back door. The patient, already drugged or poisoned — gas, perhaps, or an injection — entered the triangular room, whose one true door, virtually soundproof, he could not reopen once it closed. Perhaps Petiot lashed his victims to the rings, then watched their death agonies from the stable. The room seemed arranged especially for this purpose, though the viewer was placed inconveniently high, the white plaster wall of the stable was unblemished by dirt from the face and hands of a peering observer, and, most puzzling of all, the wallpaper had obviously been placed over the lens many years ago. There were no marks indicating a captive trying to escape his prison, nor any signs of struggle in the triangular room or elsewhere. There were no poisons or drugs in the consultation room — no needles, no gas, nothing of use to a murderer. To Massu and everyone else involved, this would remain the most puzzling aspect of the Petiot affair; and no one would ever discover how the victims were killed or what purpose was served by the triangular room, which the press found the most sinister and horrifying aspect of the case, and around which they spun the most gruesome hypotheses.

By 1:30 A.M. Massu had learned all he could at the scene, and was about to leave with two inspectors for Petiot's apartment at 66 rue Caumartin when a telegram arrived from police headquarters: ORDER FROM GERMAN AUTHORITIES. ARREST PETIOT. DANGEROUS LUNATIC. Word had filtered up through the hierarchy, and some German bureau had communicated this enigmatic order to the director of the Police Judiciaire. Massu hesitated. At the time of the Occupation, the police had been faced with the choice of abandoning their posts or remaining at them under German rule. The first alternative would have compelled the enemy to use its own soldiers as policemen; the latter, the police reasoned, kept civil disputes among Frenchmen, and incidentally left room for sabotage. The Germans, however, did not adhere strictly to their agreement to leave domestic crimes and those only to the French police, who thus sometimes found themselves forced to chase "criminals" and "terrorists" whose only crime was allegiance to France. When the Germans showed particular interest in a case, the police tactic now was to display considerable oversight and error. Thus, when Massu received his telegram and learned how eager the Germans were for Petiot's arrest, his suspicions were aroused. Pleading exhaustion, he instructed the two inspectors to wait until the following morning and went home to bed.

The next morning, the police contrived to waste several hours on irrelevant details of the case. They seemed in no hurry to capture Petiot. As they knew 21 rue Le Sueur had previously belonged to the Princess Colloredo de Mansfeld, they went to find the princess. Her house on the rue de la Faisanderie had been requisitioned by the Secretary of the Navy, and it was some time before they tracked down the sixty-seven-year-old princess on the avenue de Friedland. She informed them that she had lived at the rue Le Sueur from 1924 to 1930, that subsequently friends had lived there, that the actress Cécile Sorel had used it to store her costumes, and that she had sold the building to Dr. Petiot via the Simon agency in 1941 and had not seen him since signing the agreement of sale.

An express letter had been found at 21 rue Le Sueur addressed to "Camille," asking him to come fetch his delivery cart. Inspectors soon persuaded themselves that they believed Petiot had sublet his luxurious house to a deliveryman. They spent two hours tracking down the sender of the letter, Raymond Lion, and the intended recipient, Camille Vanderheyden, who worked with him at the Maison Lepesme. Lion, not knowing his fellow employee's exact address, had randomly written "21," whereas Vanderheyden actually lived in a small apartment at 20 rue Le Sueur, where he was nursing a head cold when the police made their dramatic entrance. He had never even heard of Petiot, and it took the police some time to make him understand why they were there. They did not tell him they were there only to waste time — but they were.

It was late in the morning when Chief Inspector Marius Batut of the Police Judiciaire arrived at the rue Caumartin with two other detectives. They stopped at the concierge's loge to ask whether Petiot was in. The concierge was out, but her twelve-year-old daughter, Alice Denis, told the police officers she had seen the doctor and Madame Petiot at 9:30 the previous evening and believed they were still at home. Batut knocked on the door of their first-floor apartment and, receiving no reply, automatically tried the latch and found it unlocked. He took this as possible evidence of a hasty departure (police later learned that, in reality, Petiot never locked his door, believing that a determined burglar would get in anyway, and by leaving the door open he would at least save himself the expense of repairing a broken lock); indeed, the apartment proved empty and the bed had not been slept in. It was several days before the police discovered that Petiot had not left in haste at all; he had been there packing only half an hour before the detectives' arrival and had persuaded Alice Denis, who had often enjoyed Madame Petiot's cakes and cookies, to lie to them about his movements.

The police did not spend the rest of the day searching train stations and circulating photographs of Dr. Petiot as one would expect. Instead they went to the Simon Real Estate Agency. They learned that Monsieur Simon was a Jew and had fled France when the Germans dissolved his business. A further search turned up a former employee of the agency and the notary who had handled the sale of the rue Le Sueur house. Petiot had purchased the building in his son Gérard's name on August 11, 1941. He paid F495,000 — F373,000 down, the balance payable in annual installments of F17,500.

Investigators then located the construction firm that had built the triangular room, installed the iron rings, and erected the wall that sheltered the courtyard from the eyes of curious neighbors. Two masons and several workers had done the job in October 1941 at a cost of F14,458.52. They had seen Petiot frequently at the time, they told the police, and the doctor had said he intended to install a clinic in the house after the war. The wall was to prevent neighbors from bothering his patients and to keep children from throwing peach pits into the yard. He intended to set up an electrotherapy apparatus in the triangular room and monitor its functioning through a viewer in the wall. The workers had found Petiot quite an amiable fellow.

The police found these details of mild interest but such information did little in helping to capture the criminal. Nor was it intended to at first — as headquarters soon came to realize. Superiors learned that the agents Teyssier and Fillion had let a prime suspect escape, and the two fled France for fear of reprisals (they did not return until after the Liberation). The Germans now told Commissaire Massu they were astonished that Petiot had not yet been caught. Massu replied that he was

surprised by their astonishment, since the files showed that the
Germans had once actually held Petiot in prison and had voluntarily released him. The impasse lasted only briefly, after which
it became all too evident that Petiot's crimes, far from being
committed in the name of France, were gruesomely personal. By
then, however, the authorities had lost valuable time, and Petiot
had vanished completely.

French newspapers during the Occupation were completely
under German control and largely printed German propaganda
as well as enlistment calls for the French Gestapo. Their circulation dropped more than 50 percent as they ceased to publish
anything of interest except amended rationing regulations.
Fewer than 18 percent of the major prewar Parisian dailies and
periodicals survived, while the rest fled to the free zone or suc-
cumbed to Nazi censorship. Those that remained and the handful of new publications were forced to collaborate actively (and
their staff members were among the most harshly treated when
the Liberation and purge finally came).

The Germans had no wish to censor the Petiot affair, and may
even have welcomed it as harmless diversion for a subjugated
Paris. On Monday, circulations shot up as every newspaper in
France exaggerated the discovery at the rue Le Sueur in an
orgy of sordid detail and carried banner headlines about the
"new Landru."° Estimates ranged as high as sixty victims, and
most reporters assumed all of them were women. Petiot, in the
speculating press, became a drug addict and abortionist, a sadist
and a lunatic who had a dozen means — each more outlandish
than the last — of murdering helpless, lovely ladies in his triangular chamber. More than one paper carried rumors that the
lower part of the bodies in the pit had been more severely dam-

° A generation earlier, Henri Désiré Landru had been guillotined for
seducing and murdering at least ten women and burning their remains in
his stove.

aged than the upper, indicating that the victims had been forced
to stand in the caustic lime and dissolve alive. Even for people
oppressed by years of war, the bizarre cruelty of the crimes
soon became the favorite topic of conversation and, later, of wry
amusement. One cartoon depicted a woman at a physician's
office door saying, "I'll only come in for my appointment, doctor,
if you swear you don't have a stove." Another showed a group
of psychics communicating with the beyond through table-
tilting: "If we put our hands on the stove instead," one of the
mediums suggested, "maybe we could contact Dr. Petiot."

The police did not find it entertaining as they began seeking
answers to a long list of questions. They methodically set out to
discover: who and where was Petiot? who were the victims and
how many were there? how and why had they been killed? how
and by whom had the building been equipped for murder?
where did the lime come from? and were there accomplices?
Experts from the police forensic lab photographed and made
scale drawings of 21 rue Le Sueur. They took fingerprints from
every available surface — and perhaps intentionally mishandled
that job; how otherwise explain the fact that no useful prints
were found at either the rue Le Sueur or the rue Caumartin?

In closets and corners of the basement, inspectors found a
jumbled collection of objects, including:

22	used toothbrushes	5	gas masks
15	women's combs	5	cigarette holders
7	pocket combs	1	pair of women's trousers
9	fingernail files	1	three-piece suit
24	tubes and boxes of	7	pairs of eyeglasses
	pharmaceutical products	2	umbrellas
3	shaving brushes	1	cane

They also found: a black satin evening gown, with golden swallows embroidered on the bosom, bearing the manufacturer's
label *Sylvia Rosa, Marseille;* a jaunty woman's hat made by

Suzanne Talbot in Paris; a man's white shirt from which the initials *K.K.* had been maladroitly removed; and a photograph of an unidentified man, which the newspapers published at the request of the police.

The large human remains had been taken to the morgue on Sunday. Policemen refused to touch the piles of quicklime, and four gravediggers from the Passy cemetery were hired to sift through them with a sieve and pack the human elements in plain wooden coffins. The examination was headed by the celebrated forensic expert Dr. Albert Paul, who had directed every major coroner's inquest in the department of the Seine since the Landru case in 1920 (when he burned human heads in a kitchen stove to observe their rate of combustion) and whose macabre humor and love of morbid detail made him as popular at social affairs as in court. Dr. Paul, Dr. Léon Dérobert, Dr. René Piédelièvre, and two professors from the Museum of Natural History, specialists in skeletal assembly and the reconstruction of fossil remains, spent several months measuring and categorizing thirty-four specimens ranging in size from a single connected shoulder blade and breastbone to the eviscerated half-corpse found on the stairs. Their final, voluminous report, with 150 pages of photographs and reams of description, was sadly disappointing.

Not even the number of victims could be accurately determined. There were:

Unpaired bones

Vertebrae	10 subjects
Sterna	7 subjects
Coccyxes	6 subjects

Paired bones

Collarbones	10 subjects
Shoulder blades	8 subjects
Pelves	5 subjects

From these remains the experts concluded that there were at least ten victims — five men, five women. But taking into account the fifteen kilograms of badly charred bones, eleven kilograms of uncharred fragments, quantities of pieces too small to identify ("three garbage cans full," Dr. Paul told the newspapers), and the fact that there were five kilograms of hair, including more than ten entire human scalps, Dr. Paul could only cautiously say that "the number ten is vastly inferior to the real one."

Identification of the victims was equally impossible based on the limited information provided by such mutilated and badly decomposed bodies. The youngest of the ten victims, the experts determined, was a twenty-five-year-old woman; the eldest, a fifty-year-old man. There were no old bone injuries that could be used for identification. The existing teeth were almost all in poor condition, though one had a porcelain cap. One woman had very small hands and feet, and the forearm of a five-foot-ten male victim was abnormally short. One man had a particularly voluminous skull, as did one woman, whose head was also round and flattened at the back. Another woman had a protruding lower jaw, which would have given her a distinctly simian appearance in life.

Radiological examinations showed no traces of bullet or knife wounds, nor any similar marks of violence on bones. Some of the long bones of the legs and arms had been broken after death, apparently either to conceal telltale deformities or to make them easier to fit into the stove for burning; the breaks were so crude that Dr. Paul gaily theorized the bones had been wedged between a door and its jamb and yanked. Photographs and full-scale drawings were made of each piece, the teguments were removed, and insect larvae were lifted and placed in numbered test tubes; then each piece was cleaned, measured, photographed, and drawn again.

Someone with an intimate knowledge of anatomy had dissected the bodies in a professional manner, though Paul noted that whereas a doctor would sever an arm at the shoulder, in this case the rib cage had been cut at the center and the whole arm, shoulder blade, and collarbone removed as a single piece — precisely, he pointed out, as one might carve a chicken. The dismemberment technique was identical to that used on a dozen batches of human remains, including nine severed heads, that were fished out of the Seine in 1942 and 1943 — a flood of cadavers that ended when the culprit narrowly escaped detection after throwing a human hand off a bridge just as a barge passed underneath. Identification of these bodies, too, had been impossible, due both to decomposition and the fact that someone had stripped away the fingerprints and expertly removed the faces and scalps in a single piece. At the time, Dr. Paul had been concerned by scalpel marks in the fleshy parts of four thighs that floated ashore at La Muette on October 29, 1942. He knew firsthand that, unlike a surgeon, a coroner switching to another instrument does not lay down his scalpel but instead uses the cadaver's thigh as a convenient pincushion; Paul had feared that one of his own students might be moonlighting. The bodies found at the rue Le Sueur bore identical marks on the thighs, and though a definite link was never proved, at least one forensic expert was convinced that the same person was responsible for the Seine and rue Le Sueur murders. This assumption did raise disturbing questions, though. Disfigurement was understandable when the bodies were to be thrown into a public waterway, but at the rue Le Sueur, when they were to be burned, what was the need for such delicate care? Perhaps the killer found the dissection not only practical, but pleasurable?

Professor Henri Griffon, director of the police toxicology laboratory, was given five jars of viscera and a kilogram of lime to examine for toxic substances. He noted that no blood was present in any specimen; the viscera were shapeless, impregnated with quicklime, in an advanced state of mummification, and exuded "a piquant and extremely disagreeable odor." His vague estimate placed the time of death at least several months to a year before the discovery, but the effects of the lime were so uncertain that Griffon would not later repeat this opinion in court. Chemical analysis could rule out poisoning by toxic metals such as lead, bismuth, barium, zinc, mercury, antimony, and arsenic, but this left innumerable other poisons as well as strangulation, asphyxiation, and a host of other murder techniques whose marks would not show or could be concealed. Organic poisons that doctors normally use, such as ouabaine, scopolamine, chloroform, strychnine, and digitalis, were eventually found at Petiot's rue Caumartin apartment, along with fifty times the amount of a doctor's normal stock of morphine and heroin, but no such substances were found at the rue Le Sueur, and no trace of them would be expected in such badly decayed corpses.

The remains were among the most horrible the forensic experts had ever seen, but despite their revulsion, they could not restrain a certain amount of professional admiration for someone who had covered his tracks so effectively. Years later, Dr. Piédelièvre included in his *Memoirs of a Coroner* a chapter on Petiot entitled "My Dear Confrère, Doctor Petiot." All of their science did not help them find one scrap of information, though they had more than enough material to study. When Dr. Paul gave his conservative estimate of ten bodies at the rue Le Sueur, he also said the number could go as high as thirty. There were from nine to a dozen more in the Seine. No one could guess how many more were never found or, at a time when bodies were common and too often meant trouble with the Germans, were found and never reported. Petiot himself later referred to sixty-three deaths — and on a few topics he was always scrupulously accurate.

2

THE FIRST IDENTIFIED VICTIMS

THE FIRST TWO tentative identifications of victims were made with embarrassing ease: the police checked department files to see whether Petiot had a record, and the bodies began to assume names — Jean-Marc Van Bever and Marthe Khaït. These two murders, apparently among the first in the series, had been simple, practical affairs, different from the rest; and perhaps by showing Petiot just how easily murder could be done, they had started him in his new vocation. At the time when they occurred, no murder charges had been brought: the police simply noted it as strange that two people connected with Petiot conveniently disappeared just before they were due to testify in court on two separate narcotics charges against him. As Massu's subordinates pieced the story together, the following tale emerged.

Early in 1942, two years before the rue Le Sueur discovery, the Police Judiciaire vice squad impounded the books of all Parisian pharmacies in an attempt to track down people who were receiving inordinately large amounts of narcotics. This

massive raid was typical of Maréchal Philippe Pétain's paradoxically moralistic Vichy government, which substituted Family, Fatherland, Work for the republican French motto Liberty,
Equality, Fraternity and elevated basic old-fashioned morality
to the level of patriotic duty. Since drug abuse ruined the
bodies and minds of Frenchmen, it was not only damaging to
the individual, but almost a crime against the State.

A raid on pharmacies was certain to catch most abusers. In
occupied France drugs were exceptionally hard to find. Borders
were effectively closed to smugglers, and pushers and other
specialists in illegal traffic found more lucrative work in the
black-market sale of daily goods. The only way an addict could
support his habit was through compliant doctors or by mis-
representing himself to a number of honest doctors as a candidate
for a drug cure. Either method left records in the dangerous-
drugs registers of pharmacies, and it was on such evidence that
the police arrested Jean-Marc Van Bever and his mistress on
February 19, 1942.

Van Bever was the son of Adolphe Van Bever, coeditor with
Paul Léautaud of a well-known anthology of French poets, and
the nephew of the painter La Quintinie, one of the founders of
the Salon d'Automne. Jean-Marc Van Bever was well brought
up and fairly well educated. He had received his *baccalauréat*
degree, spoke fluent English and some Italian and Spanish, and
had spent a year or so in law school, but after this promising
start his life fell into ruins. He squandered a F500,000 in-
heritance on various publishing and printing ventures, all of
which failed, and spent much of the decade before his arrest
drawing unemployment or welfare benefits. He had found his
first regular job at age forty-one, four months before his arrest,
when he and his sole friend, an out-of-work Italian hatter named
Ugo Papini, began delivering coal. This work brought F60–F120
a day, and by economizing Van Bever had been able to save
some F2,000–F3,000, which he always carried on his person.

Van Bever had made an abortive foray into marriage a decade earlier, and since then his only female companionship had been prostitutes. Jeannette Gaul, thirty-four, was one of these. At age thirty she had begun to use drugs, and with drugs as a lever one of her suppliers had persuaded her to quit her job as a chambermaid and become a licensed prostitute in a registered brothel. She drifted from one provincial brothel to another, and by late 1940 ended up in Paris, where she became a streetwalker, hanging about the seedier *quartiers*, picking up men — including Van Bever — and escorting them to the nearest cheap hotel. Van Bever was her paying client for three weeks in November 1941. When she fell ill, he visited her in the hospital. He persuaded her to move in with him at his hotel on the rue Piat two days before Christmas.

When she moved in with Van Bever, Jeannette Gaul gave up prostitution, but not her drug habit, which she continued to support by procuring, under guise of cures, limited quantities of heroin from five different doctors — each of whom presumably believed he was gradually weaning her from the drug. Among them was Dr. Marcel Petiot, who in late January and February 1942 had written five prescriptions in Jeannette Gaul's name and two in that of Van Bever. The latter was not an addict, and had even been trying to persuade his mistress to give up drugs. But she was more stubborn than he, and until he could convince her to change, Van Bever stood by meekly.

In France, a criminal case is first turned over to a *juge d'instruction,* or examining magistrate, who conducts the *instruction* — interrogating and confronting witnesses, gathering evidence, directing police investigations, and compiling a dossier that, should he decide that a crime has been committed, he sends to the public-prosecutor's office, where the indictment is drawn up. When this is complete, an *avocat général,* roughly equivalent to a prosecuting attorney, actually takes the case to court and argues on the State's behalf. The Van Bever and Gaul case was turned over to *juge d'instruction* Achille Olmi, who was generally seen with his mouth open and an astonished look in his eyes, and whom lawyers found to be one of the less efficient and scintillating magistrates in Paris.

Petiot in 1942 was operating as a general practitioner out of an office in his apartment at 66 rue Caumartin in the busy commercial district near the Gare Saint-Lazare. Among his other patients were about ninety-five addicts whom he was curing of their habits by means of diminishing doses of drugs. Though such cures were legal, most respectable physicians shied away from them, and there were only about twenty-five Parisian doctors who cared to deal with them at all. Petiot had previously run afoul of the narcotics laws, and though never convicted, this made him suspect from the beginning. Jeannette Gaul and Van Bever, when arrested, initially stated that Petiot had given Van Bever the two prescriptions with full knowledge that they were actually for his mistress. Both admitted that the doctor had refused to furnish him a third prescription. The whole case rested on this one point, for Petiot could possibly have been deceived by Jeannette Gaul, who had no real intention of being cured; but had he given her additional prescriptions in Van Bever's name, it would be obvious that he knew of her intentions.

When called before Olmi for questioning in February 1942, Petiot quite truthfully pointed out that his fee was only fifty francs, a quite reasonable rate and hardly the sort of sum one would charge for the illegal sale of drugs. He outlined the precautions he took to avoid abuse of his services and said he had warned Jeannette Gaul at the start that, despite any requests she might make, he would never give her more than a certain predetermined quantity of heroin. Van Bever had been presented to him as an addict, and, given certain physical signs and an awareness of the "habitual proselytism of addicts," Petiot had believed him to be one. Examination had been difficult, he said, because Van Bever had pretended to be deaf and his mistress had whispered in his ear before he answered any question. Petiot had given him two prescriptions but had finally tired of the whispering routine and grown suspicious about Van Bever's addiction, and when the latter returned a week after his second visit, Petiot refused to give him any more.

Following Petiot's statement, Jeannette Gaul changed hers and said Petiot had told the truth. Van Bever agreed, saying he had accompanied his mistress to the doctor's office in all innocence, and had been greatly surprised when he heard her telling Petiot that he was an addict. Several weeks later, Olmi heard the three again. Petiot and Gaul repeated the same story, but Van Bever now claimed he had told Petiot that he was not an addict. Jeannette Gaul then changed her statement again, saying that, after all, Petiot had really known the heroin was for her. Both maintained that Petiot had never bothered to examine Van Bever — an absolutely essential step before furnishing a prescription. Olmi didn't know what to do, and while waiting for something to occur to him, he indicted all three. Jeannette Gaul remained in jail, while the judge granted Van Bever a provisional release on March 15. Petiot had not been jailed at all. The trial date was set for May 26, 1942.

At 9:30 on the morning of Sunday, March 22, Van Bever and his friend Papini went down to the café in their building for coffee. A robust, clean-shaven man of about forty-five was waiting for Van Bever. The two seemed to know one another, and after a brief conversation, Van Bever went up to his room, came down, and was about to go out the door with the stranger when he turned to Papini. The man, Van Bever told his friend, was the husband of one of Jeannette Gaul's friends and had a letter from Jeannette that had been smuggled out of the prison. Papini asked why the stranger couldn't have brought the letter with him. "Perhaps Jeannette had some debts that they want me to pay — but don't worry, I won't pay them." Saying he would return that afternoon or evening, Van Bever bid his friend farewell and left.

Van Bever did not return that day, nor did he work or come

home Monday, Tuesday, or Wednesday. Papini entered his friend's room and noticed that everything was in its place and that Van Bever, a heavy smoker, had not even taken his tobacco pouch or a letter he had been in a hurry to post. On Wednesday, Papini contacted Van Bever's lawyer, who advised him to write to the public prosecutor. In his letter, Papini did not even mention Petiot, since Van Bever had not worried much about the case and did not think he would have any further trouble with it. Papini instead wrote that in November 1941 Van Bever had gone to Troyes with France Mignot, a prostitute who had been his mistress before Jeannette Gaul, to meet her family. When the couple had arrived at the house, the entire Mignot family had thrown itself on Van Bever, beating him with clubs, stabbing him twice, and robbing him of F1,200. Van Bever had pressed charges, and the case had been due to come up in Troyes on March 24, 1942 — two days after the disappearance. Papini feared that the Mignots had murdered his friend.

The issue grew more complex on March 26, when a stranger delivered two letters to the boulevard Saint-Germain office of Jeannette Gaul's lawyer, Françoise Pavie. One asked Maître Pavie to tell Van Bever's lawyer, Maître Michel Menard, that his services would no longer be required, while the other begged Jeannette Gaul to tell the truth — that Van Bever truly had been an addict. Maître Menard was convinced that neither the handwriting nor the style of the letters was his client's, and since he was an old family friend he could not believe Van Bever would willingly have dismissed him with a brusque note sent to a third party.

Police searched hospitals and prisons, and made inquiries at Troyes and among Jeannette Gaul's circle of friends — all without result. A drug dealer who was tentatively identified as the man who had taken the letters to Maître Pavie could never be found for questioning. Similarly, the husband of a young addict who was both a friend of Jeannette Gaul's and an occasional client of Dr. Petiot fit the description of the man who had led Van Bever away, but police never found him either. The case remained a mystery; at the time, there was no compelling reason to suspect Petiot, who denied any knowledge of Van Bever's fate and apparently stood to gain little at that stage by his disappearance. Retrospectively, however, one might find a motive in the fact that ten days after Van Bever vanished, Petiot suddenly "found" a complete report on his medical examination of Van Bever — a report so complete, he boasted to Judge Olmi, that he had even measured the length of the man's penis. Here, then, was incontrovertible proof that Petiot had diligently fulfilled the obligations of his profession. A prosecutor later wondered whether the careful report was the result not of an examination, but of an autopsy.

The drug charge came to trial as scheduled in May. Jeannette Gaul was sentenced to six months in prison and fined F2,400. Released in August, she promptly returned to prostitution and drugs, and died of tetanus three months later. Van Bever was sentenced in absentia to one year in prison and drew the same fine as his mistress. Petiot was found guilty and given a suspended one-year sentence and a F10,000 fine, which his lawyer, René Floriot, subsequently succeeded in reducing. The search for Van Bever continued over the next year, headed by Police Inspector Roger Gignoux.

The old Petiot file Commissaire Massu consulted contained another, remarkably similar case. On March 5, 1942, another young woman, Raymonde Baudet, was arrested for infraction of the drug laws. She had taken a prescription for the mild tranquilizer Sonéryl and, with the help of her lover, had removed the word "Sonéryl" with ink eradicator and substituted "14 ampoules of heroin." The pharmacist to whom she presented it immediately noticed the clumsy forgery and telephoned the police. The original prescription had been written by Dr. Marcel

Petiot, who had previously given Raymonde Baudet four prescriptions for heroin as part of a drug cure.

It is not clear what Petiot thought the danger to himself
might be from the Baudet forgery. Perhaps he was worried
about the earlier four prescriptions, particularly since the Gaul–
Van Bever case had begun only two weeks earlier. Whatever
the reason, his next actions were drastic and suspicious. Raymonde Baudet's mother, née Marthe Fortin, married three times:
to a man named Lavie, by whom she had a son; to Raymonde's
father, Monsieur Baudet; and presently to David Khaït. Raymonde had used the name Khaït with Petiot — possibly concealing the fact that she was getting drugs elsewhere under
another name — and it was "Khaït" alone that appeared on the
prescriptions. Petiot apparently reasoned that if the mother were
an addict as well and he claimed that half the prescriptions had
been intended for her, the case against him would be seriously
weakened. But to make the police believe this, he would need
the mother's help.

Several days after Raymonde's arrest, a little past noon, a man
went to the Khaït home and introduced himself as Dr. Petiot.
Marthe Khaït initially resisted the propositions he made, but
with tortuous logic he explained, cajoled, and finally persuaded
her that if she lied to the police she would weaken some of the
accusations against her daughter. Brazenly speaking in her
eldest son's presence, Petiot told her that since the police might
wish to verify Madame Khaït's fictitious narcotics use by a
physical examination, he would need to give her a dozen dry
injections in the thigh to leave convincing puncture marks. The
son, Fernand Lavie, an employee at the Préfecture de Police,
objected to this deceit, but his mother brushed him off, saying
that she had done many things for his sister in the past and
could certainly do one more small thing to help her. Petiot and
Madame Khaït went into the next room, and after a few minutes
he emerged and left.

Several days later, Madame Khaït changed her mind. She told her son that she would no longer follow Petiot's counsel and went to consult Dr. Pierre Trocmé, a trusted family friend as well as her physician. Trocmé at first could not believe a real medical man would have made such outrageous suggestions, but when he found Petiot's name quite properly listed in his medical directory, he advised his patient to tell the police everything. Later in the investigation he hid behind professional secrecy, and though he admitted having examined Madame Khaït, he would not tell police whether he had found puncture marks.

At 7:00 P.M. on Wednesday, March 25, 1942 — three days after Van Bever's disappearance — Madame Khaït put on her hat and told her husband she was going to see Raymonde's lawyer to pay part of his fee. The altruistic Dr. Petiot had offered to contribute F1,500 to the girl's defense and had also recommended the lawyer, Maître Pierre Véron — an ironic detail since, four years later, Véron would be the prosecution's most potent weapon at the Petiot murder trial. Madame Khaït took nothing with her and left a pot of water boiling on the stove for her laundry. Her husband expected her back very shortly. Perhaps she went to get money from Petiot. Perhaps, as Véron later suggested, she was planning to tell him about Petiot's false injections but, before doing so, the honest and trusting woman wished to inform the doctor that she was no longer willing to follow his plan. Wherever she went, she was never seen again.

The next morning, David Khaït found two letters under the door. One was to him, one to his stepson Fernand; both notes seemed to be in Marthe Khaït's handwriting and announced her intention to flee to the unoccupied zone of France until Raymonde's trial was over. In the letter to her husband Madame Khaït also said that, without his knowledge, she really had been taking drugs for several years. The front gate of the Khaït house was difficult to open unless one knew the trick, and their dog, which barked ferociously at strangers, had not made a sound, so Monsieur Khaït was certain his wife had delivered the letters herself. He recalled that in the past few days she had told him she thought that her disappearance during the trial would help Raymonde's case — a notion he had strongly opposed — so though he was puzzled, he was not altogether surprised.

At 10:00 the same morning, an envelope was handed to Pierre Véron's maid containing F300 toward the lawyer's fee and letters to Raymonde Baudet and Véron. At one later point Maître Véron would say his maid had formally recognized Madame Khaït; at another, that it had been a strange young man who delivered the envelope. Both letters again announced Madame Khaït's intention to flee to the free zone, and Véron also remembered her mentioning this idea during their previous meeting. Police handwriting experts compared all the letters and determined that they were indeed by Marthe Khaït but that she had written them under great stress, perhaps following someone else's dictation; the syntax was atypical, and she used none of the nicknames by which she always addressed her family.

David Khaït went to see Petiot, who claimed that Madame Khaït had spoken with him, too, about her escape plans, and who said he had given her the names of René Nézondet and some of his other friends in the free zone who could help her if and when she arrived there. Petiot hastily wrote a postcard, which he asked Monsieur Khaït to mail. It was addressed to "Gaston," at Plagne, near Loupiac in southwestern France, and Khaït thought the cryptic message was an inquiry about his wife. A few weeks later Petiot told Khaït that his friends had written saying they had seen no one fitting Madame Khaït's description.

David Khaït maintained to the end that his wife had left of her own volition, but on May 7, 1942, Fernand Lavie and Raymonde Baudet notified the police of their mother's disappearance. The case was assigned to *juge d'instruction* Achille Olmi and the investigation to Police Inspector Roger Gignoux. If Madame Khaït had been abducted, it seemed strange that her captor would have let her go home to deliver mail. Olmi sat about for hours wondering about this point and thinking how strangely the case resembled the Van Bever disappearance.

Inspector Gignoux searched throughout France for Madame Khaït, as he had for Van Bever. Raymonde Baudet had told him her mother might be using her maiden name, Fortin, or the pseudonyms Hait, Lavic, Laric, Piot, Fiot, or Lepic. At Lyon, in what seems to have been nothing more than coincidence, Gignoux found a young drug addict named Piot who chanced to be not only a friend of Raymonde Baudet, but a former client of Petiot's, but she knew nothing of the affair. Gignoux found one woman near Lyon and two railroad conductors from the Dordogne (one named Fortin) who thought the photograph of Madame Khaït resembled a woman they had seen around March or April 1942, but these, too, were written off as errors when no corroborating evidence could be found. At Plagne in the Cantal, Gignoux located the Gastons, who were distant relatives of Dr. Petiot. They had not seen him in years, though in April 1942 they had received an incoherent postcard from him — the same one David Khaït had posted — to which they had never replied.

Gignoux concluded that Madame Khaït had not fled of her own accord. In his report he pointed out the close similarities between the Van Bever and Khaït cases: narcotics, abrupt disappearance, the reception of letters from the missing persons contradicting their earlier statements, and, above all, the presence of Dr. Petiot in both cases. Though not a handwriting expert, Gignoux compared the Van Bever and Khaït letters and concluded they had been written by the same hand. If an expert could confirm this opinion, his March 1943 report boldly concluded, it would provide "irrefutable material proof that the two cases are closely linked and may be related to the narcotics cases for which Dr. Petiot was indicted. In this event, the most likely hypothesis would be that Monsieur Van Bever and Madame Khaït are being held captive or have been murdered."

Olmi sat and wondered. The Baudet drug case had come to trial on July 15, 1942. Raymonde Baudet was found guilty and sentenced to the four months she had already spent in prison, and Petiot was given another one-year suspended sentence and a F10,000 fine. Petiot's lawyer, René Floriot, subsequently managed to have the doctor's fines from both the Van Bever–Gaul and Baudet convictions combined and reduced to a grand total of F2,400. Meanwhile, attorney Pierre Véron pursued the Khaït mystery. Upon learning of the Van Bever disappearance and of Petiot's connection with it, he insisted that Olmi indict Petiot for kidnapping or murder. An investigation was made, but only halfheartedly, since so many people were disappearing in those days. David Khaït, himself a Jew, would vanish two years later and die in deportation.

Véron kept pushing, and nearly a year later Olmi grudgingly consented to search Petiot's rue Caumartin apartment. "What good is it now?" Véron asked. "Do you think he's kept them sitting in his closet?" And even then Olmi's search was so superficial and slovenly that his own secretary described it to Véron in shocked tones. Olmi went to the apartment only after warning Petiot several days in advance. He did not make routine inquiries as to whether Petiot rented a basement storage space in the building, nor did he check city-deed-office records to see if Petiot owned or rented other properties in Paris. He did not even ask questions when, during his search, he noticed a slip of paper lying in plain view — a fire insurance policy for 21 rue Le Sueur. Nor did Olmi search the entire rue Caumartin apartment, contenting himself with a cursory perusal of the doctor's office and waiting room. Opening a desk drawer, Olmi found a small fortune in gold and jewels. Petiot said they had been given to him in lieu of fees by impoverished patients; he did not, however, explain how poor people could be so wealthy. When the doctor complained about the search, Olmi made light of it, claimed it was mere troublesome routine, and joked, "I am not accusing you of killing people and burning them in your stove!"

The months went by, Gignoux's evidence built up, Véron continued to insist that an indictment should be drawn up against Petiot. A year later, on Monday, March 13, 1944, two days after the discovery at the rue Le Sueur, Pierre Véron strode angrily into Olmi's office. Olmi, who had scarcely given the case a thought since his pointless search a year before, jumped up and wailed bitterly: "I was going to arrest Petiot tomorrow — I really was! But they took the dossier away from me. I don't understand why." Had he only understood sooner, several dozen dead people might still have been alive; and there are those who maintain it is his conscience that should bear the burden of their deaths.

3

THE INVESTIGATION

ON MONDAY, March 13, 1944, the search for Dr. Marcel Petiot began in earnest. Chief Inspector Marius Batut and a subordinate requisitioned a car and some gasoline, which was rationed even for the police, and set out for Petiot's native province, the Yonne, where they thought he and his wife might be hiding with former friends and associates. They remembered the sign on the door of 21 rue Le Sueur giving an address in Auxerre, where Petiot's brother Maurice lived. Closer examination of the worn paper revealed that someone had originally written "56 rue du Pont," and that this had been erased and changed, in a different hand, to "18 rue des Lombards." The former was Maurice Petiot's home; the latter was a building that had been purchased by their father, Félix Petiot, and passed on upon his death in August 1942 to Maurice.

Number 18 rue des Lombards proved to be a curious house, built on a hill riddled with ancient Roman catacombs, and constructed, someone suggested, by an architect in the throes of delirium tremens, so tortuously was it built around its steeply sloping foundation. It was empty, except for piles of furniture and bric-a-brac reminiscent of the disordered collection found at the rue Le Sueur. In one neat room was a rumpled bed.

Inspector Batut eventually found Maurice working in his radio store as though it were a perfectly ordinary day, disturbed only by the flood of newspaper reporters who had arrived even before the police. Maurice Petiot was thirty-seven, ten years younger than Marcel, and in some ways, it later appeared, a pale copy of his sibling. The two looked similar, but Maurice was taller and thinner, more timid, his face hollow and angular, and he lacked his brother's dynamic presence and intelligence. In school he had distinguished himself only by an immoderate love of the bicycle, and his subsequent career as a bicycle salesman and radio repairman and dealer included one or two bankruptcies. In recent years, though, he had purchased quantities of furniture, art, and jewelry, reportedly sometimes at several times their value, as well as a number of buildings and properties, both in his own name and in that of his wife and two children. One could partly account for this sudden wealth by his fortuitous acquisition of large stocks of American radios and electronic parts before the Occupation, which he now sold at great profit, particularly to the Germans. But even so, it was hard to believe that this chronic failure, even helped along by luck, was covering his phenomenal expenses with business earnings alone.

Maurice told Inspector Batut he had not seen or heard from his brother since late February and was utterly astonished and puzzled by what he had heard on the radio and read in the papers about the rue Le Sueur discovery. He was obviously upset. His eyes were red and feverish from lack of sleep, he had not shaved in days, and his hands and shoulders twitched nervously as he spoke in an almost imperceptible voice. Yes, he knew that his brother owned a building in the sixteenth arrondissement, but he had never been there and had learned the exact address only from the stories in that morning's papers. As for the recent occupant of the bed at the rue des Lombards house, it had certainly not been his brother or sister-in-law in flight, but a friend from nearby Courson-les-Carrières — Albert Neuhausen, a radio distributor and repairman like himself, who often stopped in Auxerre when returning from Paris too late to make his connection home. Batut drove the ten miles to Courson. Neuhausen, he discovered, had slept at home the previous night. It was the first contradiction in a case that soon became a solid mass of them.

Batut had to return to Paris, but at Massu's request several local policemen went to stake out the Auxerre train station the next morning. They arrived when the train for Paris was less than a mile from the station, and a policeman recognized Dr. Petiot's wife, Georgette, waiting on the platform. Both she and Maurice were arrested and held at the Auxerre police station, and Massu himself drove out to bring them back to Paris. Maurice's wife Monique came to say good-bye, bringing Georgette and Marcel's fifteen-year-old son Gérard, who had been staying in Auxerre for some weeks past. As Massu's car drove off, Georgette cried that she had done nothing wrong, and told her son to behave himself, study hard, and obey his aunt until she returned.

Madame Petiot was taken to Police Judiciaire headquarters on the quai des Orfèvres. At thirty-nine, she was a beautiful woman, but now the simple elegance of her black skirt, white blouse, and astrakhan coat was in stark contrast to the disheveled curls hanging around her exhausted and tear-stained face. She could barely hold up a hand to shield herself from the photographers, and two inspectors almost had to carry her through the door.

Seated in Massu's office, Georgette Petiot claimed total ignorance of the whole affair. "I did not know the house on the rue Le Sueur very well," she told the commissaire.

I only went there once, and I didn't like it; it was too large. I don't even remember the previous owner's name. I know that he [Dr. Petiot] had some work done there, but I don't know what kind. My husband has always been a very gentle person, but he never told me anything about his business affairs, something that I complained about frequently.

Saturday morning [March 11, the day of the discovery] he saw patients at our [rue Caumartin] apartment. We ate lunch at noon. He went out at 3:00 P.M. and returned at 6:00. A patient — a foreigner, I believe — was waiting for him. We had dinner around 7:30. Suddenly, the telephone rang. I heard: "This is the police." My husband took the receiver and said, "All right, I'm on my way." He left quickly; I followed him to the stairs and asked where he was going. He did not want to tell me. I waited all night in an armchair. I didn't know what to think, and wondered if he had been arrested [by the Germans]. On Sunday morning I decided to go to Auxerre to be with my son (who was at school there), and I thought that perhaps my husband had gone there himself. I went to the Gare de Lyon to catch the 7:00 or 8:00 train, but there were no trains that day. I returned to my neighborhood, but did not want to go back to the apartment. I went to church and attended several services, then spent most of the afternoon in the waiting room of the Gare Saint-Lazare.

That evening I read in the newspapers about the horrible things they accused my husband of doing. I didn't know where to go; I couldn't return home, and did not want to go to my family in Paris. I spent the night sitting on the stairs of a building my husband owns at 52 rue de Reuilly. On Monday, I spent most of the day in a restaurant near the Gare de Lyon, on the rue de Bercy, I think. I took the 5:20 train and arrived in Auxerre at about 9:00 in the evening. When I got to the rue du Pont no one was home, but my brother-in-law arrived a few minutes later. He said that he was returning from Joigny,* and that he had been on the same train as I, though we had not seen one another. I can't tell you anything more.

---

* After Batut's visit, Maurice had gone to Joigny hoping to arrange for his nephew Gérard to be transferred to a school there — so that the youth would be more isolated from the trauma of the investigation. For whatever reason, this plan came to nothing and Gérard remained in Auxerre.

Nor could she, for at that moment she fainted.

An inspector Hernis, one of Batut's aides, was asked to check Madame Petiot's story. None of the twenty-one people living at 52 rue de Reuilly had seen her on the night of the twelfth, but this was not particularly surprising. The concierge knew her slightly, and though she had never met the doctor himself, she knew Maurice Petiot very well, since it was he who came to collect the rents every month. Henri-Casimir Alicot, owner of the Hôtel Alicot at 207 bis rue de Bercy, corroborated Madame Petiot's story in every detail. She had arrived Monday morning around 9:00, dressed in black, carrying a yellow leather suitcase, looking miserable and haggard as though she had not slept. She asked for a room and napped a bit in the afternoon; she told Alicot that she had spent the previous night awake in a staircase. She asked whether he had read the newspapers. He had. She said she could not believe it possible that her husband, so good to her, could have done such monstrous things. Alicot persuaded her to eat a bit of soup, and she left around 4:15 to catch the train for Auxerre. She told him she wanted to see her son once more as she feared she would be arrested.

Alicot also mentioned to Inspector Hernis that he knew Maurice very well, since the latter had stayed in his hotel from Wednesday to Saturday of almost every week since 1940 during business trips to Paris. The last time had been around February 19–22, when Maurice arrived with a truck, plus a driver and workman who were delivering something for him somewhere in Paris.

When Massu later questioned him, Maurice retracted his earlier statement that he knew nothing about the rue Le Sueur building his brother owned. Maurice had been to it several times to supervise some work and on occasion had paid the utility bills. Massu suspected the purpose of Maurice's February trip was to deliver the quicklime used to decompose the bodies, and he told him so. "If that's what you think," Maurice replied, "you will just have to prove it!" Prove it they did. Later that afternoon, Jean Eustache, a trucker from Auxerre who had heard of the case, contacted Massu and told him that he and Robert Massonière had driven Maurice to a quarry thirty miles away at Aisy-sur-Armançon on February 19, 1944, and picked up four hundred kilograms of quicklime, which they delivered to a large private house in the sixteenth arrondissement of Paris. Eustache could not recall the exact address, but his description of the coach door and entranceway matched those at 21 rue Le Sueur.

Faced with this evidence, Maurice admitted the journey, but claimed the sacks had contained coal, not quicklime, and that the coal had not even belonged to him. What had happened, he told Massu, was that Eustache's truck had broken down while transporting the coal and some furniture to Paris, and, since they were in the sixteenth arrondissement when the mishap occurred, Maurice had offered to let the haulers store the coal in the entrance to his brother's building on the rue Le Sueur. Eustache admitted that, yes, his truck had, indeed, broken down, but only after delivering the lime — not coal — to its intended destination. Maurice then capitulated altogether, saying he had only lied to protect the young assistant in his radio shop, Robert Maxime, whom he had sworn to secrecy.

Early in February, Maurice explained, his brother had written him from Paris asking for a quantity of lime to exterminate cockroaches and to whitewash the façade of his building. Maurice had delivered it. Then, on Saturday, March 11, toward 11:00 P.M., he had received a mysterious telephone call informing him that the police had discovered human remains at the rue Le Sueur. As the first newspaper accounts did not appear until Sunday, he had not known what to make of this peculiar anonymous communication. He mentioned it to his employee, Robert Maxime, the next day; Maxime, who knew about the lime since they had discussed places to get it, commented, "It's true that lime will destroy cockroaches as well as bodies." Terrified by this suggestion, Maurice could not bring himself to mention it to the police and risk being implicated in the affair. He asked Maxime, too, not to mention it. Maxime confirmed the incident. On the evening of Friday the seventeenth, six days after the discovery, Maurice Petiot was handed over to *juge d'instruction* Georges Berry, charged with conspiracy to commit murder, and sent to Paris's Santé prison.

Earlier that same day, Massu and several inspectors had accompanied Madame Petiot to the rue Caumartin apartment for a brief search. A thousand people mobbed the sidewalk outside, and photographers pressed in as the terrified woman tried to shield her face. As reporters followed them up the stairs shouting questions, she turned to scream: "You are assassins! You're making fun of my misery! You know that I only went to the Yonne to see my son!"

In addition to huge quantities of morphine and heroin, the search uncovered three sets of male and female human genitalia preserved in alcohol (anatomical specimens probably stolen from Petiot's medical school, as it later turned out) and a diabolical wood sculpture done by the doctor himself of a beast — half-animal, half-devil — with an exceptionally large phallus. There were no signs of the quantities of jewelry Judge Olmi had noticed the previous year, and police would later learn that, before leaving the house, Petiot had packed up all the available money and jewelry. In a locked medical cabinet they found quantities of black-market coffee, sugar, and chocolate, which Georgette was permitted to take with her to prison.

Georgette Petiot fainted again during the search and was taken to the police security ward at the Hôtel-Dieu hospital. Her health seemed so feeble that it was several days before she was officially informed that she was under arrest. For lack of any more concrete evidence, Judge Berry used her inability to verify the origin of a five-carat diamond ring her husband had given her to indict her for accepting stolen goods. It was a strange piece of judicial logic that no one but she cared to protest. She at first failed to understand the charge at all, and for several days the judge could not even persuade her to hire a lawyer. When she was fingerprinted by the Identité Judiciaire, it was found that her fingerprints spiraled in the opposite direction from all the other four million prints on file. It also appeared that a sixth finger had been amputated from both hands. Palmists assured the press that such oddities surely reflected a unique and sinister personality.

Questioned again the day after his previous interview, Maurice insisted he knew nothing about his brother's whereabouts. "Perhaps he committed suicide, or joined the Maquis, or left the country." The police did not find his sarcasm amusing. But Maurice now admitted having gone to the rue Le Sueur three or four times: the previous July to put antimite powder on the furniture in the salon (true — powder was found there); in January, accompanied by an architect, to check for water leaks that were causing troublesome moisture in a house on the rue Duret that backed on 21 rue Le Sueur (there were still leaks at number 21); and in February to deliver the lime. In January he had investigated the entire building and found nothing unusual. Since that part of the rue Le Sueur building contiguous with the house on the rue Duret included the triangular room and the stable containing the pit, Maurice and the architect had toured these rooms together. The manure pit had been covered by two heavy marble slabs, he said, which he did not attempt to move. He had tried to open the double door in the triangular room but decided it was merely decorative; he felt certain there had been no iron rings in the wall at that time. Neither he nor the architect, whom police also questioned, reported noticing anything suspicious or smelling the pestilential odor that would have permeated the building had it contained dozens of rotting bodies. Why, Massu asked Maurice, had he felt obligated to do all these chores in a building belonging to his brother? Because, he replied, Marcel had been in prison at the time: "The Germans suspected my brother of treason."

On March 15 Massu had been contacted by the German commissaire Robert Jodkum,* who was willing to furnish details of Petiot's earlier arrest by the Germans. Jodkum was the interpreter and secretary of, successively, S.S. Hauptsturmführer Theo Dannecker and S.S. Obersturmführer Heinz Röthke, who directed Gestapo subsector IV-B4 on the rue des Saussaies — the Jewish Affairs division responsible for scheduling raids and determining which Jews should be sent to camps or deported; as such, Jodkum attended or conducted interrogations, occasionally participated in arrests, and gathered information. In early 1943, a French informer had told him of an escape organization that obtained false passports and smuggled Jews and downed Allied pilots to Spain and South America. The headquarters of this network were in a barbershop at 25 rue des Mathurins, a street that intersects the rue Caumartin a few hundred feet from number 66. The barber, Raoul Fourrier, and his friend Edmond Pintard were active members of the organization, the informer said, but the leader was a mysterious and elusive figure known only as Dr. Eugène. The Gestapo had arrested Fourrier and Pintard on May 21, 1943. After threatening them and beating Dr. Eugène's real name out of the barber, Gestapo officers had gone to the rue Caumartin apartment and arrested Dr. Petiot, along with René Nézondet, who happened by to deliver theater tickets for a musical comedy. Nézondet appeared totally innocent and was released two weeks later; Fourrier, Pintard, and

* Or Jodkun, Jokum, Jodkuhn. According to the French historian and former police commissaire Jacques Delarue, "Jodkum" was a pseudonym. Robert Jodkum was arrested by the Germans later in 1944, for reasons unknown, and imprisoned at Fresnes. He was subsequently sent back to Germany, and neither his fate nor real name was ever discovered by the postwar French authorities who investigated war crimes.

Petiot were held in the Fresnes prison for eight months, until January 1944.

Massu's vision of the crimes abruptly took on a more horrifying dimension. He envisioned a new murder scenario: posing as the head of an escape organization, Petiot had lured desperate people into his home under some pretense and murdered them. Even the Germans had been fooled. But Massu was particularly puzzled by one thing: if Petiot had been in a Gestapo prison until January and, as Maurice avowed, visiting his brother at Auxerre for two weeks afterward to recuperate, and if as late as January 1944 there had been no bodies at the rue Le Sueur, as both Maurice and the architect claimed, how had the badly decomposed bodies gotten there? Was it really possible they were hidden there all the time — that the architect simply had not seen them and Maurice had lied? Surely if they were hidden there they would have given off an unmistakable stench. These conspicuous questions, which would never be answered, added themselves to the growing mountain of bizarre, contradictory detail.

Before he could investigate this new information, Massu's new theory was confirmed. That afternoon he was visited by a man named Jean Gouedo who, together with a Polish Jew named Joachim Guschinov, owned a fur store at 69 rue Caumartin. In late 1941, Gouedo told Massu, Guschinov was frightened by the increasingly harsh German treatment of Jews and toyed with the idea of leaving France. His physician and neighbor, Dr. Petiot, had told him this would be possible: for F25,000 he could obtain a false Argentinian passport and safe passage to South America. Gouedo had helped Guschinov pack on the eve of his departure. According to Petiot's instructions, all markings were removed from his clothes and $1,000 in U.S. currency was sewn into the shoulder pads of a suit. Guschinov also took a quantity of silver, gold, and diamonds worth F500,000–F700,000, another F500,000 in cash, and his five finest sable coats.

Massu summoned Guschinov's wife Renée, who told the rest of the story. On January 2, 1942, she and her husband had dined together; then he gathered his bags and consulted a map of Paris to find the street where he would meet Petiot. Madame Guschinov went with her husband as far as the rue Pergolèse, where he told her that he must continue the journey alone. They kissed and said good-bye, and Madame Guschinov had not seen him since. Massu also consulted a map, and saw that the rue Pergolèse intersects the rue Le Sueur.

Two months after her husband left, Renée Guschinov had gone to ask Petiot for news of him. The doctor had shown her a brief note in Guschinov's handwriting, undated, saying that he had traveled via Dakar and had safely reached Buenos Aires. Subsequent letters, one allegedly on the letterhead of the Alvear Palace Hotel in Buenos Aires, said that his new business there was doing well and that she should leave France and come at once. And why hadn't she gone? Massu asked. The reasons she gave the commissaire were obscure and contradictory (Petiot would later say she had found a lover she preferred to her husband). Joachim's letters stopped, and she wondered but did nothing. She was a Jew, and Jews did not like to make themselves conspicuous — which was perhaps one reason why she had not reported Joachim's disappearance to the police even now, after the Petiot affair had broken; she had been unwillingly dragged into it by Gouedo's report. Massu did not know what to make of her, but her husband's case seemed clear.

On March 17 Massu sent his men to pick up René Nézondet, whose name repeatedly came up in the Petiot investigation. Not only had he been arrested by the Germans along with Petiot the previous year, but back in 1942, when Petiot was questioned about the Van Bever and Khaït disappearances, the doctor claimed that Madame Khaït had told him of her wish to leave Paris and that he had given her Nézondet's address in Lyon, in the free zone. Inspector Gignoux had searched for Nézondet in

Lyon, but he had recently been fired from his job at the news-paper *Le Figaro* for black-market activities and had then moved to Paris. When Gignoux found him there in 1943, Nézondet said that he and a girlfriend had successfully crossed the demarcation line on the Comte de Barbantane's property and that he might conceivably have mentioned this to Petiot at some point. But no, he had certainly never met Madame Khaït or Van Bever, nor could he understand why Petiot should have given anyone his name or thought he could be of help. When Massu's men now went to Nézondet's apartment at 15 rue Pauly in the fourteenth arrondissement, they found a viewer in his front door identical to the one in the wall of the triangular room at 21 rue Le Sueur.

René-Gustave Nézondet was an amiable, loose-fleshed man just over six foot three. His left eyelid drooped when at rest, and when he spoke he unconsciously compensated by raising that eyebrow — a habit that gave him a startlingly credulous expres-sion. A forty-eight-year-old native of the Yonne, he had known Petiot for more than twenty years. When they first met, Nézon-det had been the town clerk at Villeneuve-sur-Yonne, but an injury to his right hand forced him to give up this position and he began raising trout and watercress and organizing Sunday-night dances at nearby Fontaine Rouge. After his marriage, his in-laws had insisted he see less of his friend Petiot, who was becoming actively involved in leftist politics in the village. Agreeable by nature, Nézondet bowed to their wishes, and apart from the occasions when Petiot and his wife put in an appear-ance at the Sunday-evening fêtes, he scarcely saw his former comrade until 1936, the year in which Nézondet's marriage broke up and he moved to Paris for the first time. Arriving in the capi-tal, he had learned from another old friend from the Yonne, Roland Porchon, that Petiot, too, was living in Paris. Nézondet saw the doctor a few times, and their friendship rapidly re-sumed. Petiot found Nézondet jobs at a newspaper and as receptionist for a pharmaceutical company. Later, when police questioned Petiot's concierge about his acquaintances, the only person she could remember seeing at the doctor's rue Caumartin apartment was Nézondet. Despite their close association, Nézondet pleaded complete ignorance of Petiot's alleged murders, escape routes, or anything else outside the placid life of a dedicated local doctor. As for the viewers, they had both happened to buy one the same day at a flea market.

Roland Albert Porchon, Nézondet's friend, had already voluntarily gone to the police a day or two after the discovery at the rue Le Sueur. An overweight, middle-aged man whose very face inspired suspicion, Porchon was currently running a trucking firm and second-hand-furniture shop — the latest in a long series of semilegitimate ventures. His path had occasionally crossed that of the police, and in exchange for favors or oversights, or simply out of generosity toward close acquaintances, he sometimes supplied information to the police, particularly to Inspector René Bouygues of the Criminal Brigade, a friend for several years. On March 13 or 14 he had telephoned both Bouygues and Commissaire de Police Lucien Doulet saying he had important information to give them about Petiot. But his main reason for calling, police soon learned, was to cover up his own participation in an abortive attempt to send a couple to Petiot's ostensible escape network. Nothing was simple: the investigators grew accustomed to the fact that each new character who surfaced brought along a host of others — none of whom agreed with anyone else. Porchon brought the Maries.

In March 1943, a man named René Marie and his wife Marcelle heard, through an obscure chain of friends, that Porchon knew someone who could help them escape from France. According to Porchon, he had sent them to Petiot via Nézondet. According to the Marie couple, however, Nézondet had not been involved — Porchon had sent them directly to Petiot, who told them the escape price was F45,000 per person and that they should sell all their furniture. Porchon offered them F220,000 for their possessions. The Maries were worried and uncertain what to do, and when a friend reported unsavory rumors about Petiot's professional life, they resolved not to go. Immediately after learning of the rue Le Sueur discovery, Porchon came to the Maries, they reported, and instructed them not to go to the police; he suggested several rationalizations they could give if their names were found at Petiot's apartment and if the police should come to make inquiries. Porchon had enough problems already without risking implication in a murder case, and he hoped to keep out of it at all costs. He also went to Inspector Bouygues and asked him to cover up his involvement; the police officer initially agreed, believing, he later admitted, that here was a question of an honest escape organization that patriotism demanded he protect. He knew nothing of the Petiot affair at that time. But when he confidentially told an associate at headquarters of Porchon's visit, Bouygues learned what was now involved and immediately went to Massu.

When taken before *juge d'instruction* Berry on March 17, Porchon claimed that he had known of Petiot's crimes all along. In late June 1942, he confessed, Nézondet had told him everything and had proclaimed that "Petiot is the king of criminals. I never would have thought him capable of such a thing." Porchon had asked him what he was talking about, and Nézondet told him of "sixteen corpses stretched out" at the rue Le Sueur that he had seen with his own eyes. "They were completely blackened; they were certainly killed by poison or injection." Why had they been killed, Porchon asked? "I suppose he asked them for money to pass them into the free zone and instead of helping them escape, he killed them." Nézondet had asked Porchon to remain silent about the murders and had assured him that he would go to the police himself as soon as the war was over.

Judge Berry was stunned. This was the first time anyone had admitted to knowing anything and, if it was true, the case against Petiot was suddenly blessed with firm support. But as questioning continued, Porchon showed himself to be a more and more unreliable witness. He had told Inspector Bouygues, for example, that he had once seen Petiot dressed in work clothes toiling away at foul deeds in a cellar. Called before the *juge d'instruction* again, he retracted this story, saying that he had recently undergone a minor foot operation, and that when he spoke to Bouygues he had been hallucinating as a result of the anesthetic.

Nonetheless, Porchon had certainly known something long before the police did. Commissaire Doulet, another of Porchon's many friends on the force, now remembered that the year before, on August 2, 1943, during the period that Petiot was in the Gestapo prison at Fresnes, Porchon had come to his office about some minor police matter and had told the commissaire he was about to go to the Police Judiciaire to discuss a very important case. "According to him," Doulet said, "it concerned a Parisian doctor who, under the pretext of passing young people out of the country, asked them for sums of money between F50,000 and F75,000 and then did away with them after payment. This doctor supposedly got rid of the bodies by burying them in the courtyard of his building." Porchon, according to Doulet, claimed to have heard about the murders from the Gestapo, "who did not want to interfere since it was a purely French matter."

Doulet encouraged Porchon to report immediately and without fail to the Police Judiciaire. When Doulet later asked if he had done so, Porchon assured him: "Yes, I saw a police officer whom I know well. He didn't seem to take the matter very seriously, but in the next few days I intend to give him additional information which should interest him." The officer in question, of course, was Bouygues, who now recalled that, yes, sometime in the summer of 1943 Porchon had briefly mentioned something about someone who sent people "to the other side," but had also said that this unnamed person was then arrested and imprisoned by the Germans. Porchon had never furnished additional details, nor had he mentioned Petiot's name until after the rue Le Sueur discovery, and Bouygues had completely forgotten the event until he was reminded of it. Judge Berry was dumbfounded. Witnesses rarely agree completely, but this case was truly incredible. Now, on top of everything else, he was faced with police officers who were told about mass murders and not only didn't investigate the reports, but soon forgot all about them.

Hoping someone would crack, Berry had Porchon and Nézondet confront each other in his chambers. Nézondet said Porchon's story was laughable, and to prove his point he laughed. He had never heard anything so ridiculous in his life! A day or two later, however, the police interrogated Madame Marie Turpault, a friend of Nézondet's mistress Aimée Lesage, whom the couple had once sent to Petiot for rheumatism treatments. In December 1943, Madame Turpault said, she had been at Nézondet's apartment and had asked about Petiot. "He's a real bastard," Nézondet had told her. "He's in prison right now, and he should stay there." Nézondet further said, according to Madame Turpault, that he had met Petiot's brother Maurice, who had found bodies in a pit at the doctor's house and a book with a list of sixty names. Maurice had asked Nézondet to help him dispose of the evidence and hush up the matter; Nézondet claimed he had refused to do this and had threatened to go to the police at the end of the war.

Nézondet was now confronted with Madame Turpault, and he said that she, too, was inventing fabulous stories, even though much of her tale closely resembled Porchon's testimony. Madame Turpault stubbornly stuck to her earlier statement, and added that Maurice Petiot had asked Nézondet to help him build a wall to conceal the cadavers. On March 22, Nézondet, unable to hold out any longer, announced that Porchon and Turpault were telling the truth and that he would now tell the whole story. His version, which Judge Berry's clerk copied down and added to the rest, was as follows.

In November or December 1943, while Petiot was still in prison at Fresnes, Nézondet met Maurice at the Hôtel Alicot, the same hotel where Georgette later stopped while in flight to Auxerre. Maurice was pale and trembling. He told Nézondet: "I have just come from my brother's house. There's enough there to have us all shot."

"Enough what?" Nézondet asked. "An arms cache? A secret transmitter?"

"I wish that's all it was," Maurice replied. "The journeys to South America begin and end at the rue Le Sueur. There are bodies piled in a pit, with their hair and eyebrows shaved off. I found a book where he [Marcel] wrote down the names of his victims; there must have been fifty or sixty of them." Maurice described to Nézondet the method of killing. A syringe filled with poison was somehow arranged so that it could be operated from a distance, though Nézondet did not recall the formula of the poison Maurice allegedly described, and his own descriptions of the syringe, which in some of his varying statements he claimed Maurice said had been mounted in the false doorbell in the triangular room, were incomprehensible. No mounting of any kind was found in the doorbell. Nézondet added that Maurice had also mentioned finding large quantities of clothing at the rue Le Sueur, both civilian apparel of all kinds and German army uniforms. Maurice had packed everything into crates and taken the stuff away in a five-ton truck.

A few weeks after Maurice recounted this horror story, Nézondet continued, Georgette Petiot and her son Gérard came to Nézondet's apartment for dinner. Sometime during the evening she mentioned that the accusations the Germans leveled against her husband were really not very serious, and she expected his release shortly. Nézondet drew her away from Gérard. Without mentioning Maurice's name, he informed her of the bodies at the rue Le Sueur. She fainted three times and threatened to commit suicide. Nézondet, with a peculiar notion of assuagement and tact, advised her to get a divorce and find a lover. When Georgette pulled herself together she went to Maurice, who was in Paris on business, and recounted Nézondet's incredible story. Nézondet was summoned by them the next day to explain himself. Maurice now feigned ignorance of the whole matter, according to Nézondet, and so he remained silent. He assumed Maurice's attitude must mean he wished to protect his sister-in-law from knowledge that might endanger her sanity. When Judge Berry questioned Aimée Lesage, who had been present at the dinner, she supported everything her lover had said about the evening's events. She suspected Madame Petiot had contrived her fainting spells and was really neither so surprised nor horrified as she seemed.

Georgette Petiot told Judge Berry that this 1943 incident really had happened, but that when Nézondet refused to repeat his extraordinary claims in front of Maurice she had concluded that he was lying. When he had suggested she take a lover she thought he was offering himself for the role, and she surmised that his slanders against her husband were only a weird means of attaining this end by forcing her into a divorce.

Nézondet also now told Judge Berry that he had gone to the police about Petiot. Inspector Gignoux had questioned him about Madame Khaït in July 1943. At that time Nézondet had simply said that Petiot was in prison, without mentioning anything about Maurice's alleged confidences. When the Germans released Petiot in January 1944, Nézondet said he had been extremely worried and uncertain. He knew that Petiot had killed, but since Maurice had told him about German army uniforms at the rue Le Sueur, and since the Germans had released Petiot, he wildly theorized that his friend was killing German deserters with the approval of the Gestapo. But he wasn't sure. Nézondet had gone to the Police Judiciaire and told Inspector Gignoux that Petiot was now free, vaguely hoping that the police would keep an eye on him. According to Nézondet, Gignoux told him: "The Petiot affair is over; besides, we can't follow him." And another inspector in the room muttered to himself, "I wouldn't be surprised if there were thirty or forty victims in this case." All of this led Nézondet to believe the police were completely aware of what was going on. Gignoux and the other inspector denied having said any such thing and said that though Nézondet had come to tell them of Petiot's release, they had not understood the point of his visit. Curiously, immediately after telling the Police Judiciaire about Petiot, Nézondet, by his own admission, told Petiot that he had spoken to the authorities — perhaps thinking that the doctor would not dare harm him with the police in the picture. Since, as he told inspectors, he feared for his life, he and Aimée Lesage had insisted on meeting Petiot and his brother in a public café.

The investigators found Nézondet impossible to figure out. Maurice Petiot naturally denied the whole extraordinary tale, and the entire Petiot family called Nézondet a buffoon and a lunatic. "He was very upset when the Germans arrested him," Maurice explained gently, "and his mind has never completely recovered from the shock. Nézondet always used to keep me well entertained because he told a lot of amusing stories. This time I don't think he's very funny." Maurice's wife Monique recounted to police and reporters that when Nézondet lived in Lyon, he had reportedly discovered the location of a buried treasure by dowsing with a pendulum. He had bought the field under which the treasure lay, only to have his pendulum change its mind and indicate that the treasure was in an adjacent field. Rather than purchase that field, he began digging a tunnel underneath. Nézondet did not deny this story; he dryly commented: "So? That doesn't prove that I'm a buffoon."

For a week, the investigation remained at an impasse. Though the police could never prove that Maurice had truly told him of the bodies at the rue Le Sueur, Nézondet was charged with non-denunciation of a crime — an offense instituted by the Germans in October 1941 to discourage the French from concealing Resistance activity. Technically the law concerned only those who were witnesses to a crime or who learned of projected crimes, and Nézondet's lawyer argued that his client fell into neither of these categories. Nonetheless, Nézondet was to spend fourteen months in the Santé prison. The court was using any possible pretext to keep everyone connected with Petiot in custody until the maze of complicity could be untangled. Besides, Commissaire Massu assured Aimée Lesage, her lover was really much safer imprisoned by the French than at the mercy of the Germans.

4

THE ESCAPE NETWORK

THE GERMAN REPORT had presented Massu with two other key names: Fourrier and Pintard, who had been arrested for helping Petiot with his "escape network." Edmond Pintard was fifty-six years old, but the flesh had shrunk on his stooped, large frame, his teeth were broken and discolored, and he looked much older than his age. In the twenties, as a vaudeville actor, he had performed song-and-dance routines at various cabarets under the stage name of Francinet. But changing times and the war had squeezed him out, and he now earned an irregular living doing odd jobs and working as a free-lance cinema makeup man for Paramount. The rest of the time he loitered about cafés in the less desirable *quartiers* of Paris and reminisced about the old days. He responded to Massu's questioning like an indignant, wronged innocent.

"Monsieur le Commissaire, do you have any idea who you're talking to?"

"Yes, I do. Edmond Pintard, makeup artist, currently threatened with indictment for complicity."

"Complicity? Me? The great Francinet? Yes, the great Francinet, a personal friend of every music-hall director in Paris, specialist in songs for weddings and banquets. My name, Monsieur le Commissaire, was on the Morris columns in letters *that* big. If today you find me a mere makeup artist, it is because I chose to retire at the height of my glory."

"How much did Dr. Petiot give you to be his recruiting agent?"

"You dare . . ."

"I dare say that if you keep telling me the story of your life, I'm going to get very angry. We are not at the theater here, and in this file that you see here on this desk there are the names of nine people, innocent men and women, who were murdered through the diligent care of your friend Petiot. Murdered and perhaps tortured before being neatly dissected and dropped into a lime pit. I don't suppose you have ever smelled the fragrance of burning human flesh, have you? I asked how much Petiot paid you. I don't believe I heard your answer."

Pintard was quickly broken and confessed everything. As he left, he begged: "Monsieur le Commissaire, could you ask the photographers to leave me alone? The people who know me . . . I'm ashamed . . ."

"I can't do anything about it," Massu replied with a shrug. "They're only doing their job." And the photographs of Pintard that appeared in the papers, like those of Fourrier, Nézondet, Porchon, and the others, would show them leaving interrogations tired, unshaven, and frightened, giving readers the impression that Petiot was aided in his work by a band of crazed derelicts.

Raoul Fourrier, the sixty-one-year-old barber, was as short and square as Pintard was lean. The beret thrust down about his ears would have made him look comical but for his tightly clenched teeth and the terrified expression in his eyes. He was crushed in advance. Droplets of sweat ran through the deep wrinkles of his neck, his eyelids fluttered uncontrollably, he never lifted his head or raised his voice above a low monotone as he told his story. Aside from the question of money — for each witness wished to retain a vestige of pride and present himself as a patriot rather than an opportunist — Fourrier and Pintard told exactly the same tale of how they had unwittingly sent a dozen people to their deaths. Their story, as follows, was borne out in every detail by the few surviving witnesses as well as by the German dossier Robert Jodkum surreptitiously loaned to Massu.

Fourrier had known Dr. Petiot for seven years. Since the rue des Mathurins, where his barbershop was located, is near the rue Caumartin, the doctor went to Fourrier for shaves and haircuts, and in turn the barber consulted him for medical problems. In May 1941, Petiot was in the shop waiting his turn when Fourrier told a story about a team of bicycle racers who were caught when they tried to cross the demarcation line into the free zone while pretending to race.* While the other patrons laughed, Petiot quietly told Fourrier he always kept a packed suitcase near the door in case he needed to flee. He had an organization that could get people safely to South America. Fourrier asked the price. "Twenty-five thousand francs per person, false papers supplied, all costs included. If you know people who need to escape . . ."

France was divided into an occupied zone in the north and a free, or unoccupied, zone in the south until November 1942, when the Germans overran France all the way to the Mediterranean coast. The demarcation line, however, remained in effect until February 1943, and special permission to cross the line was generally given only for such emergencies as the sickness or death of a close relative. It was dangerous but comparatively easy to cross the line by using forged papers on

---

* The same tactic was successfully used for a different purpose in August 1941, when a hundred cyclists "raced" across the Belgian border carrying four tons of black-market wheat on their backs.

public routes or by sneaking across poorly guarded border areas, as Nézondet had done.

Leaving France altogether was more difficult and became virtually impossible after the autumn of 1942 without the aid of a large network with numerous refuges across the country and carefully planned relays. The refugees' prime goal was Spain, from which ships would take them to England, North Africa, or South America, but the guidance of skilled mountaineers was required to cross the Pyrenees through Andorra, and alert coastal patrols made travel from France to Spain by small boat extremely dangerous. It has been estimated that only 30 percent of those who set out for Spain ever got there, though not all of the others fell victim to German patrols. There are terrible stories of *passeurs* who charged up to a million francs for the crossing, then demanded more when they reached the most dangerous part of the mountains or even killed their charges outright for their money. An honest network's price in 1942 could go as high as fifty thousand francs, and the price rose quickly in time; thus, Marcel Petiot was offering a fairly good deal.

Fourrier mentioned the escape network to his old friend Pintard. They apparently saw an opportunity to make some easy money, since Pintard set about actively recruiting customers. At a favorite café on the rue de l'Echiquier, around the corner from Pintard's rue d'Hauteville apartment and near the major prostitution area on the rue Saint-Denis, he ran into an underworld figure named Joseph Réocreux. Réocreux, alias Iron Arm Jo, alias Jo le Boxeur, had built up an impressive résumé in his thirty-two years: prison sentences totaling five-and-a-half years for three separate thefts, a one-year sentence for pimping, which was his current means of livelihood, and revocation of his citizenship and right to travel for twenty years. He was presently sought on a 1940 assault charge, and there were four other warrants outstanding that could not be served since he was known to be under German protection in exchange for services rendered — either supplying prostitutes or information or both. He was notoriously strong and fearless, and had been known to fight and vanquish three assailants simultaneously.

Recently, Jo le Boxeur and his copain Adrien "le Basque" Estébétéguy, disguised as Gestapo officers, had pulled off several robberies in the provinces, and his popularity with the occupying forces was on the decline. Faced with a sheaf of French warrants as well as possible prosecution by the Germans for impersonating an officer, Jo le Boxeur decided it would be a good time to leave the country together with his employee and current mistress Claudia "Lulu" Chamoux, whose identity papers gave her residence as the rue l'Echiquier café. With them would go another copain, François "le Corse" Albertini, a well-known pimp with a miraculously pristine police record, and François's mistress Annette "la Poute" Basset, alias Petit. Jo le Boxeur, after hearing about the escape route, told Pintard that he was very interested in knowing more. Could he give him details? Pintard saw the chance for a tidy profit and quoted the price as F50,000 per person — exactly double the rate Petiot had quoted to the barber Fourrier. Jo agreed: it was not excessive, and he had anticipated more difficulty due to his suspicious background.

At that time, Pintard had no direct contact with Petiot, whom he knew only from Fourrier's references to "Dr. Eugène." He arranged a meeting through Fourrier, and it was at the Brasserie Molard near the Gare Saint-Lazare that Petiot met Jo le Boxeur. When Petiot learned that Fourrier and Pintard were trying to charge double his price, he furiously threatened never to deal with them again. He insisted that they were all working for a noble cause that held no place for thoughts of personal gain. Fourrier swore it would never happen again, and Pintard, in terror, apologized to a menacing Jo.

Jo le Boxeur, with good reason, did not trust Pintard, yet his friends were astonished to hear this hardened professional say that "Dr. Eugène's" eyes had made him extremely uneasy and

that despite his initial enthusiasm he was now reluctant to leave
Paris. He vacillated, and persuaded François le Corse to leave
first. They swapped mistresses, perhaps to insure honor among
thieves, and early one Sunday morning in September 1942,
François and Lulu Chamoux arrived at the rue des Mathurins
barbershop with their luggage. Around 9:00 A.M. Dr. Eugène
came to meet them, and Fourrier and Pintard watched from an
upstairs window as they walked away with their suitcases. Several times Petiot glanced furtively about to make sure they were
not being followed.

Jo le Boxeur still hesitated, and Petiot complained to Fourrier
that Jo knew too much and should be pushed into leaving.
Several weeks after the departure of François le Corse and Lulu,
Petiot gave Fourrier a letter; he wanted it returned to him as
soon as possible. Pintard showed the letter to Jo. It was from
François le Corse and said that they had arrived safely in
Argentina. Jo's confidence was now restored. He concealed
plaques of gold in the heels of his shoes, sewed F1.4 million
into the shoulder pads of his suit, loaded Annette La Poute
and another, unidentified prostitute — Mademoiselle X — with
jewels, and early one Sunday morning, they, too, departed. Several days later a puzzled Fourrier noticed Jo's gold watch on
Petiot's wrist. Oh, the doctor said, Jo had given it to him out of
gratitude — a sentiment most of Jo's friends had rarely discerned in him.

Several weeks later, Pintard passed a telegram from Jo le
Boxeur around the rue de l'Echiquier café saying that all had
gone well, and the great Francinet soon had another group eager
to make use of his agency. Adrien "le Basque" Estébéteguy was
a close friend of Jo's and boasted a similar police dossier (one
police report on him, with typical understatement, called him
"an individual of more than doubtful morality"): eight prison
sentences and seven warrants outstanding on charges including
theft, fraud, possession of firearms, and eight counts of assault —
four of them against French policemen. Most of the warrants

had never been served because Estébétéguy, too, was under Nazi protection.

Early during the Occupation, the Germans had seen the value of employing Frenchmen not only as informants but as sleuths and agents in their purchasing offices, which bought or requisitioned gold, jewels, and other valuable or useful materials to fund the war and nourish the Reich. A former criminal named Henri Chamberlin, better known under his alias Henri Lafont, was the most powerful and feared of these agents, and he had rapidly earned the position of head of the French Gestapo office at the rue Lauriston, near the Etoile. A clever man, Lafont was nonetheless initially hampered by his small-time criminal experience and lack of education, but his skill as a leader emerged when the Germans persuaded him to hire the superb organizer Pierre Bonny, who had become famous as "the greatest policeman in France" during the Stavisky affair of the thirties and was later drummed out of the force after numerous scandals.

The Lafont-Bonny gang was among the most effective weapons of the occupying forces: it was efficient, and the French were frightened and humiliated by the collaboration of their countrymen. The Germans were not particular about the methods the French sleuths used, and through dubious requisitions, outright theft, and shakedowns, Lafont's service systematically accumulated valuables, often retaining more than the 20 percent commission authorized by the Germans. To carry out his agency's specialized task, Lafont had originally formed a nucleus of twenty-seven hardened criminals the Germans released at his request from the notorious Fresnes prison. Adrien Estébétéguy was among the first.

Adrien le Basque's team was assigned to General von Behr's Service for Recuperation of Jewish Property, which requisitioned furniture, money, apartments, and land, directly turning over 80 percent of the take to the German government and 20 percent to Lafont at the rue Lauriston. This was the theory, at least; Lafont quickly discovered that Estébétéguy not only frequently denounced Frenchmen to suit his personal convenience but also had an unpleasant tendency to substitute gilded copper for confiscated gold ingots. Lafont did not mind swindling the Germans himself, but he found it rather "indelicate" (to use his own word) for one of his own men — and one who owed him his freedom at that — to perpetrate the same frauds on his benefactor. Estébétéguy was dismissed, and though he quickly transferred his allegiance to Wehrmacht Intelligence, he realized that the Gestapo was by far the more powerful service and that the loss of its protection seriously undermined his immunity from French justice.

On December 14, 1942, Estébétéguy and three cohorts disguised themselves as Gestapo officers and stole a large sum at the Hautefort farm of Emile Joulot in the Dordogne region. They announced they had come for Gilbert Saada, a young Jew from Nice staying with Joulot. Saada, they claimed, was suspected of owning a secret radio transmitter. While one of the gang guarded the two men, the others went off to find the radio; instead they took $2,300 in gold dollars, 530 louis d'or, $7,000 and F500,000 in paper money, and some of Saada's silk shirts, along with a suitcase to put them in. Taking Saada as their prisoner, they drove off in a black Citroën registered in the name of a licensed Paris prostitute named Gisèle Rossmy. Saada was released in Toulouse for a promise of F200,000, which the captors said they would return to collect in one month's time.

In addition to Estébétéguy, two of the other false policemen, Charles Lombard and Auguste Jeunet, also happened to be members in good standing of the rue Lauriston French Gestapo. Curiously, Saada, Joulot, and several others who had been in the farmhouse during the robbery formally identified the fourth robber as Joseph Réocreux, alias Jo le Boxeur, even though he

had disappeared two months earlier.* Henri Lafont, angered
that his men were still using the Gestapo for their own ends,
flew into a rage and personally reported the crime to the French
police. One can assume that he obtained full details through his
contacts, and though, for his own reasons, he disguised the name
of one of the agents in his report, he agreed that the other three
robbers were Lombard, Joseph Réocreux, and Estébétéguy, and
he told police he no longer considered them to be under his
protection.

Thus in early 1943 Adrien le Basque found himself falling
into disfavor on all sides and resolved to leave the country with
his friend Joseph Didioni Sidissé Piereschi, alias Dionisi, alias
Zé. Piereschi had spent three years of his youth in a penal colony
after committing a murder at age eighteen. He deserted from
the army twice during the First World War, breaking jail while
serving his second term. Later convicted of stealing military
supplies, of arms trafficking and of pimping, during the Occupation of France he operated brothels reserved for the Germans.
He had recently escaped from a Marseille prison, where he had
been serving five years for a daylight holdup of a train station
that netted F983,000. At forty-four, he was well known as a
pimp and had fifteen girls working for him, though his true
specialty was luring new girls into brothels and holding them in
his power. Seeking to emigrate with Estébétéguy and Piereschi
were their respective mistresses, Gisèle Rossmy and Joséphine-
Aimée Grippay. Joséphine, alias Paulette, was twenty-four and
beautiful; her dark complexion and the slant to her eyes had
earned her the nickname of Paulette la Chinoise. She had been
a professional and very high-class prostitute since she left home
— "to follow her destiny," as she had told her mother — at age
sixteen. Recently, she and Piereschi had told friends they

* Police investigators working on the Petiot case later also found evidence
that Annette Basset, who had left with Réocreux, sent her mother a money
order on November 1 — a month after her disappearance. This puzzle was
never solved.

planned to take F800,000 in savings and open a brothel in South America. When she packed her clothes now for the departure, she included a black satin evening gown with golden swallows embroidered on the bosom — the dress later found under the basement stairs at 21 rue Le Sueur.

Gisèle Rossmy had led a mixed life. At age twenty she had given birth to an illegitimate child, now fifteen and being raised in an orphanage. She subsequently found a job as a typist and stenographer, which paid well, but dreamed of the fame to be found on the stage. She quit her job and, under the stage name Gine Volna, obtained a few rôles in small theaters and cabarets, and it was in such a setting that she met Adrien le Basque, some twenty years her senior. They lived together for several years, moving from one apartment to another as the neighbors complained of the noise made by their unsavory guests. Materially she could not ask for more, since Adrien drenched her with jewels and they lived in great luxury, but he forbade her to visit her family and former friends, and when he was drunk, which was often, he mistreated her shamelessly and she would hide in the concierge's loge. She had often thought of leaving, but she could think of nowhere else to go, and when he decided to leave the country she agreed to go along. On the last Saturday of March 1943, Gisèle Rossmy had dinner with a friend who later reported that she seemed sad at the prospect of leaving Paris the next day. As Réocreux and Albertini had done before them, Estébétéguy and Piereschi each escorted the other's mistress; Paulette la Chinoise and Adrien le Basque had already gone the day before.*

Petiot told Fourrier that his group had devised a secret sign to signal safe arrival: the traveler would draw a sun surrounded by flames on a F100 note, tear the bill in half, and send one

---

*Adrien's brother Emile Estébétéguy, who also worked at the rue Lauriston and was later shot with Lafont at the end of the war, believed Lafont had known about Petiot and had sent his brother to him as a convenient means of disposing of Adrien. There is no evidence to support this, and Lafont, who generally admitted his crimes, denied it.

portion back to Petiot's escape organization. Shortly after Adrien le Basque and his three companions left, Petiot showed Fourrier half of a F100 note with a flaming sun. "They have arrived," he said. "My men got them through." Police ultimately found the other half of the bill at the rue Caumartin.

The most curious fact about these disappearances was that all the escapees who left the barbershop on the rue des Mathurins did so during the day — the nine pimps and prostitutes left at 9:00 on a Saturday or Sunday morning. Petiot did not take them to his apartment around the corner, but headed off to the west, toward the Etoile, two miles away, and the rue Le Sueur. Yet none of the neighbors on the rue Le Sueur — who remembered every truck that came and, many of them, even Madame Petiot's sole visit three years earlier — ever saw a stranger enter the house. They were willing to swear that no one had. At night there was a 10:00 curfew, and bands of people with suitcases could scarcely have walked the streets without being noticed by a German patrol. It was never learned how the victims arrived at the rue Le Sueur, if, in fact, they did.

Pintard's open soliciting at the rue de l'Echiquier café in a milieu that included informers was effective for volume traffic but not well suited to secrecy, and it was not long before the Gestapo heard about the escape organization. Early German reports indicated that agents of the Reich had little difficulty spotting Pintard and Fourrier but were completely baffled when it came to identifying the ingenious medical doctor who directed what they believed was a highly effective escape network. A Gestapo security file dated April 8, 1943, stated:

There is a great deal of talk in public about an organization which arranges clandestine crossings of the Spanish border by means of falsified Argentinian passports.

I have consequently, through a man in our confidence, learned the conditions for traveling to [South] America. A group leaves for Spain every three weeks. The interested party must pay F50,000 and provide ten photographs and his address at the first interview. Inquiries are subsequently made to determine whether the person does, in fact, live at the indicated address. It is probable that these inquiries are made by a French police inspector. Finally, the interested party is notified three or four days before the convoy's departure and must go to a place whose location is concealed until the last moment. There, he is taken in charge by a member of the organization and lodged at a hotel or in a doctor's apartment. The daily rate is F400. From this moment on, the parties are not allowed to write to or contact anyone. After several days, the subjects are taken to the train station and turned over to two other members of the organization, who give them their false passports in exchange for the F50,000. All liquid cash — particularly foreign currency — and jewels must be surrendered, and are returned only at the Spanish border. Each traveler is free to take with him as much money as he chooses.

It is assumed that this organization is directed by high French officials.

Another report, this one from Robert Jodkum's Jewish Affairs sector of the Gestapo, added:

According to my informants, the doctor in question does not deal solely with Jews, but with anyone who comes to him, and it is said that he has abetted the escape of certain suspicious persons, notably terrorists, and even army deserters.

The voyagers travel on neutral ships leaving from a port in Portugal. They are sent there by rail via Irún. . . .

The long and fastidious investigation which I have made shows that this network is organized in a remarkable fashion and takes infinite precautions to avoid crossover or communication between adjacent cells in the network's hierarchy.

It would be interesting to be able to organize a surveillance all along the railway trajectory to the frontier and discover the method of crossing the border.

Members of a foreign embassy are certainly collaborating on the furnishing of false passports. A later report will deal more specifically with this point.

Robert Jodkum resolved to crack the organization, and to do so he recruited, or rather blackmailed into service, a Jew whose credentials as an enemy of the Germans would be above all suspicion. Yvan Dreyfus was a wealthy Jew who headed a large radio and electronics importing-and-distribution company in Lyon. When the war broke out in 1939, he had returned from studies in the United States to enlist in the French army; when the Germans disbanded the French military forces in 1940, he used his company to supply the Resistance with transmitters and to repair damaged air-dropped material. The Gestapo had arrested him at Montpellier while he and nine others were trying to flee and join de Gaulle's forces in London. He was currently in prison at Compiègne awaiting deportation.

Yvan's wife Paulette did everything imaginable to force the release of her husband. Since the camp at Compiègne was the staging area for most deportations to Germany and eastern Europe, Madame Dreyfus had every reason to fear for his life. With the proper connections and the right amount of cash, however, one could often negotiate the release of prisoners who were not dangerous saboteurs. After long months spent questioning friends and acquaintances, she was put in touch with a Monsieur Dequeker, a merchant employed by the Germans as an administrator of confiscated goods. He was also a director of the Théâtre des Nouveautés.

Dequeker asked for and received F100,000 merely to have the file opened. Soon afterward he demanded an additional F700,000; he told Paulette Dreyfus that his codirector at the theater, a former lawyer named Jean Guélin, had important connections with the Gestapo, notably with Robert Jodkum, who held a high post in the very sector that was handling her husband's case. This was, in fact, a lucky break for Guélin. It was he who had first told Jodkum about the escape organization and Dr. Eugène. He had learned of it through the director of the Banque Régionale Parisienne, Marcel Chantin, who knew

Fourrier. For the past several months Guélin had been a regular customer at the rue des Mathurins barbershop, improving his appearance while picking up any tidbits he could. He had spent weeks trying to figure out the best way to insinuate a convincing agent into the organization. If worked properly, he told himself, this just might be the chance he was looking for.

Madame Dreyfus, of course, knew none of this. In late April or early May 1943 she met Guélin in front of Le Fouquet's on the Champs-Elysées and was told that the release of someone like her husband could not be obtained for less than F4 million. She managed to work the price down to F3.5 million and told Guélin to go ahead.

Guélin's first move was to send an intermediary to Dreyfus at Compiègne. The man chosen was Pierre Péhu, a former police commissioner who had been removed from his post by the Vichy régime and was presently doing secretarial work for Guélin while hoping for reinstatement. Péhu went to Compiègne one Sunday afternoon armed with the code word *pomme* — the Dreyfuses' nickname for their young daughter — to convince the prisoner that his wife was really a trusting accomplice in a plan for his release. As far as Dreyfus was told, nothing more was involved than bribery. He was willing to cooperate, but balked when Péhu produced two typed letters for him to sign. The first swore that he would do nothing further that might be detrimental to the Reich; in the second, he would expressly promise to furnish any and all useful information concerning clandestine passages of Jews out of France. Dreyfus, appalled by the suggestion that he should betray his people and country for his own freedom, refused to sign. Péhu assured him that the letters were really without importance — merely a formality so that Jodkum could, if need be, justify the release to his superiors by proving that Dreyfus had been released for services rendered to the Reich rather than in return for a bribe; unfortunate, but that was the way things worked in these hard times. Péhu as-

sured him the letters would, of course, never be used, and Dreyfus could have them back to destroy once the negotiations were
complete. Dreyfus signed.

Péhu gave the letters to Guélin, who in turn showed them to
Madame Dreyfus. She was horrified; she could not believe that
her husband would have signed them, but Guélin assured her
also that they were a meaningless formality. He mentioned,
incidentally, that he would need another F500,000 for Jodkum
and F200,000 for Péhu. This latter cost was slightly elevated
because Péhu had incurred travel expenses and had worked on
Sunday. She hesitated, but finally delivered the money to
Dequeker. Several days later, Dequeker phoned her and she
demanded to know if her husband was free. Not yet, he replied,
and furthermore they needed another F1 million — which she
obstinately worked down to F400,000. Guélin and Dequeker
realized by now that they had milked her for everything she
was willing to give. Finally, in mid-May, Guélin informed
Paulette Dreyfus that her husband had been released and was
at the rue des Saussaies Gestapo office; it was time to pay the
final installment of F3.5 million. She could come along if she
wished. She declined and simply turned over the money.

That evening Yvan and Paulette Dreyfus were reunited in a
hotel near the place de la République, and they celebrated over
dinner with Guélin and a few friends. But the freedom was only
relative: Paulette was in Paris illegally, and Guélin had not yet
returned Yvan's identity papers nor surrendered the two compromising letters. Moreover, Guélin began speaking of actually
exposing an escape organization. Once again, it would only be
to give Jodkum justification for Dreyfus's release. The escape
organization was already well known and scheduled for arrest;
thus, Guélin claimed, Dreyfus's assistance would be quite superfluous, but it would look good to the Germans. Madame Dreyfus called Dequeker, who seemed the least antipathetic of the
bunch, to beg him to leave her husband out of their plans. But
Dreyfus initially played along.

No one ever really knew why or whether Dreyfus finally agreed. Perhaps he intended to fool Guélin and actually escape through the organization he was supposed to expose, though he never mentioned this to his wife. It is true that when Guélin arranged through Fourrier to meet Dr. Eugène at the barbershop on May 15, Dreyfus would not permit Guélin to enter the dim back room while he spoke to Dr. Eugène, and Guélin got only the quickest glimpse of the mysterious network leader. Or perhaps Dreyfus did cooperate, seeing no other way out, though one can scarcely imagine that a man of indisputable courage and resourcefulness could not have found some means of escape during his several days of liberty. Or perhaps he was biding time and when he left his wife four days later on May 19 he really believed, as Guélin told Madame Dreyfus, that he was only going to the rue des Saussaies Gestapo office for his papers — though he had with him ten photographs, and Guélin had brought two of his own suitcases as props. One can scarcely doubt the courage, patriotism, and integrity of Yvan Dreyfus, but the circumstances surrounding his departure that Wednesday afternoon were so compromising and inexplicable that Pierre Véron, the lawyer the Dreyfus family later hired to present their case (and who, coincidentally, also represented the Khaïts), had little hope of persuading a post-Liberation jury that Dreyfus's murder had been anything but the justifiable execution of a French traitor.

Guélin, in any event, did not take Dreyfus to the rue des Saussaies, but to the barbershop on the rue des Mathurins. He was again denied the opportunity of meeting Dr. Eugène. Fourrier insisted that Guélin wait in his apartment while he and Dreyfus walked toward the place de la Concorde. Halfway there, reported the Germans who were following them, Fourrier turned back and Dreyfus fell in with a man fitting the description of Dr. Eugène: thirty-five to thirty-eight years old (Petiot was actually forty-six), five feet eight, thin, chestnut hair, clean-shaven, dressed in a blue suit with white stripes, nervous and habitually rubbing his hands together. The two men chatted amicably as they headed up the Champs-Elysées toward the Etoile and, incidentally, the rue Le Sueur. Halfway along the avenue, Petiot and Dreyfus neatly eluded their pursuers. Robert Jodkum was annoyed yet intrigued by the cleverness of his prey, but he had another pigeon ready to depart the following week and then, he felt sure, he would break the entire organization.

Robert Jodkum, however, was not the only Nazi intelligence official to have learned of the escape network. Herr Doktor Friedrich Berger, head of the rue de la Pompe Gestapo office — subsector IV-E3 in charge of security for the occupied territory — was equally ambitious and just as well informed, though he was more interested in simply stopping the network than in tracing its ramifications. A French acquaintance of his, Charles Beretta, was enlisted for the task. It is uncertain whether Beretta had been collaborating for some time or whether, as he claimed later when under indictment on that charge, he had truly been seeking escape, had been arrested by the Germans during a routine check, and when he mentioned Berger's name in an attempt to extricate himself, was blackmailed by his friend into following his original plan but with a new aim. In any event, it is clear that Beretta had been arrested by the Nazis and sent to Germany in June 1940, that he had returned to France with a false postal-worker's identity card, and that his wife had been arrested in April 1943 and sent to the prison camp at Drancy, in the northeastern suburbs of Paris, where she was now under threat of deportation. Assuming he really was innocent, his position under German domination would indeed have been a tenuous one: his wife's fate and his own freedom depended upon the Germans' goodwill. On the other hand, whether he was forced to participate in the Petiot affair or not, he subsequently went on to collaborate with a wild abandon rarely seen in victims of blackmail. He denounced many Jews on his own initiative and helped capture an escaped French prisoner. Moreover, he told the Germans the time and place of a secret meeting of a Resistance group at Montargis in Brittany; when German troops raided the meeting, the Frenchmen opened fire and were wiped out on the spot. Beretta carried out his present task with great efficiency, as his reports showed.

Sunday 5/16
Subject: Clandestine passages

This past Friday the 14th, as arranged, I went to Fourrier's barbershop at 25 rue des Mathurins at 11:30 A.M. The Doctor was there with Fourrier and an unknown third party.

I was asked several questions:

1. My family name, given names and address;

2. They checked my military and other papers;

3. Checked my identity card; all this to verify the truth of what I had told them.

Had I not been able to furnish proof that I am really a prisoner of war on parole from prison [this was true, and was one of the facts Berger felt made Beretta convincing as a candidate for escape], the Doctor would have canceled the deal.

All of this took place in a small isolated office at the back of the apartment, and lasted one hour and fifteen minutes.

In addition, the sum of 100,000 francs was requested. I pretended that I would not be able to raise such a sum, and we finally compromised at 60,000 francs. This amount should cover expenses for the voyage to Spain and the preparation of false papers. (False passport, etc.)

The Doctor showed me a passport, but he did not let me take it and study it closely.

I gave him ten photographs (5 full-face, 5 profile).

We were supposed to meet again that same evening at 7:00 at my home, but no one came. This morning a new appointment was made for tomorrow evening, Monday the 17th, at my house, at which time I am to pay the agreed upon 60,000 francs.

Thursday evening I will be notified to prepare 2 suitcases and a blanket, and I will be taken to a spot whose location I will know only at the last moment, and from which I will be sent on to a train station for my definitive departure.

According to the Doctor, it is at this moment that I will be given my false papers.

Beretta attached a diagram of Fourrier's apartment.

At 7:00 the next evening, Fourrier and Pintard arrived at Beretta's; he gave them only F10,000, hoping to show his precarious financial position. He said that he earned his money through the black market and that collection of debts was sometimes difficult. He promised to pay the remaining F50,000 at 7:00 the following evening. As it turned out, all of the money that Beretta paid had been furnished by the Gestapo; the serial numbers had been noted, Beretta had signed a receipt, and in each report concerning a payment, he copied down the serial numbers again. He was a fine, thorough traitor, and the Germans had no cause for complaint.

The next day Beretta paid Fourrier and "Francinet" an additional F45,000, once again claiming that difficulties with his debtors had made it impossible to come up with the whole sum. The remaining F5,000 was later handed over in a telephone booth at the Café de la Renaissance near the métro station Strasbourg-St. Denis (a map of the area was appended to his report!). During one of their conversations, the boastful Fourrier pulled a notebook out of his pocket, saying it contained the names of everyone they had sent to Spain. Seven other people, he claimed, would be traveling with Beretta when he left on Thursday.

It was Friday, May 21, two days after Yvan Dreyfus vanished, when Beretta arrived at the rue des Mathurins with a light bag containing underwear, one change of clothes, and "all the money he owned," as Dr. Eugène had instructed. An instant later, the Gestapo burst in and arrested Beretta, Fourrier, and Pintard. They forced Petiot's name and address out of the terrified Fourrier before taking them all to prison, and soon found the doctor at home at the rue Caumartin with his wife. As the Germans were searching the apartment, René Nézondet arrived to deliver tickets for that evening's performance of *Ah, la belle époque,* a musical comedy about the joys of life in 1900 playing at the music hall Bobino. Though he protested ignorance and waved the tickets in front of them, the officers pushed him and Petiot downstairs and into a waiting car. Petiot turned as he left and called, "Don't worry!" to his wife, who apparently understood nothing of what was going on until several days later, when Gestapo agents returned for a more thorough search. They told her that her husband was guilty of smuggling people out of the country — notably a Jew named Dreyfus, who had either escaped or been killed.

Herr Doktor Berger's satisfaction with the Beretta coup lasted only a few hours before he discovered he had ruined another subsector's carefully laid plans and had eliminated all possibility of tracing the entire escape organization. With profuse apologies, Berger sent his four prisoners — Petiot, Nézondet, Fourrier, and Pintard — to Robert Jodkum at the rue des Saussaies for questioning. Beretta was sent with the others as a plant, in hopes that he might learn something, but during a routine search he was unable to conceal the Gestapo card and revolver he was foolishly carrying, and the others recognized him for what he was. Guélin appeared, too, pretending to have been arrested on some obscure charge, but Petiot did not trust him any more than Beretta and treated him with quiet disdain.

Petiot was questioned and beaten all night. The next day he was driven to Fourrier's, where the Germans hoped to capture other group members when they came to collect Madame Dreyfus. Guélin had made arrangements with Fourrier and Petiot for her departure that Saturday and had even paid F50,000 of the Gestapo's money for her passage. He had not, however, brought up the matter with Paulette Dreyfus herself, and neither she nor the Resistance comrades Jodkum expected arrived.

Petiot was then returned to Jodkum's office and savagely beaten once more — by Péhu, he later affirmed. He was taken to the prison at Fresnes, seven miles south of Paris, but was almost immediately returned to the rue des Saussaies for more beatings. He confessed that he was part of an escape organization, but maintained that he knew nothing about its other members or operation, and that the actual passages were effected by a man known as Robert Martinetti, whom he had no way of contacting. Petiot was sent to the German army center for counterespionage on the avenue Henri-Martin and was there tortured for three days without a break. He was plunged into a freezing bath until he was almost drowned, his head was crushed in iron bands, his teeth were filed down three millimeters, and he was beaten so severely that he spat blood for a week and had dizzy spells for six months. The Germans showed him a dead man, and a man writhing in agony on a stretcher, his face beaten to an unrecognizable pulp; he was told they were members of his group.

Periodically over the next six months, Petiot would be taken from the Fresnes prison, where he, Fourrier, and Pintard were held, to the avenue Henri-Martin or the rue des Saussaies for questioning. Petiot repeated the same story about Robert Martinetti again and again, but steadfastly refused to supply further details. The Germans searched the rue Caumartin apartment once more, as well as 52 rue de Reuilly, the only other one of Petiot's properties they seem to have located. This was a curious oversight, since there were bills and other documents concerning 21 rue Le Sueur at Petiot's home, and a quick check in the Paris municipal archives would have given them a complete list of his properties. The Germans were thorough in everything else, and even arrested a woman Petiot had sent to a rest home on May 1, believing that this establishment — filled only with old people and women — might be part of the escape route.

Nézondet, who had loudly proclaimed his innocence and waved his theater tickets, was released from Fresnes after two weeks since there was no evidence that he was implicated in the "network." He was taken to the rue des Saussaies for final processing. When it was complete, the Germans jokingly asked whether he wanted to go straight home or return to Fresnes for a visit. Nézondet placidly said that he *would* like to go back and get his shoelaces, handkerchiefs, and tobacco. "Damned if that isn't the first time we've seen anyone ask to go back to Fresnes!" said a Gestapo man, and they gave him F100 and a pack of cigarettes and sent him home.

The Germans cautioned Nézondet to stay away from Petiot's family and apartment. Several days before leaving Fresnes, he had been momentarily left alone with his friend Petiot, who had whispered, "Tell my wife to go where she knows to go and dig up what is hidden there." Just before Nézondet's release, left alone again, Petiot told him to forget the errand — it was no longer important.

Nézondet, for some unexplained reason, decided to ignore Petiot's injunction, and one afternoon in June, as she was about to leave for Auxerre to visit Maurice and his family, Georgette Petiot received a mysterious telephone call asking her to prepare a sandwich and go to the entrance of the Gare Saint-Lazare métro station. She followed the strange instructions and to her surprise found Nézondet, who had not been fed before his release from Fresnes; while devouring the sandwich, he gave her news of her husband and passed on Petiot's original message. She said she did not understand what her husband meant, but nonetheless she mentioned it to Maurice when she arrived in Auxerre.

Georgette also told Maurice what the Germans had said to her when they searched the rue Caumartin apartment: that Marcel was suspected of having either smuggled Yvan Dreyfus out of France or murdered him. Maurice was acquainted with several members of the Dreyfus family, all of whom were in the radio business, like himself, and in a curious, rather incoherent attempt to help his brother, he wrote to Yvan Dreyfus's father.

June 17, 1943

Monsieur,

I obtained your address through the director of S.I.R., since I knew that your son was director of this firm's branch in Lyon. — My brother has been arrested by the German police in Paris, and I think it is because he helped your son.

According to what the police told my sister-in-law my brother stands accused of assassinating your son.

I can scarcely see how this is possible, since such things are not easily done in Paris, and particularly considering my brother's character — a doctor well loved by his patients, among them some people who are presently offering the most unbelievable things and even their lives to save that of my brother. And my brother has, before my eyes, during raids, sheltered Jews with their entire fortunes in his own apartment. (They were neighbors of his whom I know well: they are still living in the same building.)

Finally, my brother earned about 500,000 [francs] a year in his profession, a profession which he adored, and he did not need any money since he lived very modestly (he was even accused of being miserly).

His only expenses were for the purchase of art objects and especially of books, but he has always had this passion and has not been spending more than he spent before.

I have always known my brother to be likeable, regular in his habits, and never liable even to raise his voice in anger — nonetheless he has had periods of extreme exhaustion and depressions which he overcame with difficulty.

What's more, people say that we resemble one another closely, and your relative Camille Dreyfus (American apparatus import — rue Saulnier) can tell you who I am.

All of these reasons must lead one to believe that the accusation is false.

I can see only one way to save my brother from this serious accusation, which is that your son must be found. I have asked everyone I know, and the only response they will give is: if I knew where he is I wouldn't say.

This is why I am writing to you. If you know where your son is, tell him to change hiding places if he doesn't want to be found, and tell witnesses who have seen him since May 20 to go to the police or a government official who can take their deposition.

If he is overseas and you have letters from your son, send them to me or remove the return address and send them to the police, since I do not want to have anyone else implicated in this affair — too many people are in trouble already. . . .

Maurice wrote to other members of the Dreyfus family as well, and his strange letters were turned over to Paulette Dreyfus, who never answered them. Maurice also pursued Nézondet's message to Georgette. The only hiding place he could think of was the rue Le Sueur, and he went there in late May to investigate. He told police that he found nothing, but it was during this visit, according to Nézondet's statement to Judge Berry, that Maurice supposedly found mountains of clothing and a pile of bodies. The most recent body, Nézondet reported, the one lying on top of the mound, Maurice had recognized as that of Yvan Dreyfus. In this case, at least, one must begin to doubt Nézondet. It seems unlikely that Maurice would have written to the Dreyfus family asking the whereabouts of someone he already knew to be dead. In addition, Maurice would have recognized Dreyfus with difficulty, since the two had never met.

Petiot suffered his eight months of prison stoically. He was allowed no visitors, no mail, no tobacco, no Red Cross packages, no newspapers, clean clothes, or soap, and was poorly fed and periodically interrogated. Cellmates would later testify that his courage and spirit were incredible. He spoke to them of his Resistance organization, which he called "Fly-Tox," and indeed seemed to have intimate knowledge of Resistance operations. He had methods for smuggling messages out of the prison, and he gave his companions names of people to whom they might appeal for help in the event that they escaped. None had the chance, since they were all later sent to German labor camps, where some of them died. It was miraculous that Petiot was not shot for the evident sarcasm and loathing with which he invariably addressed the Germans, and his utter unwillingness to treat his jailors as anything but worthless enemies, even at great personal risk, was a source of amusement and inspiration to his fellow prisoners.

Finally the Germans decided to release him, but they demanded a large sum of money for his liberty. A woman Resistance member who was being questioned on charges of espionage in Jodkum's office while Petiot was there said Petiot acted proud and scornful to the German officer and said he didn't give a damn whether they released him or not — that he had terminal cancer and whatever they did to him could scarcely matter. Negotiations for his release were conducted through Maurice, who pretended his brother and he had less money than they actually did and gradually worked the release price down to F100,000.

No one involved with the Petiot case has ever quite understood the doctor's curious release by the Germans, who ordinarily preferred certainty to justice and shot people for much less than actually admitting participation in a Resistance group, as he had. Some of Petiot's opponents would later insinuate that he had agreed to work for the Gestapo, or else that he had told them the truth — that he really murdered his primarily Jewish candidates for escape — and the Gestapo were willing to tolerate a free-lance comrade who was, in his own modest way, doing some of their work for them. This is scarcely believable. On the other hand, one can suppose the Gestapo intended to keep Petiot under surveillance after releasing him, in hopes of discovering secrets he had not revealed under torture. The Germans were not particularly successful: just two months later, one of those secrets — in the form of piles of bodies — was found in the basement of Petiot's house.

When, in April 1944, Judge Berry asked Maurice Petiot about his brother's unexpected release, Maurice described the circumstances:

A policeman in the commissaire's [Jodkum's] group told me it was he who had arranged for my brother's liberation, and that there was practically nothing left in his dossier (in fact, they could not even find my brother's papers to return to me when the commissaire asked for them). This policeman added that he was disgusted by the whole thing, and that out of eight people they held at the time of my brother's arrest, only two were left . . . the others had disappeared.

Besides, even under torture my brother admitted nothing — he had spent eight months in solitary confinement [sic], and after everything he had gone through, the German commissaire did not think he could do anything more against Germany.

When I went with the money, the commissaire showed admiration for my brother, and he told me there were only two things they could do with him: convict him and deport him to the salt mines, from which he would never return, or execute him; or else free him — they could no longer just hold him in prison.

He said to me: "Your brother is sick, you will take care of him; I cannot bring myself to liquidate a man such as he. He has been deceived by his ideals, but I am giving him the chance to return to his patients, as long as he behaves himself." He said this despite the fact that during their last interview, my brother had shouted out his hatred for the German régime.

Fourrier and Pintard were released on January 11, 1944. They had told all they knew, and the Germans realized this amounted to nothing at all. Petiot himself was discharged two days later. Maurice and Georgette went to Paris and awaited him at the Hôtel Alicot on the rue de Bercy, and he accompanied them back to Auxerre for twelve days to recuperate. Georgette was surprisingly understanding and uninquisitive. Since she considered Nézondet dishonest and scheming, she did not mention his revelations about the corpses at the rue Le Sueur. She told Judge Berry:

I did not speak about it to my husband, because I did not want to reveal the shameful attitude of his friend and cause trouble between them. I simply asked my husband for an explanation of the Dreyfus case and the disappearance with which they accused him. He replied, "You can't fight a war without killing men any more than you can make an omelette without breaking eggs," and added that he had done nothing wrong, and that the best proof of this was that the Germans had let him go. With that, my complete confidence in him was restored.

Judge Berry found Georgette's blind trust in her husband uncanny considering his past, but could only conclude that she was telling the truth when she said that Marcel couldn't stand people meddling in his affairs and did not like questions; consequently, she never asked any. Throughout the investigation, despite all the facts gathered, the question of just who Petiot was remained unanswered. No image of a human personality emerged, no motive surfaced; one could scarcely even imagine simple greed or sadism in a person who seemed to exist only as an incredibly dexterous performer. Petiot had fooled the French, the Germans, the Resistants, the courts, psychiatrists, his friends, and his own wife. He had acted as a solitary enigmatic force amidst a world in which he did not participate, and which he regarded only with scorn.

5

THE WEIGHT OF THE EVIDENCE

VAN BEVER, Madame Khaït, Guschinov, Dreyfus, the nine pimps
and prostitutes — thirteen was a rather impressive number of
murder victims, but scarcely the final total. Petiot had mentioned at least three other "passages" to Fourrier, and only the
case of Guschinov, the rue Caumartin furrier, matched a previously identified victim. The objects found at the rue Le Sueur
represented a large number of people, but few of the items were
useful for purposes of identification, and those that were only
led back to known victims. The man in the photograph found
at the house was identified as Joseph "le Boxeur" Réocreux.
Sylvia Rosa, a Marseille dressmaker, recalled making the black
dress with golden swallows for a licensed prostitute named
Paulette; she easily identified Joséphine "Paulette" Grippay from
a police photograph. A small, round woman's hat with a feather
made by Suzanne Talbot in Paris, on the other hand, had been
sold to the Princess Colloredo de Mansfeld in 1934. The police
report on the hat demonstrated remarkable thoroughness, com-

ing to the plodding conclusion: "The investigation [of the hat] was not pressed further, given that the princess is alive and once lived in the building on the rue Le Sueur. Consequently she cannot be considered as one of Dr. Petiot's victims, and one may plausibly believe that she left the aforementioned hat behind when she sold the building."

Interviews with Petiot's neighbors in the rue Le Sueur provided some interesting information. Many of them claimed to have seen Petiot several times during the period when he was, in fact, in prison. At least one neighbor supplied an intriguing hint of mistaken identity. One day the previous year she had called over Dr. Petiot to give him some mistakenly delivered mail, only to realize at the last minute that it was really another man who closely resembled the doctor: Maurice Petiot, whom some of the neighbors had seen delivering the lime. They were equally certain that some time the previous summer he had come to 21 rue Le Sueur and removed a large number of suitcases. A woman who lived directly across the street was sitting in her window with her daughter during the removal, and they had counted forty-seven suitcases and trunks; she felt sure this was not the total figure, since she had noticed Maurice only after the loading began. The removal van was a battered gray truck with a side panel reading TRANSPORTS — AVENUE DAUMESNIL.

Commissaire Massu sent a special inspector to search the entire avenue Daumesnil, which stretches for more than two miles past the place de la Bastille, the Gare de Lyon, and off into the suburbs. The detective checked all garages and trucking firms in the neighborhood and inquired at the local commissariat — all without success. But in the course of his search he grew friendly with the truckers, one of whom thought he had heard that someone at the Hôtel Alicot on the nearly rue de Bercy had once asked two drivers to pick up suitcases in the sixteenth arrondissement. These drivers identified Maurice Petiot as the man who had approached them, but they had been unable to do the job and did not know who had. The owner of a garage next to the Hôtel Alicot said that the Manjeard Company had brought a load of suitcases to her garage, and that from there they had been taken to the Gare de Lyon by an Arab known as the Frizzy (he denied it). At the Gare de Lyon baggage office, records showed that on May 26, 1943, five days after the Germans arrested his brother, Maurice Petiot had dispatched forty-five suitcases, weighing a total of 683 kilograms, to Auxerre.

Confronted with this evidence, Maurice admitted having removed clothing from the house. When Georgette had given him Nézondet's strange message, he had gone to the rue Le Sueur, believing this was the only possible place where his brother could have hidden anything. He had found nothing unusual, though he was surprised, he admitted, by the large quantity of clothing. Even this could be explained by Marcel's almost irrational drive to purchase everything and anything at auction — he had once bought a lot consisting of three hundred gabardine raincoats. Maurice removed the clothes because, quite simply, he feared the Germans would take them when they searched the building, as he was sure they would. As to the present location of the suitcases, the same driver who had helped with the lime, Jean Eustache, had driven them to Courson-les-Carrières, where they were stored in the attic of Albert Neuhausen, the mysterious friend Maurice first claimed had spent the night at his rue des Lombards house in Auxerre.

Inspector Batut drove to Courson and arrested Neuhausen's wife Simone and Léone Arnoux. The latter was the former maid and mistress of Georgette Petiot's late father, and it was learned that she had made several mysterious trips between Auxerre and Courson, and had removed some items from the suitcases for herself and for Maurice's family. Albert Neuhausen was not at home — he was on a business trip in Paris, staying at the now familiar Hôtel Alicot, where he was arrested the next day and charged with accepting stolen goods and obstructing justice. The people of Courson gathered in the square across the street from the Neuhausen residence as a crew of policemen lowered forty-nine trunks and suitcases from the attic window to the sidewalk. The Gare de Lyon baggage tickets were still attached to them; police discovered that eight of the forty-five suitcases sent from Paris were missing, meaning that twelve new suitcases had been stored with the others, and the missing ones must be hidden elsewhere.

The contents of these forty-nine bags were astonishing and would have filled the shelves of a small store. Among 1,760 items the Police Judiciaire catalogued at the quai des Orfèvres headquarters in Paris were:

5	fur coats	96	collars
48	scarves	104	detachable cuffs
26	women's hats	3	nightshirts
79	dresses	9	sheets
22	sweaters	13	pillowcases
42	blouses	87	towels
29	brassieres	3	tablecloths
77	pairs of gloves	3	cultured-pearl necklaces
311	handkerchiefs	5	fingernail files
14	men's raincoats	5	pairs of eyeglasses
66	pairs of shoes	1	hatpin
28	suits	13	tram tickets
115	men's shirts		

Considering that at least Van Bever and Madame Khaït had left home without luggage, and that Petiot had told the other escapees to travel light, what were police to make of three-quarters of a ton of clothing? If such a vast collection of clothes really belonged to the dead, it obviously represented a great many victims. Nor was this all: combined with articles found at the rue Le Sueur, the rue Caumartin, and in Maurice's two houses at Auxerre, police would end up with a final tally of eighty-three suitcases, plus umbrellas, canes, and assorted other objects. The total weight of the evidence against Petiot was nearly three tons.

Léone Arnoux, Georgette's father's mistress and maid, refused to cooperate with the police. As she did not believe Dr. Petiot guilty of murder, she said, there could be no victims, and hence the contents of the suitcases were not stolen goods and she was not guilty of receiving them. She defended her right to remove articles for the use of the Petiot family. One of these items, a gaudy silk tie with Adrien Estébétéguy's initials, had been around Gérard Petiot's neck when police questioned him at his uncle's house in Auxerre. At one point Léone Arnoux said Monique Petiot, Maurice's wife, had asked her to hide the suitcases; later she said her instructions were just the opposite. Albert Neuhausen claimed to know nothing about the suitcases; Maurice had simply not wanted to keep them in his own house because he was afraid the Germans might come there, too. He had never gone near them, Neuhausen said at first, but when suspicious sheets and clothing were found in his bureau drawers, he admitted having taken a few things out to dry after melting snow leaked through the roof and damaged some of the suitcases, and he had apparently forgotten to put them back.

There was also a question about whether Georgette Petiot knew of the existence of the suitcases. Apparently, while staying at Auxerre, she had asked Maurice to stop at the rue Caumartin apartment during a trip to Paris and bring some of her clothes to her. He packed them in a suitcase that was inadvertently mixed up with those sent to Neuhausen's house. At one point Maurice and Georgette had gone to Courson to find her misplaced things, and on this point the *juge d'instruction* spent weeks interrogating Georgette, Maurice, and Madame Neuhausen — separately and together — trying to determine whether

Maurice had gone to the Neuhausen attic alone, or whether Georgette had accompanied him and consequently knew more than she cared to admit.

It soon became evident that the longer the investigation continued, the more it got bogged down in small details, getting farther and farther away from the few large, central questions. Dozens of small discrepancies arose, and though police had everyone in the case confront everyone else, all parties involved repeatedly changed positions in a bizarre ballet of facts. No two witnesses ever quite agreed on anything, and the exact roles of all the secondary participants could never be determined. While the court held him at the Santé prison, Nézondet had even tried to smuggle a letter out to his mistress, Aimée Lesage, in which he wrote: "Since I am dealing with nothing but bastards, I have made a decision. There is no reason for me to charge Maurice with anything, particularly since I'm not sure that he told me he had seen any bodies. . . . I am going to write to the judge and tell him that I exaggerated in my testimony about Maurice. That way, they won't be able to convict anyone." The letter was intercepted, and when Judge Berry confronted him with it, Nézondet calmly returned to his former position. He had simply been depressed and disgusted on the day he wrote the note, he said, and his original statement had been the absolute truth. Judge Berry began to wonder whether such a thing could exist.

The contents of the pile of suitcases should have furnished police with tangible clues about further victims, but the investigation was partly baffled by the circumstances of the Occupation. Communication with other parts of France and with foreign countries was difficult if not impossible. The clothing bore more than two dozen different laundry marks and forty-eight different sets of initials — only a handful of which corresponded to the initials of those victims ultimately identified. Judge Berry, in the desperate hope of identifying more people, sent letters to every police department in France asking them to check every laundry in their area. The results were nil. A few suits and shirts bore manufacturer's labels, and many of them were identified as having belonged to Estébétéguy, Réocreux, Piereschi, and their companions. Henri Lafont, Estébétéguy's former French Gestapo chief, voluntarily came to Police Judiciaire headquarters and identified Adrien le Basque's silk shirts. The only new lead was that several shirts and a suit were marked *Wolff* or *Made for M. Wolff*.

M. Wolff's clothes had all been made in Amsterdam, where it would be difficult to pursue an investigation. As Massu was pondering this problem, an anonymous letter arrived. These were not uncommon: ever since the discovery at the rue Le Sueur, dozens of reports had rained on police headquarters about sightings of fearsome strangers. Scores of people reported missing friends and relatives, but at a time when thousands of people, particularly Jews, vanished without a trace, these reports were difficult to follow up and were scarcely worth the trouble. This particular letter, however, seemed to merit closer scrutiny. Its author said she had known a family of Jews from Holland who had fled to Paris in August 1942. Several weeks after their arrival, they had a close brush with the Gestapo and sought to leave the country. They had met a medical doctor who said he could get them to South America. They were to convert their assets into gold and precious gems. The doctor had come to fetch them in December, and they had never been heard from again. The family consisted of "Madame W. . ." (about age sixty-three), her son "Maurice W. . ." (thirty-six), and his wife "L.W." (forty-six). The writer also suspected that "the family B. . ." — consisting of two elderly people and a couple in their twenties — had followed the same route in January 1943. Only initials were given, the letter was not signed, and the only clue was a Vincennes postmark on the envelope.

Massu informed the newspapers about the letter and asked

them to print his appeal for the anonymous author to come forward and tell the whole story; he assured the writer that her identity would be kept secret (and when she came forth it was, even from the other investigators on the case, until another witness mentioned her name). The correspondent, Ilse Gang, showed up at the quai des Orfèvres headquarters of the Police Judiciaire several days after the commissaire's appeal; between her testimony and that of Eryane Kahan, arrested six months later, Massu would be able to piece together the circumstances of nine more disappearances.

The Wolff story, one of the saddest cases, typifies the situation of Jews under the Occupation and the circumstances that facilitated Petiot's incredible plan. The Wolffs were a wealthy Jewish family from Königsberg in Germany. The patriarch, Sally Wolff, had run the Incona Lumber Company, which had branches in several major European cities. When Hitler came to power in 1933, Sally's son Moses Maurice Israel Wolff, known as Maurice, moved to France with his wife Lina. When, three years later, Sally, his wife Rachel, and their other son Heinrich moved to Amsterdam, Maurice and Lina joined them there, and after Sally died in 1940 the two brothers took over management of the company. Heinrich disappeared during the war (years later it was learned he had fled to New York), and Maurice continued running the business until it was liquidated under German occupation as a Jewish firm.

In June 1942, the German attitude toward Jews everywhere in occupied territory grew more severe. One day in June, the Germans ordered all Amsterdam Jews to report to the nearest police commissariat to register for "work in Germany." Few reported, and the following weeks and months saw mass raids and the deportation of thousands of Jews directly from the Netherlands to Auschwitz and Buchenwald. The Wolffs — Maurice, Lina, and Maurice's mother Rachel — sold all their possessions at a great loss and left Amsterdam on July 12, 1942, with an estimated F309,575 worth of valuables and cash in various currencies. Under the name Wolters they crossed the border into Belgium without difficulty. Since the French frontier posed a more serious obstacle, Rachel and Lina waited in Antwerp while Maurice tried to cross into France with the money.

Maurice Wolff was arrested at the border by French customs officials on July 23 and taken before the court at Rocroi, in the Ardennes. His court-appointed lawyer, Maître René Iung, was sympathetic, and Maurice gradually told him his whole story. Iung arranged to smuggle Rachel and Lina over the border and hid them in his house at Rocroi for nearly a month, after which the customs director concealed them in a convent near Charleville for several days before arranging their departure for Paris. Iung discreetly explained the situation to the court officials at Rocroi, and though they could not just release Maurice Wolff without arousing German suspicion, when the case came up ten days later, they sentenced him to exactly the time he had already spent in jail, forgot about the money he had, which they should have confiscated, and set him free. Wolff joined his wife and mother at the Hôtel Helvetia on the rue Tourneux, just off the avenue Daumesnil in Paris. When Maître Iung went to Paris a few weeks later to bring them their money, jewels, and original identity papers, he found them living under the name Walbert.

On September 2, 1942, the Wolffs were visiting Lina's old friend Ilse Gang in her apartment near the Etoile and were about to return to their hotel when its proprietress telephoned to say that another of her guests, a young Jewish girl, had been arrested earlier that day for not wearing the mandatory yellow star. She felt sure the Germans would now search the entire building. The Wolffs stayed at Madame Gang's for three days, then moved to the Hôtel du Danube on the rue Jacob in the Quartier Latin. On October 1, the Germans announced they would requisition that hotel on the fifth; the Wolff-Walberts moved several doors away to the Hôtel Jacob. On the fifth, it turned out that the Hôtel du Danube was requisitioned not by some innocuous administrative office, but to house personnel from the rue des Saussaies Gestapo bureau. Whenever the Gestapo moved to a new place, they carefully checked out the occupants of the adjacent buildings. The Wolffs had to flee again. As Jews who had entered France illegally, they would be deported as soon as they were found. The Wolffs asked Madame Gang if she knew of an apartment for rent, and Madame Gang in turn asked a friend of hers, a dental surgeon, who asked one of her patients, Eryane Kahan. Kahan was able to find a place in her own building at 10 rue Pasquier, a small street intersected by the rue des Mathurins.

Rudolphine "Eryane" Kahan was a fifty-year-old Rumanian Jew who looked half her age. Police were never able to determine her source of income, though Petiot would claim she had told him she "liked business better than whoring," intimating that she had experience in both. If nothing else, she was an opportunist, and when a new venture presented itself, she pursued it with vigor. The Wolffs told Eryane of their wish to leave France for Switzerland or America; she, too, she said, felt the Gestapo was after her and wanted to leave. Around November or December 1942, Eryane's physician, Dr. Louis-Théophile Saint-Pierre, a shady individual with a police record for swindling and abortion, chanced to mention to her that another of his patients had heard of an escape organization. Eryane met the patient, Robert — really a pimp named Henri Guintrand, alias Henri le Marseillais — who led her to a café near the Madeleine and introduced her to Pintard. She told him of the Walberts' wish to escape, and Pintard escorted her to the rue des Mathurins. Dr. Eugène-Petiot arrived ten minutes later. He questioned her at length about herself and the Walberts, showing particular interest in their state of mind and financial situation. During the conversation Petiot apparently learned that Fourrier and Pintard had once again quoted double his asking price; he burst into a violent rage, threatening to drop the two if they sullied a noble cause with their own petty greed again. Eryane was very impressed and quite convinced. Dr. Eugène — the only name by which she knew him — told her the Walberts could leave, but since he was unable to take more than three people at a time, and also because she was such an intelligent person and fluent in several languages, she could be of further use to the escape organization. He would prefer that she wait until a subsequent trip.

Petiot met the Walberts the next day in the apartment of Adrienne Ginas, the concierge at 10 rue Pasquier. They sat drinking tea and spoke of music and the arts. As the Wolff family's lawyer later put it, Petiot appeared to be "a man of vast culture and fine sentiments, whose magnanimity and character fully explained his devotion to the noble cause of clandestine passages." Petiot told the Wolff-Walberts they could take all the money they wished and two suitcases apiece, and that they would have to remain hidden in a Paris house for a few days before their departure. They should not carry identification papers or clothing bearing marks or labels — instructions none of them heeded, since they left carrying sheets, tablecloths, handkerchiefs, and clothing with embroidered initials or name tags. The women's jewels were sewn into the shoulders of Maurice Wolff's jacket.

One day at the end of December 1942, the Wolffs spent the afternoon with Ilse Gang. They told her about the doctor, who was coming for them that evening. Ilse Gang heard nothing further of them, though two months later a woman in dark glasses now known to be Eryane Kahan stopped at her home and asked if she would like to follow the Wolffs. She refused.

Two weeks after the Wolffs left, Dr. Eugène saw Eryane again. He said the Walberts had left safely and asked whether she knew a couple named Baston, some friends of the Walberts who were also interested in leaving. Eryane did not know them;

two weeks later, though, Madame Ginas told her that a couple named Baston had moved into the Wolffs' old apartment at 10 rue Pasquier. Petiot was apparently already in touch with them. They were nice people, Madame Ginas said. The Bastons wished to depart accompanied by four relatives from Nice.

The story of the Baston group is complex, and it took some time for the police to decide just how many of them there had been, since the six people in the group used ten different last names. All of them were German or Polish Jews who had long resided in the Netherlands and adopted the nationality of that country, though each had a set of false papers giving his birthplace as Belgium. Gilbert Baston was the general representative in the Netherlands for the French perfume company Rigaud, and though he had been known to French friends as Baston for over ten years, his real name was Basch. His wife was Marie-Anne Basch, though she also used the name Baston, as well as the two parts of her originally hyphenated maiden name, Hollander and Schonker. The relatives from Nice were Mrs. Basch-Baston's parents and her sister and brother-in-law. Chaïma Schonker, her father, used the pseudonym Stevens, while his wife Franziska used both of them, as well as her maiden name, Ehrenreich, and the pseudonym Eemans. Brother-in-law Ludwig Arnsberg, the former Netherlands representative of the French firm Jean Patou and the German company Junge and Gebhardt, used the name Anspach, while his wife Ludwika also called herself Hollander and Schepers.

The Bastons had been in Paris for some time, but they were growing increasingly worried about the German persecution of Jews. Old friends of the Wolffs, they had frantically moved with them from one hotel to another and had followed their escape plans with interest. The Stevens and Anspach couples, on the other hand, had only fled Amsterdam in August 1942, when they paid a *passeur* F1 million to smuggle them into France and across the demarcation line to Nice. Since then they had been hiding in Nice, using false names and pretending to be Catholic, while waiting for the opportunity to escape to Switzerland or South America. They dressed modestly to avoid attention, though they still possessed valuable furs, jewels, and, one assumes, a great deal of cash. They stayed at the four-star Hôtel Continental on the rue Rossini, which was largely filled with wealthy Jews in flight, but also with officers of the Italian army's intelligence service. (This curious cohabitation with the enemy was not so strange as it seems. By July 1943 fully one-fifth of the surviving Jews in France had fled to the eight southern departments held by Italian troops. Mussolini did not share or approve of Hitler's racist ideas, and though the Italians generally simply overlooked German orders on the Jewish issue, they were occasionally more active in their opposition. When a diligent Vichy prefect in the Alpes-Maritimes ordered raids on Jews, the Italian consul at Nice posted *carabinieri* in strategic positions with orders to arrest or shoot any French policemen who bothered the Jews. After the Italian armistice in September 1943, the retreating troops even took many Jews with them to protect them from the advancing German army.)

When the Stevenses and Anspachs learned from their relatives of the chance to leave France altogether, the Belgian consul in Nice put the four people in touch with Robert Malfet, a middle-aged former chauffeur who now specialized in clandestine passages. He took them to Paris in early January 1943. But when Inspector Batut began searching for traces of the four fugitives a year and a half later, he found four receipts from the Cook Travel Agency showing that the Stevenses and Anspachs had, under the names they had been using all along, gone to Paris by wagon-lit on September 26, 1942, and again on January 6, 1943; this last time they went with Malfet's help, and their destination was the rue Pasquier. What, police wondered, were they doing in Paris during their first visit? If they were so frightened, why and how did they cross the demarcation line several times? Above all, why did they buy their tickets at a travel agency and travel openly on a regular train? It made no sense at all. Nor was Robert Malfet's role very clear. When the police arrested him in 1944, they found in his Nice apartment F315,000, expensive jewelry, clothing that was not his, and fifty-five newspapers concerning the Petiot affair, which he claimed his wife was using to line the kitchen shelves. Meanwhile, six people left the rue Pasquier: the Arnsberg-Anspachs in early January 1942, the Schonker-Stevenses around January 8–10, and the Basch-Bastons a week later. None of them was seen again.

When Malfet dropped the group off he had met Eryane Kahan. She arranged to meet him again the next day at the Café Weber near the Madeleine, and as they sat over drinks she inquired about his work and connections. She, like Fourrier and Pintard, was out to recruit. She spoke of "the doctor" and the trips to South America, gave him her telephone number, and encouraged him to send people her way. He did. Robert Malfet presented three more candidates in April 1943. Michel and Marie Cadoret de l'Epinguen and their young son wished to leave the country, and they were placed in contact with Malfet through a circuitous grapevine. He presented them to Eryane Kahan, who was posing as Petiot's secretary; she told them the price would be F50,000 per person. They paid F50,000 in advance to Malfet and were given an appointment with Dr. Eugène. "I went to this appointment at the rue Pasquier and we were introduced to the doctor," Cadoret said.

The doctor gave us details about the method of passage, pointing out that we would leave when space was available and that he was helping us only as a special favor. Next, he told us that the organization required all potential travelers to remain hidden for forty-eight hours — the time necessary to prepare official documents and to fulfill the health regulations of the country where we would land.

He specified that we would have to receive injections. He also specified that the place where we would be hidden was a beauty salon near the Etoile. Finally, he advised us to take the maximum amount of money but not more than fifty kilograms of luggage.

In the course of their conversation, Madame Cadoret de l'Epinguen, herself a doctor, mentioned the difficulty of procuring pharmaceutical products in those hard times, and Petiot began a rambling discourse on certain obscure South American drugs. His manner of speaking was strange, and she noticed that his hands were covered with a thick layer of dirt — unusual for a medical man. These factors, combined with a vague mistrust of Eryane Kahan, caused the Cadorets to change their minds. They called Eryane, but before they could inform her of their resolve, she told them that Dr. Eugène had changed *his* mind and no longer wished to occupy himself with their case. Their money was returned by Malfet, and they eventually found another means of leaving the country. They did not return to Paris until 1945, and consequently knew little about the Petiot affair, which was not covered appreciably by the foreign press. One evening they chanced to dine with the friend of a friend, Maître Pierre Véron, and they recounted their abortive escape attempt via "Dr. Eugène."

"Good God," said Véron. "That was Dr. Petiot!"

6

DEPARTURES WITHOUT END

FROM JUNE 1944 to August 1945 the police identified five more missing persons who had in some way been in contact with Petiot. The last three were brought to their attention only weeks before the definitive act of accusation was drawn up — seventeen months after the rue Le Sueur discovery and only seven months before the beginning of the trial. By that time, the police were no longer really looking for new victims; the bodies and clothing yielded virtually no useful information. Had they continued to search, even more victims may have been found. Petiot would eventually be accused of twenty-seven murders; he boasted sixty-three, and the attorney general surmised there may have been as many as a hundred. Reports were never filed on nine of the twenty-seven identified victims, and there were other people Petiot had told Fourrier and Pintard he had "passed" whose descriptions fit none of the known travelers.

Nelly-Denise Bartholomeus was a young Parisian girl who sold handbags and belts at Lancel, near the place de l'Opéra.

During the 1940 Christmas season she met Jean Hotin, a farmer from Neuville-Garnier in the Seine-et-Oise, and they married on June 5, 1941, when she was twenty-six and he twenty-seven. A month after the wedding, she apparently discovered that she was several months pregnant. War deaths and a declining birth rate were ravaging the population of France, and to counteract this trend the Vichy régime had made abortion a capital offense. But Jean's father, the mayor of Neuville-Garnier and a wealthy landowner, held the family honor above the law and gave the couple money for an abortion, justifying the expense by saying the loss was the same as for a dead cow. Denise went to Paris and spent several days at the home of Madame Mallard, a midwife.

Neuville-Garnier is a small town, and suspicions arose about Denise's treatment for "pneumonia." A year later, the Hotins decided that Denise should return to Paris and procure a doctor's certificate proving that she had not had an abortion — though it is unclear just how her family intended to exhibit this document. On June 5, 1942, the first anniversary of her marriage, she climbed on the train to Paris alone, without luggage and without even a hat.

Two days later an ominously strange letter, heavily underlined, arrived postmarked from Paris.

Dear Parents,

I cannot come home this evening as planned. Having seen Madame Mallard, I learned that inquiries had been made: she will say that I was treated for pneumonia — *which is true*. If I told Mme Grédely something else it was because I was mad at you but, of course, I never had a miscarriage *because I was never pregnant*. I cannot come home for the time being (though I have done NOTHING wrong). If anyone asks you where I am, say that I am with my family in Bordeaux, and that I will return sometime soon. Don't worry, I hope everything will work out. . . .

Three weeks later she still had not returned, but another letter, also mailed in Paris, arrived for her husband.

Mon petit Jean chéri,
I am very sad about being away from you. I can't come home. I don't know when I will be able to. I am so sad. I embrace you tenderly, and I love you.

Both letters were signed "Lily," the name she was known by in her family, and appeared to be in her hand. There were no more, and she never came home.

Jean did not worry. In fact, after a surprisingly brief delay he became engaged to someone else and filed for divorce from Denise on grounds of desertion — a project his father whole-heartedly supported. Denise's parents grew concerned about her, but in response to their persistent queries the Hotins would only say, "No, she is not here," or, "Your daughter is just fine but we don't know where she is." Denise was very close to her own parents, and it was impossible that she should not write. In September, the Bartholomeuses went to the police. Nothing much was done.

In January 1943, six months after his wife's disappearance, Jean Hotin stopped at Madame Mallard's in the course of a business trip to Paris. He casually inquired whether by any chance she had seen his wife? Yes, Madame Mallard replied, she had sent her to a Dr. Petiot for treatment on June 5, 1942. Hotin went to 66 rue Caumartin. He read the sign on the door that listed office hours, which did not begin for another half hour, and since he had a train to catch, he left. Apparently he scarcely gave Denise another thought until he spoke to the police in May 1944.

The people of Neuville-Garnier were unanimous in saying that Jean's parents had always disliked Denise and that Jean had gradually come to share their point of view. Denise loved Paris, was bored in a small town, and had no desire to spend her days working in the fields. Many people believed Jean himself had murdered her and that when he finally went to the police almost two years later it was simply because a dead wife was more readily divorced than one who was only missing. Certainly his search had been unconvincing, and he had never actually reported her missing until the Petiot affair broke. Madame Mallard had died by 1944; her daughter vaguely recalled having heard Petiot's name at some time, but apart from that there was nothing to support Jean's contention that his wife had gone to see Petiot at all. It turned out, too, that the sign Hotin would have seen on Petiot's door in 1943 did not show the office hours he claimed.

At 8:30 A.M. on June 20, 1942, an unknown man telephoned Paul-Léon Braunberger, a physician, age sixty-two, at his home at 207 rue du Faubourg Saint-Denis. The caller asked Dr. Braunberger to be at the métro station Etoile at 11:00 A.M. A patient whose name could not be revealed, living on the rue Duret, urgently required medical attention. The rue Duret meets the avenue de la Grande Armée at a small open intersection formed by the joining of three streets: the rue Duret, the rue Pergolèse, and the rue Le Sueur. The caller appeared to know Braunberger, since he neither gave nor requested a description when he offered to pick him up at the meeting place and conduct him to the patient's nearby home.

Braunberger was not altogether surprised by this unusual request. He and his wife had long since sent their money and valuables to a friend in Cannes in preparation for possible flight, and a few days earlier the German authorities had notified him that, being a Jew, he would shortly be barred from his practice. In these dangerous times everyone had troubles and reasons for secrecy, and he did not question the telephone call. The doctor left shortly before the appointed hour. He went on foot, carried only his medical bag and a minimal amount of cash, and he was never seen again.

At 11:30 A.M. of the same day, an express letter was delivered to the home of Raymond Vallée, a family friend and patient of Dr. Braunberger's. Vallée immediately took it to Braunberger's wife Marguerite. It was written on the doctor's letterhead and appeared to be in his handwriting, though the terminology was uncharacteristic and the letters shaky; police graphologists would eventually surmise it had been written under constraint. "I was almost arrested and barely managed to escape," the letter read.

> Tell my wife that I am not coming home, and that she should put all her most valuable possessions in two suitcases and prepare to leave for the free zone and overseas. I will let her know where she can join me. She should say nothing to anyone, and tell my patients I was taken ill in the suburbs and could not travel.

On June 22 and 23, Madame Braunberger herself received two similar letters; they gave the same explanation and added that she should destroy the letters and be ready to leave on the following Saturday. On the twenty-fourth, Raymond Vallée received a registered letter in Braunberger's hand that said:

> My dear friend,
>   I know that your cousin, the doctor, recently purchased a house near the Bois de Boulogne in which he does not intend to live until after the war. Would you do me the great service of speaking with him and making arrangements to have all my furniture and property moved to his house. I am counting on you. Please have this done within 48 hours. Thank you.

Vallée and Madame Braunberger ignored this preposterous request. Vallée was quite puzzled. In the course of a single letter, Braunberger switched from the formal *vous* to the informal *tu*, which indicated a degree of familiarity the two men had never attained. For that matter, there was no reason why

Braunberger should have confided in Vallée at all, since it turned out that in fact Braunberger detested the man. He only visited him out of consideration for his wife, and when Vallée came to his office for treatment or consultations, Braunberger had often taken a perverse pleasure in making him wait as long as possible. But strangest of all was the mention of the house near the Bois de Boulogne. Vallée was quite certain he had never spoken to Dr. Braunberger about any such thing. Yet the house did exist; among Vallée's relatives there was only one doctor, the husband of his wife's cousin — Dr. Marcel Petiot, who had indeed purchased a building at 21 rue Le Sueur, not far from the Bois de Boulogne.

On June 30, the Braunbergers' maid picked up the telephone and an unidentified man's voice told her: "I am calling to give you news of the doctor. I passed him into the free zone; he was a bit crazy. He started doing stupid things in the métro and almost got us caught. Madame can get out of trouble on her own — I'm not going to pass her, I was too badly paid." The maid asked how the doctor was and where he had gone. "I left him en route to Spain and Portugal." She begged the caller to come and they would pay him better for his services. "Not likely. I have a letter I was supposed to bring you, but I would just as soon mail it."

The letter arrived on July 1:

Ma Chérie,
Follow the person who brings you this letter; he will tell you how to come and join me. I shall see you soon. All my love.

The handwriting was more tortured than ever, and in this letter, as in the previous ones, Marguerite noticed that her husband did not call her, as he invariably did, "Ma chère Maggie." It also seemed odd that he had repeatedly asked her to bring her valuables, when he knew as well as she that they had all been long since sent ahead to Cannes. She became even more confused on July 3, when a German soldier came to her building and asked the concierge whether a doctor fitting Braunberger's description lived there. The visit had no apparent purpose and was not repeated.

On September 12, after several months had passed and her husband had neither communicated further nor contacted their friends in Cannes, an alarmed Madame Braunberger reported her husband missing. The police did not investigate. In 1942 it was hardly worthwhile or wise to hunt for missing Jews, and to close the case the police fictitiously noted that the doctor returned home several days after the original report was filed. Petiot's name did not come up at the time, since the oblique mention of his house was merely another detail in a series of uncanny events. What connection could there be? As Madame Braunberger told police later, her husband and Petiot had met only once, at a party at Raymond Vallée's house almost ten years earlier. The two physicians had discussed cancer cures, and after they left, Braunberger told his wife he had just met either a genius or a lunatic. They had not made any effort to see one another again. At the time it did not seem suspicious, but retrospectively, after March 1944, Raymond Vallée found it peculiar that Petiot should quickly have learned of Braunberger's disappearance and inquired several times whether they had received news from him. And if Petiot had been involved in the affair, it no longer seemed so odd that Vallée should have received the first letter, since he was the only friend of Braunberger's whom Petiot knew.

The story grew even more complex the following year. In April 1943, the wife of Roger Allard, one of Braunberger's patients who had been involved in clandestine passages himself and who had even offered to help the Braunbergers if they needed it, told the doctor's cook, "I know who passed the doctor; a friend of one of my cousins told her, 'It was my father who passed Dr. Braunberger.' " Madame Braunberger telephoned Roger Allard, who said the father of the friend who had spoken to his cousin was named José or Josian; he was not personally acquainted with him and did not know his address. Some time later, Braunberger's brother met Roger's mother, Andrée Allard, and told her, "We know that it was your son who passed my brother, and you don't want to tell us where he left him."

She replied: "It was not my son, it was Josian who passed him. The doctor cried out when crossing the demarcation line and was almost caught." This was almost the exact phrase the mysterious telephone caller had used when he spoke to the maid, and Madame Braunberger and her brother-in-law were now convinced that the Allards were involved. When asked where Josian lived, Madame Allard said she believed he was a railroad employee and lived on the rue Ordener, near the freightyards at the Porte de la Chapelle. She promised to ask Roger for details.

Finally, Roger Allard told the Braunbergers that his cousin's friend's father had passed not Dr. Braunberger, but a Dr. Ascher. The subsequent police investigation the following year only served to add another layer of confusion to this twisted tale: the Allards' stories became increasingly bizarre; police eventually found, in Dr. Braunberger's own address book, a patient named Chauzan who lived at 67 rue Louis-Blanc near the Gare de l'Est. "Chauzan" sounded similar to "Josian," but investigators found that no one of either name had ever lived at that address. Nor was Chauzan or Josian found among the railroad employees, listed in the city-hall files, or inscribed on coal-ration lists. One more strange fact surfaced during the investigation. Braunberger's nurse informed the police that a man named Francinet had regularly called at the doctor's house to deliver wine, but a few months later she changed her mind and strenuously denied ever having said such a thing or heard such a name.

Aside from the mention of the doctor's house in the first letter, there was little tangible link between Braunberger and Petiot, and even less imaginable motive. After the discovery of the suitcases at Courson-les-Carrières, newspapers published relatively complete inventories of the clothes found there and in Paris. Among the items were a size-40 men's shirt, blue with white stripes, made by David, 32 avenue de l'Opéra, and a man's hat with the initials *P.B.* made by A. Berteil on the rue du Quatre-Septembre. Madame Braunberger asked to see these items and positively identified them as articles her husband had worn on the day of his disappearance. They would play a significant role in the trial.

On August 13, 1945, the French minister of justice received a letter from the American Joint Distribution Committee in New York; a Jewish refugee living in Bolivia had asked the committee to look into the whereabouts of members of his family in Paris — Kurt, Margeret, and René Kneller. The committee had written to the Knellers' landlady at 4 avenue du Général-Balfourier, but she was no longer there. Police found another inhabitant of the building, Christiane Roart, who was also René Kneller's godmother. She told them that the unfortunate family had departed with Dr. Petiot, ostensibly to flee the country. For some reason she had never reported this to the police, though she must have suspected her friends' fate after she recognized a photo of their doctor in the newspapers.

Kurt Kneller was a Jew born at Breslau in 1897 who emigrated from Germany to France on June 10, 1933. In France, he worked successively as codirector of the Cristal radio-and-home-appliance distribution firm and as technical consultant to a battery manufacturer. On December 6, 1934, he married Margeret (Greta) Lent, thirty-three, originally from Berlin, and their son René was born at Issy-les-Moulineaux on May 8 of the following year. Kneller requested French citizenship in 1937 and served honorably in the French Foreign Legion from September 1939 until the disarmament a year later. Police checked Kurt Kneller's record thoroughly. His loyalty to France seemed impeccable, and the closest he had ever come to illegal activities was once when he had overdrawn his bank account.

Since June 1941 Jews had been circumscribed from most professional posts and forbidden access to theaters, restaurants, swimming pools, cafés, racetracks, public parks, and libraries, and they were not usually permitted to own a telephone. On July 8, 1942, they were forbidden entry to department stores and most other wholesale and retail shops except between 3:00 and 4:00 P.M. — hours when most businesses were closed. Mass raids had already begun, though the Germans, hoping to arouse French antagonism as little as possible, started with immigrants rather than native French Jews and began publicity campaigns presenting them as aliens who stole food and jobs from the French. These people were stripped of their citizenship and deported as parasites on the national economy.

On Thursday, July 16, 1942, German officers came to the Knellers' apartment. Greta was visiting Mademoiselle Roart upstairs, and upon glancing down the stairwell to see who was at her door, she realized the family was in danger. When her husband returned home they left seven-year-old René with Mademoiselle Roart and went to stay with Clara Noé, a friend who lived around the corner on the rue Erlanger. The next day Kurt told Christiane Roart that his doctor was going to help them escape the country. He asked her to prepare their suitcases, which someone would fetch later that day, and to keep René until Saturday, then bring him to Madame Noé's apartment. That afternoon, a doctor whose name Mademoiselle Roart did not know but whom she later identified from mug shots as Dr. Petiot, came to her building with a handcart and an elderly man to help him. He played with René while they spoke for a few minutes, then left with two large and four small suitcases

containing the most important of the Knellers' possessions. He
wanted to remove all of the furniture as well, but the landlady
would not permit him to do this.

At 6:00 P.M. on Saturday, July 18, Mademoiselle Roart took
René to the rue Erlanger; the same evening the doctor came for
Kurt Kneller, who was to be followed the next day by his wife
and son. The doctor asked Clara Noé to walk some distance behind them as far as the Etoile to make sure they were not
shadowed. She accompanied them only about halfway and, seeing nothing suspicious, hurried home. The next morning
Madame Noé was out buying milk for René's breakfast when
the doctor returned for the mother and son; by the time she
returned home they were gone. Clara Noé was pleased to have
the Knellers out of Paris; she learned that the Gestapo visit to
the Knellers' apartment had been part of a massive two-day raid
in which 12,884 Jews had been arrested and herded into the
Vélodrome d'Hiver, where they spent three or four days
cramped in the grandstands without food before being shuttled
to the camp at Drancy and loaded into freight cars bound for
the east. Of the total 150,000 native and foreign Jews deported
from France during the war, only 3,000 adults and 5 or 6
children returned.

In the weeks that followed the Knellers' departure, Mademoiselle Roart, Madame Noé, and another friend of the Knellers'
received postcards from Greta. She said they had safely passed
the line, though her husband was sick and had almost lost his
mind. The grammar was strange and the words uncharacteristic.
The cards were signed "Marguerite," whereas Madame Kneller
had never changed to the French form and still spelled her
name "Margeret," and the handwriting was fine and spindly —
not at all like Greta Kneller's, said Madame Noé, but very similar
to newspaper photographs she later saw of Dr. Petiot's prescriptions. Mademoiselle Roart said Kurt Kneller had shirts with
his initials on them — similar to those found at the rue Le Sueur

with the letters *K.K.* removed, and she positively identified a pair of child's pajamas found in Petiot's building as those worn by René on the last night he spent at her home.

The Knellers vanished on July 18 and 19. Three weeks later, on August 8, 1942, in the Seine near Asnières, barge men discovered the head, legs, feet, vertically sectioned thorax, upper arm, and pelvis of a seven- or eight-year-old male child, along with the head, femurs, pelvis, and arms of a middle-aged woman. A man's head was found some distance away three days later. All three victims had been dead for several weeks and their remains were putrified beyond all possibility of further identification.

PART TWO

7

MARCEL PETIOT: THE DOSSIER

WHO WAS DR. MARCEL PETIOT, the "Vampire of the rue Le Sueur," "the new Bluebeard," "the second Landru," or, more simply, "the monster"? The French judicial system, unlike many others in the West, holds that the life history and previous record of an accused criminal provide an essential context within which to evaluate the case at hand. The presiding magistrate at a trial opens by presenting a brief biographical sketch of the accused, and the jury's opinion of the evidence is weighted by this knowledge. Within days of the discovery in the rue Le Sueur, the court assigned detectives to piece together Marcel Petiot's life story. They interviewed thousands of former patients and hundreds of old neighbors from the various towns where he had lived. Inspectors sifted through school, military, and professional records, court files and old newspaper accounts, and dutifully followed up all rumors and clues no matter how unlikely or bizarre. Rarely has a man been honored with such a professional team of biographers, and rarely has the picture of him that emerged been so grim.

Marcel André Henri Félix Petiot was born at 3:00 A.M. on January 17, 1897, the son of Félix Iréné Mustiole Petiot, a post and telegraph employee, age thirty, and his wife Marthe Marie Constance Joséphine Bourdon, age twenty-two. They lived at 100 rue de Paris in Auxerre, an ancient town of about thirty thousand inhabitants located one hundred miles south of Paris in the rural Burgundian department of the Yonne.

The Auxerrois have a wealth of extravagant stories about Petiot's youth, some of them true, some doubtless invented as suitable for a future killer. People assured inspectors that he developed a cruel streak at an early age. One day when he was five, while he was sitting on the kitchen floor snipping his nursemaid's tape measure into individual centimeters and storing the numbers in a matchbox, the neighbors' gray kitten strayed in. He grew fond of the cat and threw fits and almost crushed it in his embrace if anyone tried to take it from him. But despite his affection, one day the nursemaid found Marcel standing beside a tub of boiling water she had prepared for her laundry; he was dipping the kitten's hind paws in the water and beaming rapturously as it howled with pain. That night the maid let him take the cat to bed; she thought that Marcel was upset by his behavior and felt remorse. The next morning she found his hands and face covered with scratches, and the kitten was dead, suffocated in his bed. A favorite pastime of the same period was to steal young birds from their nests, poke their eyes out with a needle, and delightedly watch them hurl themselves against the bars of a cage.

His schoolmasters agreed that Marcel was extraordinarily intelligent, but strange, solitary, incorrigible, and unable to show sustained interest in his work. At age five, he could read like a child of ten. His precocity showed in other ways, as when he was caught passing obscene pictures around the classroom or making indecent proposals to a male schoolmate. At eleven, he interrupted a history class on African civilization by firing a shot into the ceiling with a revolver stolen from his father, and he spent one recess period standing a classmate against a door and throwing knives into the frame around him, with astonishing accuracy. His parents once consulted a doctor about his eccentricity and such physiological or mental abnormalities as convulsions, somnambulism, and a tendency to wet his bed and trousers between ages ten and twelve, but the medical man could only tell them that time and hope might cure what he could not.*

Petiot's mother died in 1912, when he was fifteen and his brother Maurice was five. The father accepted a job at the post office in the village of Joigny, some fifteen miles away, and his two sons stayed with their aunt Henriette Bourdon in Auxerre. Before the end of the year Marcel was thrown out of school for disciplinary reasons. He went to stay with his father at Joigny, and was thrown out of school there, too. Returning to Auxerre, he was once again thrown out of school, this time for more than mere unruly behavior and "over-excitation." Using a stick with glue on the end, Marcel, now seventeen, had stolen mail from a postbox — possibly to cash money orders, perhaps out of mere curiosity, conceivably, as was once suggested, to blackmail townsfolk who wrote of their indiscretions. He was eventually caught, and in February 1914 was charged with damaging public property and mail theft.

French courts at that time, even as now, commonly recommended psychiatric examination of accused lawbreakers, particularly when there were any unusual circumstances, such as, in this case, the youth of the offender. On March 26, 1914, a court-appointed psychiatrist found Marcel to be "an abnormal youth suffering from personal and hereditary problems which limit to

* It is interesting to note that an early psychiatric description of the psychopathic personality listed four childhood symptoms characteristic of that disorder: somnambulism, enuresis, cruelty to animals (particularly decapitation), and arson. Petiot was never accused of arson — at least not as a child — but otherwise his record was perfect.

a large degree his responsibility for his acts"; another physician concurred on May 6, adding that the only cure for what ailed Marcel would be one mainly oriented toward his "adaptation to discipline and social life." Following these diagnoses, and abetted, perhaps, by his father's intervention with the postal authorities, charges against Marcel were dropped on August 14 because, according to the court judgment, "the accused appears to be mentally ill." Félix Petiot was so upset by Marcel's repeated delinquencies and unrepentant nature that he wanted nothing further to do with his son. Petiot was sent to Dijon to complete his schooling; he finished only the first part of his *baccalauréat* examination before unspecified problems forced him to return to Auxerre, where he was once again expelled from school. Finally he received his degree from a special school in Paris on July 10, 1915.

Petiot was inducted into the Eighty-ninth Infantry Regiment in January 1916 and was sent to the front in November. He served with neither distinction nor dishonor until May 20, 1917, when, in bitter fighting in the Aisne, hand-grenade shrapnel ripped open his left foot. He was evacuated to a military clinic in the Orléans insane asylum for treatment of this injury and of a bronchial condition brought on by a poison-gas attack. His wound healed well, but he began to exhibit symptoms of mental disorder and was sent to a series of rest homes and clinics to convalesce. He returned briefly to his regiment, then was almost immediately sent back to a clinic. There he was involved in an obscure incident involving stolen blankets and was placed in the military prison at Orléans. Renewed indications of mental unbalance caused his transfer to the psychiatric unit at Fleury-les-Aubrais, in the same region, where a doctor diagnosed him as suffering from "mental disequilibrium, neurasthenia, mental depression, melancholia, obsessions and phobias," and concluded that Marcel could not be held legally responsible for his acts.

After a month of treatment and another month's convalescent leave, Petiot was returned to the front in June 1918. He had a nervous breakdown, fired a revolver at his foot, and was transferred to a depot behind the lines. In July he went into convulsions at the Dijon train station; he spent the afternoon unconscious in the railroad infirmary and was granted another three-week leave. In September, he joined the Ninety-first Infantry Regiment at Charleville as a machine gunner, but was unable to accept discipline, complained of incessant headaches, and claimed to be in constant dread of another fit. In March 1919 he spent two weeks at the psychiatric division of the Rennes military hospital, where the medical director found him the victim of neurasthenia, amnesia, mental unbalance, sleep-walking, severe depression, paranoia, and suicidal tendencies. He recommended his discharge from the army.

This recommendation was examined by the Commission de Réforme, which governs discharges and pensions. They approved, and on July 4, 1919, Petiot was released from the army with a 40 percent disability pension. The case was reviewed in September 1920 and his disability rating increased to 100 percent; the examining psychiatrist, concluding that Petiot was suffering from severe depression, suicidal tendencies, hyper-emotivity, and utter inability to perform any physical or intellectual work, recommended that the patient might be best off placed under continuous surveillance in a psychiatric hospital.

Petiot was examined again in March 1922, and immediately afterward he wrote to the Commission de Réforme that he "purely and simply refused to accept any disability pension at all so as to avoid being subjected again to what I find a more than disagreeable bit of exhibitionism." Nonetheless, he continued to receive a pension for years and underwent the disagreeable examination again in July 1923. Both of these last two reviews upheld the earlier conclusions, with the added notations that Petiot showed complete indifference about his future and had bite scars on his tongue from bimonthly epileptic seizures. Curiously, his pension was now reduced to 50 percent disability.

When in 1920 the commission psychiatrist found Petiot incapable of any work and suggested his placement in a mental hospital, Petiot was indeed already at a mental hospital, in the town of Evreux, sixty miles west of Paris in the Eure. He was not there as a patient, however, but as a medical student serving his internship and preparing a thesis on an incurable, progressive nerve degeneration called Landry's paralysis. (Some newspapers later misunderstood their informants and wrote that Petiot had written his thesis on the mass murderer Landru.) Truncated and accelerated medical programs designed for former soldiers enabled him to complete his schooling in eight months and his internship in two years; the police in 1944, unable to piece together a full set of records, suspected Petiot had accelerated his program even further through unscrupulous means. In any event, he received his degree from the Faculté de Médecine de Paris on December 15, 1921.

Petiot was proud of his new position, though his friend Nézondet believed that he wanted it only for the power it conferred: the power of healing, the power over life and death, the prestige, the control over people who gave him their trust and confided their secrets. Félix Petiot was proud, too, and wrote to the son he had banished in disgrace years before. Marcel went to see him. He listened to his father's apologies and praise, he dined with him, and when dinner was over and Félix prepared to sit down to a long talk, Marcel rudely announced that he was expected elsewhere and walked out of the house.

8

DR. PETIOT AND MR. MAYOR

ARMED WITH HIS PARIS MEDICAL DEGREE, Petiot moved to the town of Villeneuve-sur-Yonne, an old historical village on the banks of the Yonne River built in 1165 as a royal residence for King Louis VII. Villeneuve was only twenty-five miles from Petiot's native Auxerre, and with a population of forty-two hundred served only by two aging physicians, it appeared the ideal spot for an ambitious young doctor of twenty-five to set up practice. He rented a small house on the rue Carnot with three rooms and a garden, and spent several weeks distributing tracts he had printed up that announced his arrival: "Dr. Petiot is young, and only a young doctor can keep up to date on the latest methods born of a progress which marches with giant strides. This is why intelligent patients have confidence in him. Dr. Petiot treats, but does not exploit his patients." At first this boastful flier attracted only those patients already dissatisfied with the other two doctors, as well as hypochondriacs always eager for new treatments and a virgin ear, but Petiot quickly began to lure away even the more devoted patients. He was a gentleman to the ladies, paternal to the children, and a sympathetic listener to the men. While maintaining his exalted position, he nonetheless made the people of the village feel he was just one of them.

Patients without money were treated for a fraction of the cost or for free, and he was known to open his office on Sunday for those whose work prevented them from coming during the week, and to travel great distances late at night to treat sick children. His treatments were successful and his tone reassuring. He seemed able to diagnose an ailment and write the necessary prescription even before the patient had a chance to describe his symptoms: "No, don't tell me. I know all about it. You have this, this, this, and that. Take a bit of this and you will feel better in no time." More often, Petiot would persuade his patients that there was really nothing wrong with them at all. Many of his patients were flattered by the interest Petiot took in their lives. Something about him drew out their confidence, and he enjoyed hearing about their social lives, their finances, their small worries in life. A patient would sometimes realize, after being ushered to the door with a prescription in his hand, that during the entire consultation he had spoken about nothing but his life and had never mentioned his ailment.

As it turned out, Petiot was not quite so self-sacrificing as it seemed. It was learned later that he enrolled virtually all of his patients in Medical Assistance without their knowledge, so that he was reimbursed by the State for those who did not pay, and was paid twice for some who did. Although patients went to see him in ever increasing numbers, local pharmacists occasionally complained about his prescriptions, which all too frequently contained potent doses of narcotics. Once a pharmacist telephoned Petiot to correct a prescription that called for a near-lethal dose of a dangerous drug. Petiot replied that since the pharmaceutical companies and druggists watered down the products, it was only by prescribing excessive amounts that he could compensate and obtain the required dose. Another pharmacist refused to fill a prescription for a child that would have killed an adult. When he complained to the doctor, Petiot replied: "What difference does it make to you anyway? Isn't it better to do away with this kid who's not doing anything in the world but pestering its mother?" Still, not one of his patients seems to have died, and none complained.

In his private life, Petiot was taciturn and distant. The main feature of his personality seemed to be scorn: scorn for people, institutions, sickness, danger, life, and the law. Beneath his seductive charm and professional devotion, there appeared to be nothing but cold amusement and detached interest. A turbulent inner life there was, which made him nervous and tense, and sometimes plunged him into sudden despair and fits of weeping. The cause of these crises was never communicated to those around him. He did not smoke, drink, or frequent cafés, had few friends, and shared none of the simple problems, joys, and casual conversations that draw people together and form the tissue of daily life. When he did speak, his talk did not seem to emerge from amiability, but from a desire to manipulate people. "To succeed in life," he once told a friend, "one must have a fortune or a powerful position. One must want to dominate those who might cause one problems, and impose one's will on them."

A conversation with Petiot was a debate in which he always seized the upper hand. René Nézondet described him in his 1950 book about Petiot:

Logic and common sense were his personal enemies and had no place in his mind. Even when faced with firm evidence, he did not know how to give in. On the contrary; he was always prepared with ten answers to prove that you were in the most complete error. I, who had time to study the depths of his mind, I am convinced that his greatest pleasure was to play with men's minds. . . . He knew how to create doubt, even though you often suspected that he was saying the opposite of what he truly believed. He forced his way of seeing things upon you. When you asked his advice, he was never at a loose end. He invariably replied: "But it's exceedingly simple, you have only to . . ." Then he launched into endless explanations, definitions and rationalizations. He laid out a veritable encyclopedia of ideas, so simple to comprehend that ninety-nine times out of a hundred, you hadn't understood a single thing, but out of politeness or in order not to seem more ignorant than he, you did not press the matter.

Petiot lived very modestly — too modestly perhaps, villagers thought, for a man in his position. An old woman came to clean house and prepare meals. His clothes were not in the latest style except for his neckties, in which he took some pride. Besides being poorly cut, his suits were often covered with grease stains; he made his own automobile repairs and never troubled to change before burying himself in the engine or sliding under the car. His light-yellow sports car was his only luxury and also the greatest danger to the townspeople. He would drive without headlights, and over several years caused dozens of accidents; and though the car gradually lost bumpers, mudguards, paint, and all respectability, Petiot himself was, miraculously, never injured.

Mostly Petiot kept to himself when not working. He read voraciously — generally police stories and pulp literature, which he would devour at a rate of three hundred pages an hour, reading a page at a time and fixing it so firmly in his memory that he could quote long extracts of unbelievable tripe. He went out little, and then mostly at night. He could see well in the darkness, was able to pick up a pin in near-total obscurity, and often walked the streets for hours long after the lights were out and the village asleep. He seemed born of the night, it was said, and his personality changed when he plunged into his element. He was more alive, his movements supple and feline, his carriage different, his face more relaxed, his smile more frank and open. It hardly seemed that he slept at all. His peculiarities conspired to make people uneasy at the same time that they trusted him. At certain moments he overflowed with a sort of exuberant vitality that scarcely seemed to come from within him. Nézondet likened him to a man possessed.

Though his style of living was far from lavish and he scarcely needed money, Petiot displayed an acquisitive streak — a need to accumulate and possess that would grow with the years. He was a kleptomaniac, and frequently took something besides himself when he left a house after a visit. Maurice Petiot told Nézondet he always searched his brother's pockets at the door before bidding him farewell. The items the doctor stole were never very expensive or important, and the village people excused or overlooked his quirk. In later years, Petiot's wife and son surreptitiously returned stolen objects to their rightful owners and Marcel apparently never missed them. But these small thefts seemed indicative of other, still largely hidden aspects of Petiot's personality. The Mongins, from whom Petiot rented his rue Carnot house, had given him a one-year lease, and it was understood that at the end of that time he would move elsewhere and they would move back into the house. But when the lease expired, Petiot refused to leave; the couple had to evict him with a court order, and when they regained possession they discovered that he had removed a number of ornaments and pieces of their furniture and had replaced an antique stove worth F25,000 with a clever imitation. When the Mongins threatened him with a lawsuit, he pointed out that, being a certified lunatic, no court would find him legally responsible. They were convinced he had robbed them out of sheer perversity, since most of the things he had taken were of no use to him whatsoever.

Much worse suspicions were aroused several years later, in

1926. One of Petiot's patients was an aged woman, a Madame Fleury, who had a beautiful twenty-six-year-old housekeeper named Louise, or Louisette, Delaveau. When Madame Fleury made an extended visit to Paris, Louisette decided to stay behind. A few days later the people of Villeneuve were surprised to discover that Petiot had dismissed his old housekeeper and Louisette had moved in. Ostensibly she was employed only as cook and housekeeper, but soon it was common knowledge that she had also become his mistress — a surprising change for Petiot, who had never previously shown much interest in any of the women who lavished their attention on the eligible young bachelor. Soon after Louisette moved in, the house next door to the Fleury home was burglarized, and several days later the Fleury house itself was robbed and set on fire to cover the traces of the burglary — incidents significant, perhaps, in the light of later events.

For several months the communal life chez Petiot went on more happily than anyone would have suspected, and Nézondet himself noticed that Petiot seemed calm and relaxed for a change. The only problem was that Louisette seemed to be gaining weight, and gossips murmured that she was pregnant. Then on the Monday after Pentecost, in mid-May, Louisette disappeared. Several days later, while attending a funeral in the village, Petiot asked a local gendarme if the people of Villeneuve were not concerned about Louisette's departure; his manner of asking was so odd that the officer mentioned the incident to his chief. Someone then reported he had recently seen Petiot loading a large trunk into his car. A similar trunk, containing a decapitated and unidentifiable young female corpse was found floating in the river not long afterward. The brief police search for Louisette ended, however, without official suspicion seriously cast on the respectable Dr. Petiot.

René Nézondet fended off unpleasant rumors. He said he had met Petiot on the street one day. He was weeping in a state of utmost misery, bemoaning the fact that Louisette had abandoned him. Throughout lunch, Petiot stared straight ahead, his hands trembled, and he barely spoke as he seemed to search for some kind of solution to his woeful state. Suddenly he appeared to find it. He calmed down, poured himself a drink, and announced to Nézondet: "I think I will get involved in politics." Nézondet also angrily rebutted local newspaper stories that he and Petiot had been seen late one night pushing a corpse-shaped package in a handcart. He said that Petiot had an automobile and he had a van, and if they wanted to tote corpse-shaped parcels about under cover of darkness they would not do so in a wheelbarrow.

Nézondet thought Petiot was joking when he announced his intention to run for office, but several weeks later his friend's name appeared on the ballots as Socialist candidate for mayor of Villeneuve-sur-Yonne. The campaign was long, hard, and not always scrupulously honest. At his best, Petiot was an excellent speaker and actor who knew how to amuse, cajole, and seduce an audience that was already largely indebted to him for his medical services. At one performance he dragged himself painfully onto the platform with the air of a man crushed by guilt and sorrow, and said, "I confess that I am guilty of a serious crime." The crowd gasped, and waited breathlessly while he stood, head bowed, eyes moist, seemingly overcome by emotion. "I stand accused of loving the people too much. I confess: it is true."

As the campaign neared its close, the tireless Petiot seemed to be everywhere, and his tactics took on a more perfunctory tone. On the evening of a major electoral debate at the town hall, Petiot furnished a supporter with a length of copper cable and a set of detailed instructions. Petiot spoke first and had timed his speech to the minute. At 9:45 P.M., as his opponent stepped to the podium, Petiot's aide short-circuited the main power supply of Villeneuve-sur-Yonne. The town and hall were blacked out, a few small fires were started, and the opponent's speech came to a swift end. On July 25, 1926, Marcel Petiot was elected by a landslide.

Not everyone was pleased with the new mayor. Besides the small but vocal political opposition, some townspeople took umbrage at Petiot's campaign tactics and his blatant dishonesty. A Monsieur Gandy wrote to the Commission de Réforme complaining that during his campaign Petiot publicly boasted of having feigned insanity to fool the army into discharging him with a pension. The commission went back over the medical records and upheld their earlier decisions. Petiot really was sick, though as their conclusions depicted it, his sickness was curiously flexible:

The very fact mentioned by Monsieur Gandy — the alleged admission of a fraud perpetrated to obtain a pension — is but another manifestation of the subject's mentally unbalanced state. . . .

This form of mental disorder can very easily escape detection by lay persons who are inclined, as Monsieur Gandy, to attribute the same significance to the words and actions of someone mentally ill as they would to those of a perfectly normal individual.

In addition, to fully appreciate this sort of infirmity, one must take into consideration the fact that in the course of its evolution, the affliction can show rather long periods of remission which might lead lay persons to believe it has actually been cured.

As far as the degree of invalidity, the previous evaluation of the experts and the commission is equitable.

In conclusion, there is no cause to review Monsieur Petiot's pension, and the matter should be closed.

Petiot was officially established as a part-time lunatic. Conveniently, he was quite sane enough to carry on a normal political and professional life, but not always sufficiently responsible to be prosecuted for his misdemeanors. This would serve Petiot well again.

As mayor of the town, Petiot's petty offenses took on greater breadth. City funds were stolen from the town clerk's (Nézondet's) desk, and rumor accused the mayor. An ultrapatriotic band whose music and political orientation were distasteful to Petiot and his friends discovered one day that their bass drum had been stolen. A few days later Petiot founded another band and donated a similar, freshly painted drum. He complained that a stone cross at the entrance to the town cemetery — a cross eight feet high and weighing nearly twelve hundred pounds — was ugly and obstructed the hearses. One Christmas Eve he warned the police that the cross just might vanish that night. The police laughed. The next morning the cross was gone. When Petiot was questioned, he laughed: "I don't believe I have it on me. Besides, what on earth would I ever do with it?"

Dr. Eugène Duran, a physician from Villeneuve who was called as a character witness during the police investigation in 1945, would state: "Petiot, Marcel, was a politician to the depths of his soul, knowing how to flatter the people and make them love him. Nonetheless, his altruism was but an appearance, since his overriding passions were money and personal power. He was very intelligent, but had occasional mental lapses which made him seem truly abnormal. . . . He was never honest as a mayor, as a doctor, or as an individual." Former city-hall employee Léon Pinau said he had quit his job for fear of being dragged into some awful scandal by the mayor and because he could not tolerate Petiot's many thefts and innumerable exhibitions of odd behavior. Once, he said, Petiot hurled himself off the express train from Paris, which did not happen to stop in Villeneuve-sur-Yonne.

If Petiot did leap from the train, it may have been to make a point, for at the time Monsieur Pinau resigned, Petiot was trying to persuade the railroad company to schedule more stops in his town. However unorthodox his methods, Petiot did get things done. He installed a sewer system, completely renovated the elementary school, and constantly lobbied for State-funded improvements — sometimes beginning work on them before the necessary authorizations came through. An anti-Petiotist newspaper complained that Villeneuve did not really have a municipal government: it had nothing but Marcel Petiot, filling the roles of mayor, municipal council, street commissioner, commissioner of everything else, director of public works, municipal court, and representative for the canton. Nor was the newspaper far wrong. The municipal council, theoretically a balancing power, functioned merely as a rubber stamp. In 1926 Petiot decided to revive an 1881 proposal to construct a slaughterhouse. The municipal council gave its unanimous approval. The following year, after plans had been drawn and approved, Petiot abruptly changed his mind and the councillors voted thirteen to seven against it — solely, it appears, to prove their complete sympathy with the mayor's decisions and their willingness to obey his every whim. Some time later, when Petiot was in disfavor, a new municipal council unanimously voted the project in again and castigated its predecessors for a ridiculous action that simultaneously proved their unthinking allegiance to the mayor and their complete disregard for the wishes and interests of the townspeople. Petiot's rule was absolute, efficient, and highly irregular. Twenty years later, the Villeneuvians were still sharply divided among themselves. Some bemoaned the loss of the best mayor they had ever had — the only one who got things done. Others claimed with equal vehemence that he was the most unscrupulous scoundrel ever to sully their town.

Petiot himself loudly proclaimed his innocence of all crimes and irregularities. He accused nameless "political enemies," who resented his progressive Socialist stand, of resorting to slander because they had been impotent against him in an honest election. Many people believed him. Petiot seemed able to convince people of almost anything, and some credited him with hypnotic powers. Once when he was arrested for driving without headlights and led before the judge, he was so commanding that Captain Mourrot, the confused and intimidated arresting officer, who began with clear certainty of the charge, ended up by strangely testifying that Petiot's headlights had indeed been lit but that no one could see them.

On June 4, 1927, Petiot married Georgette Valentine Lablais, twenty-three, the beautiful daughter of a wealthy landowner from the nearby town of Seignelay. Monsieur Lablais, who initially opposed the marriage, was commonly known as Long Arm because of his powerful connections. From 1918 to 1936 he owned one of the most expensive restaurants in Paris — on the rue de Bourgogne, right next to the Chambre des députés (now the Assemblée Nationale) and amidst half the ministries in France — and many of the country's most influential politicians were his steady customers and friends. It was intimated that Petiot, scarcely a wild romantic, had been partly attracted to Georgette by the possibility of using her father's influence to his own benefit, since his own political ambitions did not seem limited to a small town. At first, though, the couple led a quiet existence, and their household was augmented by the birth of Gerhardt Georges Claude Félix Petiot on April 19 of the following year. Petiot never did use the influence apparently at his disposal; or perhaps he never had the opportunity.

At 8:00 P.M. on March 11, 1930 — fourteen years almost to the hour before the rue Le Sueur discovery — an incident erupted that was to trouble Villeneuve for many years. Armand Debauve, the director of the local dairy cooperative, returned home that evening to find his house on fire. He raised an alarm and smashed into the kitchen, where he stumbled over the body of his wife Henriette. She was carried outside and artificial respiration was begun before someone noticed that one side of her head had been completely smashed by blows with a heavy instrument. As firemen extinguished the blaze and police examined the grounds, Marcel and Georgette Petiot drove by. They stopped for a few moments, but to the great indignation of spectators who believed the mayor's and a doctor's place was at the scene of the tragedy, they continued on to a movie theater in nearby Sens, where other patrons noted Petiot's unusually nervous and distracted air.

The great depth of the wounds and the area over which blood had spattered testified to the viciousness of the assault on Madame Debauve. The killer had poured gasoline around the house and set it alight in a poor attempt to conceal the crime. Recent footprints led from the dairy across marshy fields, along the river, and toward the town of Villeneuve, confirming the suspicion that the killer was someone from the town. Only someone who knew the terrain well could have negotiated the path in the dark. It was obvious, too, that the criminal knew that Armand Debauve went to a café every evening and did not return home until 7:30 or 7:45. The heat of the fire had stopped the kitchen clock at 7:13.

The murderer also seemed to know that on the second Wednesday of every month the Debauves made payment for the milk they had collected from neighboring regions. That day would have been March 12, meaning that on the evening of the crime an entire month's take, F235,000, would be in the house. The murderer had not found the money, which was hidden under a kitchen counter; instead he had tried to force open a safe in the bedroom with an engraving tool taken from the dairy toolshed. Police found the tool buried in the folds of an eiderdown quilt where the killer apparently laid it while he searched a closet. He took F20,000 from the closet, leaving three distinct bloody fingerprints on a cardboard box during his search. The only other objects missing were a hammer and a wallet containing several hundred francs. The hammer, which perfectly fit Madame Debauve's skull wounds, was subsequently found in a small stream the killer had crossed in his flight. By the time it was discovered, the hammer was so covered with rust and slime that it was impossible to lift any fingerprints or detect traces of blood.

In a town of forty-two hundred inhabitants, it was frightening to know that a neighbor was the author of such a brutal crime. There were dozens of denunciations: anonymous messages composed of cut and pasted newsprint, a groundless accusation of his former mistress by a jealous man whom she in turn accused, muttered stories about mysterious strangers glimpsed lurking in the trees by the river, and speculations such as those about a local café owner, Léon Fiscot, who suddenly paid long-standing debts the day after the crime. The twenty-one employees of the dairy were fingerprinted, as were most others whom popular opinion accused, but no solid leads turned up. A series of newspaper articles in *Le Petit Régional* made snide comments about the inefficiency of the police, cast aspersions on the character of Madame Debauve, described in intimate detail the nature of the wounds made by each blow, and concluded with the observation that the crime would doubtless remain unsolved, as had the Fleury theft and arson, several other burglaries, and the disappearance of Louisette Delaveau. People were offended by the ironic tone of the articles. An inspector helping to investigate Petiot's past read them in 1945 and was sufficiently impressed to make inquiries at the newspaper's offices. The anonymous author of the articles, it turned out, had been Dr. Marcel Petiot. It seemed surprising that Petiot could have known all the details of the wounds, since they had never been made public and the man who had been coroner at that time never cared for Petiot and would not have been likely to discuss the case with him.

Some weeks after the crime, Monsieur Fiscot, who had himself been a suspect, was heard to say that he had seen Dr. Petiot near the Debauve house at the time the murder was committed and that he intended to speak with the Brigade Mobile of Dijon, which had taken charge of the investigation. There were already vague rumors that the forty-five-year-old Madame Debauve had been young Dr. Petiot's mistress. Fiscot suffered from rheumatism. One afternoon he met Dr. Petiot, who sympathized with the man's misery and said he had just received a miraculous new drug from Paris that did wonders for just that ailment. Fiscot let himself be led to Petiot's office, where the doctor gave him an injection. Three hours later, Fiscot was dead. This struck some as an odd coincidence, but it was established that Fiscot had died of an aneurism. By another odd coincidence, the doctor who determined the cause of death, signed the certificate, and authorized burial was also Marcel Petiot.

A month after his wife's death, Armand Debauve went to the police. He informed them that a Maurice Parigot had told him that a Victor Tissandier had told *him* that Petiot knew who had murdered Madame Debauve. The Villeneuve gendarme who received this information, Urbain Couraux, was reluctant to question the mayor or to involve himself in the affair in any way. He reasoned, and wrote in his report, that "since Messieurs Tissandier and Petiot have not deemed it opportune to confide their information to the local gendarmerie, it is obvious that they prefer to deal directly with the Police Mobile. . . . We thus think it prudent not to approach Messieurs Parigot, Tissandier and Petiot and risk disclosing their revelations prematurely." It is difficult to imagine how the information could be spread about if it was heard only by Couraux, but the gendarme chose not to press the matter. Instead he sent a letter to the regional commissaire in Dijon outlining the situation. What action resulted will never be known. In 1944 the Paris police tried to locate the Debauve dossier but were unable to find it; they were immediately suspicious that Petiot, as mayor, had contrived to spirit it away. Subsequently the folder was found; it had been filed not under *D*, for Debauve, as they expected, but under *M*, for murder. The last item in the file was Gendarme Couraux's report. Certainly the Brigade Mobile must have investigated, but their results are not there. In any event, by the time the dossier arrived in Paris on April 5, 1946, Petiot's trial had just ended and by then no one particularly cared whether he had murdered one person more or less.°

At the time of the Debauve affair, Petiot was involved in another legal matter, a less serious one than murder, but one that would have more definite consequences. On January 29, 1930, the Tribunal de Première Instance in Sens, a local court dealing with minor offenses, sentenced him to three months in prison and a F200 fine for attempted fraud. About a year earlier, in December 1928, the police had investigated a report that Petiot had stolen some tins of oil from the Villeneuve-sur-Yonne railroad-station platform. As it turned out, Petiot had ordered the oil for himself from a firm in Issoudun, and it had been duly sent. The trucker charged with taking the cans from the station to Petiot's house, however, did not like Petiot (he was a political enemy, the mayor later claimed) and left them sitting on the platform for nearly a week. Petiot seized an opportunity when the baggagemaster was absent to pick up his order himself. This was irregular, but not altogether illegal, except for the fact that Petiot subsequently claimed he had never received the oil at all and demanded reimbursement of the money he had already paid.

The court did not find the crime a serious one, but felt obliged

---

°Apparently the Paris police did not try to compare the fingerprints in the Debauve dossier with Petiot's. At the author's request, William H. Kelly, Temple University criminalistics instructor and former fingerprint expert for the Philadelphia police, did compare copies of the two sets of prints. Both sets are fairly clear, and could be used for identification, but whereas the Police Judiciaire's file card on Petiot shows first-joint, or fingertip, prints, those left in blood at the scene of the Debauve murder were made by the second joint of the fingers, and there is very little overlap for comparison. Both sets show similar loop-type patterns on the right index, middle, and ring fingers, but there are not enough common points to conclude with any confidence that the prints either do or do not match. Had someone been curious in 1946, he could have taken a set of second-joint fingerprints from Petiot and solved this mystery.

to be particularly severe since it had been committed by the town's mayor and chief representative of administrative order. Petiot, finding that the evidence against him was too strong to be denied, may have resorted to his tactic of pleading temporary insanity: one can scarcely imagine that the court would spontaneously have ordered a psychiatric examination in such an unimportant and obvious case. The appointed psychiatrist concluded that Petiot had not been in a "demented state" at the time the crime was committed, but that for some unspecified reason his responsibility could be considered as "attenuated." Though Petiot's guilt was clear and he was found guilty, this medical opinion persuaded the court to suspend the prison sentence.

On February 6, 1930, as a result of Petiot's conviction, the departmental prefect suspended him from his mayoral duties for one month. This was the harshest penalty a prefect was entitled to impose, but he petitioned the president of the Republic to increase this suspension to three months. Minister of the Interior Pierre Laval authorized the extension a week later. Petiot, however, appealed the original case, and on April 16 the Appeals Court reversed the earlier conviction, concluding that there was insufficient proof that the oil had ever been delivered to the Villeneuve station or, if it had, that Petiot had taken it. Petiot's certified mental state also contributed to the court's justification for acquittal, a seemingly superfluous point in light of its stand on the evidence. Mayor Petiot resumed office.

During the next year the prefect heard various complaints about the mayor of Villeneuve-sur-Yonne. Irregularities in Medical Assistance applications and payments, the disappearance of city-hall property, peculiar purchasing orders for scholastic material, and the mysterious evaporation of gasoline that ran the town's water pump were but a few. They were absurdly small complaints for the most part, but what they lacked in quality was made up in quantity. Then in mid-July 1931, in the course of a routine audit, the departmental auditor from Auxerre found gross improprieties in the town records. The prefect was informed and the affair was turned over to the public prosecutor to determine whether there was cause for criminal proceedings.

The inspectors charged with the investigation found several additional irregularities, notably concerning 138 alien-registration applications and F2,890 in related fees that had been held at the city hall for several years rather than forwarded to the appropriate authorities. The consequence was that a number of resident aliens found themselves without the identity papers so necessary in France. The prosecutor decided that there had been negligence, but nothing serious enough to merit criminal prosecution. The prefect was not content, however, and on August 26 he and the auditor went to question Petiot. The mayor denied all knowledge of the matter; he laid the blame on his secretary and provocatively added that if either the foreigners or the public treasury took action against him, he was completely covered and would simply refer them to his insurance agent. The secretary totally supported Petiot, insisting that the mayor knew nothing about the matter in question and that if he himself had made any mistakes, it was because he was old, ill, and overworked.

Petiot accused the prefecture of political compromise and "permanent hostility" toward himself, and claimed he was now forced to defend "my tranquillity, my honor and my life," though it is hard to see how the latter was endangered. In an indignant letter to the prefect in Auxerre, he wrote:

Monsieur le Préfet,

I can no longer resist the pleasure of handing you my resignation. I am not well known at the Préfecture, and you obviously take me for a man against whom one can do anything with impunity. You will see by the present letter that the reality is nothing of the sort. When things go too far, I, too, know how to protest.

The prefect was unimpressed by such juvenile sword-rattling, particularly since Petiot could "no longer resist the pleasure" of resigning on August 27, and the prefect had suspended him from office on the evening of the twenty-sixth. Again, the prefect was entitled to inflict only a one-month suspension. This time he asked the president of the Republic for Petiot's definitive removal from office. Once more, it was the soon-to-be-infamous Minister of the Interior Laval who answered in the president's stead. Petiot's removal was finalized on September 9.

The municipal council of Villeneuve met on the last day of August and unanimously decided to resign in sympathy with the mayor. The proceedings of their meeting were published in a "weekly" bulletin, "Les Amis de la Constitution," which, in fact, appeared solely on this occasion. The council repeated Petiot's charges of obstructionism and hostility on the part of the prefecture, and pointed out that the constitution gave the voters the right to evaluate and choose their officials. For the prefect to override the will of the people was nothing short of dictatorship.

According to law, when the municipal council resigns in a community of fewer than thirty-five thousand inhabitants, a three-member delegation must be appointed to serve for two months, after which new elections must be held. One of the first duties of the delegation in this case was to check records and insure that the city hall was in order. They found that the files were a mess and the accounting slovenly; there were unusually large expenses for books and office supplies and irregular gasoline allotments, and a number of bills bore corrections and erasures, or had been crossed out and written over in Petiot's own hand. Major public-works projects had been undertaken without the necessary approvals and supervision, and the money for them frequently passed from hand to hand in a dizzying fashion that seemed, now and then, to lead back to the mayor. The provisional delegation asked the prefect and treasurer to investigate these irregularities, but it would seem that no action was taken, since in May 1932, Maître Henri Guttin, the most bitter anti-Petiotist among the three delegates, again brought the matter up with the prefect and public prosecutor.

French elections are held in two rounds one week apart; the dates for the 1931 mayoral election to replace Petiot were set for November 15 and 22. One of the prime candidates was Henri Guttin, who wished to remain in office after the dissolution of the provisional delegation and undo the evil he felt Petiot had wrought on the community. The main issue in his platform seems to have been a strong personal attack on Petiot. Among other charges he pointed out that a search of Petiot's secretary's house had uncovered a duplicating machine stolen from the city hall, which, adding insult to injury, had been used to print the single issue of the municipal council's "weekly" bulletin. He was joined vociferously by much of the press, which raked up mountains of scandal about Petiot and insisted that, contrary to the ex-mayor's claims, prefects do not go about impeaching small-town mayors on mere whim.

The other chief candidate for mayor was Dr. Marcel Petiot. The fact that he had been thrown out of office in no way prevented him from running for the same post a mere two months later. The electoral campaign was all the more heated for its brevity, and during the entire week before the election Petiot reportedly did not sleep at all. People who had never previously taken an interest in politics were drawn into the impassioned battle, and the town found itself sharply divided. Once again, Petiot overwhelmed Villeneuve with his speeches, and he was more seductive than ever as he enumerated the great improvements he had made in the town. Slowly he convinced many voters that he was, in reality, the victim of a vicious campaign: he was a Socialist, and his efficiency embarrassed corrupt politicians. It is testimony to Petiot's extraordinary personality that he could persuade people of his innocence in the face of repeated and almost irrefutable proof against him. Maître Guttin and several others complained to the telephone company about leaks of official conversations with the gendarmerie; Petiot, far from denying it, publicly boasted in one campaign speech that he had an efficient private police force at his disposal that "kept him posted on everything that happened in the community, and particularly of all the telephone conversations concerning him."

In the November 15 preliminary election, Guttin was defeated, leaving the field to Petiot, five of his sympathizers, and a single member of the opposition. The campaign grew more feverish yet in the week before the second round, which would determine the winner. On November 22, in an abrupt voting reversal, Dr. Eugène Duran, Petiot's medical and political competitor, won a resounding victory. Petiot may have been disappointed, but he did not act like a defeated candidate. Being mayor was not his only ambition, nor was it the only office for which he had run. A month earlier, on October 18, 1931, he had been elected the youngest of the thirty-four general councillors serving the entire Yonne — a position comparable to congressman in the United States. He had received 1,054 votes to his opponent's 810, and out of the eight communes voting, he had lost, by a small margin, in only one — and that the farthest from Villeneuve. In his own town, he had won by 528 to 467.

As a general councillor, wrote Pierre Manière, a recent prefect of the Yonne who studied the case, Petiot gave the impression of a man "dynamic, conscientious, attentive to all departmental problems and particularly to those concerning his electors. [He presented] a sympathetic and reassuring image — one that he maintained throughout his participation in the departmental assembly and that hardly led one to suspect any hidden Machiavellianism in his character." He relentlessly pursued programs of public safety and convenience, and was meticulous in carrying out the committee work assigned to him. In his role as general councillor, there was not a single reproach leveled against him, and given his industry, ambition, and ability to persuade, people felt he could have become a minister had he wanted.

If his new position did not show the same irregularities as the old, Petiot had in no way totally reformed. Soon after his election, he was accused of stealing electricity. As mayor of Villeneuve, one of Petiot's duties had been the supervision of the power system. In exchange for this duty, he was provided with electricity free of charge. On September 9, 1931, the date of his official revocation as mayor, Petiot announced that he was giving up his rights to free power and asked that an individual electric meter be installed in his home. He did not, however, wait for power-company employees to make the installation, but instead performed the work himself, and did it in a defective and dangerous way. A Monsieur Mouret, the director of the electric company, consequently decided to inspect the meter on June 18, 1932. He was not allowed to enter the house. The same thing happened on June 27, so on June 30 he sent a registered letter of complaint, which Dr. Petiot refused to accept. On July 15, Mouret obtained a court order stating that unless company inspectors were allowed to enter the building within forty-eight hours, the power would be turned off. Petiot responded with a series of letters to the prefect; he disputed the validity of Mouret's appointment as director and claimed that the whole incident was further evidence of his persecution by political enemies. Since he still would not admit the inspectors, his electricity, according to Mouret, was shut off at 1:00 P.M. on July 19. Petiot claimed this was not true — his power had been turned off on July 4, well before the court order was even obtained.

Neighbors were surprised to see lights in the supposedly powerless Petiot house and to hear the radio playing. Complaints were lodged, and on July 26 and 27, Maître Guttin, Petiot's old foe, decided to find out what was going on. Guttin's tactics, if not evidence that Petiot did have rabid political enemies, at least indicate the peculiarity of politics in Villeneuve-sur-Yonne in that era. On the twenty-sixth, Guttin arranged with Mouret to have the power to several houses in Petiot's neighborhood turned off at 9:00 A.M. Guttin climbed to the attic of a building that faced Petiot's house and watched to see whether Petiot's lights went off at the same time or whether Petiot had his own generator. Guttin thought a light in the back remained on, but could not be sure that it was not a reflection from an adjacent building. The next morning the same performance was repeated while Guttin and two witnesses stationed themselves down the street. This time he claimed he distinctly saw an electric light going off and on. Later that evening, a company inspector discovered a wire running from the main power line to Petiot's attic window. A few days later, another wire appeared in front of Petiot's house running to the lines on the rue Carnot. Criminal charges were filed on August 20, 1932.

Petiot fought the case for all he was worth. "He protests," wrote a prosecutor later, "he denies, he becomes indignant, he refuses to answer, he paints himself as a victim, he portrays himself as the object of vicious, suspicious and scurrilous political attacks, he qualifies as idiotic the testimony of expert witnesses, he sidesteps the questions, he changes the subject. After the hearing, while the case was under deliberation, he did not hesitate to approach the magistrate who was sitting in judgment." Petiot spoke plausibly, as long as the facts could not contradict him and he could manufacture the ones he chose. "I questioned him," said the assistant prefect who began the investigation, "I spoke with him, and at the end of an hour I was convinced of his perfect innocence. Two days later, I had ironclad proof of his guilt."

The court, finally, was not deceived. The evidence was overwhelming. The judge found Petiot's explanations "pure fantasy" and his two defense witnesses vague, uneasy, and suspicious. On July 19, 1933, Petiot was sentenced to fifteen days in prison and a F300 fine. Petiot appealed to the Cour d'Appel de Paris — the highest appeal court in the country — where the case lingered for more than a year. On July 26, 1934, the earlier conviction was upheld, though the jail sentence was suspended and the fine reduced to F100. "I've been convicted," Petiot said, "but that doesn't prove that I'm guilty."

As a result of his conviction, Petiot temporarily lost his right to vote, and since according to French law a person without voting rights is not entitled to hold an elected post, Petiot was officially removed from office as general councillor on October 17. Certain of his fate well before the administrative details were complete, Petiot repeated his earlier performance and addressed a letter to the departmental assembly on October 10: "I have the regret to inform you that my current professional obligations and my absence from the department no longer permit me to fulfill my duties as General Councillor. In consequence, I would ask you to accept my resignation as of this day." In fact, Petiot had not fulfilled his duties for some time; in January 1933 he and his family had moved to Paris, and he had not attended any assemblies for an entire year. Nonetheless, several years later, when it suited his convenience, Petiot would still list among his current occupations "General Councillor of the Yonne."

9

THE DOCTOR IN PARIS

THE PETIOT FAMILY moved into an apartment at 66 rue Caumartin in the Saint-Lazare district of Paris. Located next to the Printemps and Galeries Lafayette department stores, the neighborhood was a busy commercial district during the day, while at night it was deserted except for the busy café life around the Gare Saint-Lazare. The doctor passed several months without working while he rallied a new clientele. The tract he printed and personally placed in every mailbox in the *quartier* was far more extravagant than the one he had circulated at Villeneuve-sur-Yonne. He boasted of many credentials, real and imaginary, and even played on the fact that accents in French are often not placed over capital letters, to advertise his experience as an *INTERNE* (an intern) at a mental hospital where he had, in reality, been an *interné* (a patient). He offered painless childbirths and drug cures, mysterious nonanesthetic pain relief that helped sciatica, rheumatism, neuralgia, ulcers, and cancer pain. With X rays, ultraviolet rays, infrared rays, electrotherapy, ionization therapy, diathermy, aerotherapy, surgery, artificial fevers, and a host of other techniques, he claimed he could remove, relieve, and generally cure fungi, red spots, goiter, tattoos, scars, tumors either benign or malignant, arteriosclerosis, anemia, obesity, diabetes, cardiac and renal deficiencies, arthritis, nervous depression, senility, colds, pneumonia, emphysema, asthma, tuberculosis, appendicitis, ulcers, syphilis, bone diseases, ailments of the heart, liver, and stomach, and even plain fatigue. He mounted a huge brass plaque outside his building listing so many improbable credentials that another doctor in the area complained to the medical association and he was forced to take it down.

However preposterous his claims may have been, Petiot once again attracted, retained, and pleased a huge clientele and gained a reputation for selfless devotion. He would ride his bicycle fifteen miles in the night to treat a poor patient in the suburbs, and his wife claimed that if she hadn't done his accounting for him he would never have billed anyone at all. When in 1944 the police interviewed two thousand of Petiot's former patients they heard nothing but praise about him, and as late as 1960 a gynecologist who took an office in Petiot's old building and received several dozen former patients was told how wonderful Petiot had been to them. It was impossible, they said, that such a fine man and doctor could ever have committed a crime. But apparently police did not hear out everyone, for occasionally there were complaints. Rumor had it that Petiot performed abortions and that under guise of furnishing drug cures he was actually supplying drugs to addicts. In 1935, Madame Anna Coquille lodged a complaint with the police about the mysterious death of her daughter, Raymonde Hanss, age thirty, who had gone to Petiot the previous year to have an abscess in her mouth lanced. She had not regained consciousness after the anesthetic was administered; Petiot had driven her home, where she died several hours later. Madame Coquille requested an autopsy. The coroner found the circumstances suspicious and refused to authorize burial until a thorough investigation had been made, but although significant quantities of morphine were found in the body, the case was dismissed. Madame Coquille tried to reopen it in 1942, but after so many years the court was unwilling to hear witnesses and upheld the earlier ruling.

Nor was this Petiot's only involvement with narcotics before the Gaul and Baudet cases in 1942. On July 30, 1935, he was investigated for infraction of the narcotics laws. There were several other police inquiries, and Petiot himself claimed that, during one of them, he had offered to denounce a narcotics dealer who had come to see him in exchange for having the charges dropped. No firm evidence was found in any case, and far from being the subject of lingering suspicions, Petiot was able, in 1936, to apply successfully for the position of *médecin d'etat-civil* for the ninth arrondissement of Paris, which gave him certain minor administrative duties, a degree of prestige, and entitled him to sign death certificates. It would seem that Petiot used even this position for unscrupulous ends. In December 1942, when called to attest to the decease of a prominent attorney, he was suspected of removing F74,000 from the drawers of the lawyer's desk while the bereaved widow was absent from the room.

In 1936 Petiot ran into more serious difficulties. At 12:30 P.M. on April 4, a store detective at the Joseph Gibert bookstore on the boulevard Saint-Michel noticed a man pick up a book from the outside racks, slip it under his arm, and stroll off. The detective accosted the man, who produced papers in the name of Dr. Marcel Petiot, feigned surprise at finding the book under his arm, and insisted he must have taken it in a moment of absentmindedness. He offered to pay for the book, an elementary text on electricity and mechanics worth only twenty-five francs, and hoped the store could forget the whole thing. The detective,

René Cotteret, said he would just as soon they take a little stroll to the nearest police station and he firmly held the doctor's arm. At that point, Petiot threatened to "bash his face in," grabbed Cotteret by the necktie and throat, and began to strangle him; he then broke loose and fled three blocks, where he disappeared into the Odéon métro station.

Cotteret lodged a complaint for theft and assault at the commissariat de police. The commissaire telephoned the rue Caumartin apartment designated on the papers Petiot had produced, and a man's voice told him Dr. Petiot was not there and had been out of town for several weeks. The commissariat in Petiot's *quartier* was asked to make inquiries, and Petiot himself opened the door when two policemen arrived and requested him to appear at the commissariat at 3:00 on April 6. At 4:00 P.M. on that day, Petiot, claiming he was too upset and confused to answer questions lucidly, arrived bearing a letter he said would explain everything. Sobbing, he begged the commissaire not to tell his wife and mentioned that he had suffered from depression and spent time in mental hospitals. He said he was disgusted with life and would rather commit suicide than spend more time in an asylum.

If the police found Petiot's manner strange, they found his letter even more so. On the day of the so-called theft, the letter related, Petiot was wandering in the Quartier Latin, exhausted, depressed, and obsessed with the problem of what sort of pumping mechanism to use to attain an alternating positive pressure and suction in a machine intended to cure chronic constipation. He included an elaborate description and diagram, and to prove he was an inventor offered receipts from medical-equipment suppliers and mentioned that he had recently invented a perpetual-motion machine "based on a very simple principle and which will run until the end of time." Engrossed in this problem, he may inadvertently have picked up the book, though he had no intention of buying and certainly none of stealing it, since he had already leafed through it and found it useless for his purpose. Insisting that he had offered to pay and had willingly given his name ("and if I hadn't given it, you never would have found me"), he denied the assault charge and said he had refused to go to the commissariat simply because there had been no crime, he had nothing to say, and because his wife and eight-year-old son had been waiting for him to take them to the train station and he was already late when stopped. A few days after presenting this strange letter, he was questioned in person at home. He repeated the same story, showed police inspectors his army discharge papers to prove his mental abnormality, and added that he had been suffering from migraine on the day of the "alleged" theft.

The commissaire found Petiot's behavior peculiar — even dangerous, in a man responsible for people's lives — and he ordered a psychiatric examination before deciding what legal course to pursue. The appointed psychiatrist, Dr. Ceillier, found Petiot agitated, anxious, depressed, weeping, sobbing, and constitutionally unbalanced. He reviewed the army records, commented on the impossible inventions of constipation cures and perpetual-motion machines, and expressed concern over Petiot's letterhead, which looked like alphabet soup and was little more meaningful. Dr. Ceillier and his colleagues found their subject "dangerous to himself and to others" according to the 1838 formula,* and since Petiot refused to enter a hospital of his own free will, he recommended forcible internment in a psychiatric institution. Consequently, René Cotteret dropped the

---

* France's Law of 1838, one of the earliest legal attempts to humanize the situation of the mental patient, required the opinions of two psychiatrists, the authorization of a government official, and periodic reports from a mental hospital to institute and maintain the forcible internment of a patient. One of the law's main purposes was to avoid the prevalent abuse of internment such as by parents wishing to rid themselves of promiscuous or boisterous children by declaring them insane. It also contained a set of conditions for such legal internment — chief among them that the person must be medically diagnosed as dangerous to himself, to society, or both.

assault charge, and Petiot was found not guilty of shoplifting by reason of insanity.

Georgette Petiot arranged to have her husband interned not at a regular state mental hospital, the usual procedure in such cases, but at the Maison de Santé d'Ivry, a private sanatorium on the grounds of an old estate just outside Paris run by Dr. Achille Delmas. Delmas was a notoriously easygoing psychiatrist. A decade later, for example, the poets Roger Gilbert-Lecomte and Antonin Artaud were placed there by friends because of Delmas's willingness to give supervised doses of narcotics to incurable drug addicts without trying to cure them. Petiot may have thought Delmas would be an easy dupe. The court acquiesced in the choice, but insisted that state-appointed doctors from outside the clinic must periodically examine the patient and evaluate his progress.

As soon as Petiot was officially interned on August 1 and the police charges had been dropped, he demanded his release and persuaded Dr. Delmas that, if he had ever been suffering from a disorder, it was temporary and had now disappeared. Delmas was convinced. He had initially diagnosed Petiot as cyclothymic, an old term for someone suffering from a form of mild manic-depressive psychosis, but rest and daily hydrotherapy seemed to have banished his few abnormalities, so Delmas petitioned the court for Petiot's release. On August 18, only two weeks after Petiot's admission to the hospital, the court psychiatrist, Dr. Rogues de Fursac, found the patient calm, lucid, and free from delirium; on September 2, he stated that though Petiot was "chronically unbalanced," he was not presently delirious, depressed, overly excited, or conspicuously abnormal in any way, and recommended his release.

Several months passed; Petiot was not released and he soon began to fire a barrage of letters at the judge, the procureur de la République, and even the president of France complaining of his unjust and inhumane treatment. The court appointed three well-known psychiatrists — Drs. Claude, Laignel-Lavastine, and Génil-Perrin — to examine the patient. They were instructed to recommend either further hospitalization or immediate release.

"When one compares Dr. Petiot's various statements with each other," their report began, "and examines his version of objective facts, one finds obscurities and contradictions leading to strong doubts as to his good faith at any point during this affair." They went on to note that although Petiot had pointedly told the police and the court that his army hospitalizations had been for psychiatric reasons, as soon as his internment was a certainty, he had denied it all, claiming to have been treated for suspected syphilis in nonpsychiatric military wards that just happened to be located in mental hospitals. Speaking to the psychiatrists, he maintained that he had never had troubles with the law previously, despite firm evidence to the contrary. When asked about the death of his patient Raymonde Hanss, he replied — in a mocking tone that offended the panel — that the girl had killed herself by stupidly taking ten times the prescribed dose of her medication and that her mother was a nasty German who had accused him out of spite. The psychiatrists did not like Petiot, did not believe him, and strongly suspected he had feigned insanity to obtain his acquittal. "But in our present report," they concluded,

it is not our job to shed light on these obscure matters. . . . The aim of the preceding exposition was to present the true nature of Petiot, who is an individual without scruples and devoid of all moral sensibility. . . . This picture of an amoral and unbalanced person corresponds closely to that depicted by Dr. Rogues de Fursac who, in August-September 1936, deemed that Petiot was no more or less sick, no different than he had been throughout his life, and, we might add, from what he shall be for the rest of it. . . .

At present, though, we are simply presented with a hospitalized subject, and we are required to evaluate his current state to determine whether he exhibits mental disorders necessitating the continuation of his internment. As did Dr. Rogues de Fursac, we find that he does not. Petiot is free from delirium, hallucinations, mental confusion, intellectual disability, and pathological excitation or depression. In consequence, he does not fall within the limits of the Law of 1838 and should be released.

Petiot, they knew, was far from insane, and they had no wish to keep him. What irritated them was that he had used a transparent ruse to elude justice. It was too late to do anything about his acquittal now, but they took the unusual step of adding a warning in hopes of preventing such a thing from happening again.

, . . it is in the public interest that we draw attention to his very peculiar situation, and point out that in the event of a future criminal indictment, the present internment should not weigh excessively in the deliberations of whatever panel of experts may be assigned to evaluate him. Such panel should go back to the beginning and examine in detail the question of Petiot's criminal responsibility.

Perhaps Petiot was told of this warning, which was placed in his permanent police dossier, for he never used the same tactic again. For the moment it did not matter much, and on February 20, 1937, after seven months in the hospital, Petiot was again a free man.

For the next several years Petiot was on his best behavior — at least he was not caught doing anything wrong except for cheating on his income taxes. The legal results of this fraud were negligible, but Petiot's attitude toward it was interesting. For years he reported less than one-tenth of his earnings. In 1938, with an average annual income of F300,000–F500,000, he declared only F29,700. From this he deducted F16,600 as office expenses, leaving a mere F13,100 — scarcely more than his annual rent at 66 rue Caumartin.

The controller finally noticed this trend and fined Petiot

F25,000 for fraud. Petiot defended himself with embarrassing fervor. He claimed that his returns were accurate. Business was terrible, he wrote to the controller, even though he worked incessantly. He made house calls on foot. He had not taken a vacation or bought a new suit in three years. He was so poor that he had not smoked or entered a café in five years, and didn't even have a bedroom to sleep in (he had several). He said he was ashamed to admit that he supported his family only through loans from his family, his in-laws, and friends, and even so had to insist that his wife and son spend vacations with relatives in order to cut expenses. His income had suffered further when he was hospitalized for eight months (which, of course, he was — though not during that tax year), and he constantly dreaded the next catastrophe, which would wipe him out.

The controller did not relent, and the fine had to be paid. Petiot seethed with anger, but he was fortunate that the controller's office did not make an investigation. Even six years later, Judge Berry was able to piece together Petiot's true 1938 financial status. Petiot owned several houses and properties in and out of Paris, though most of them were purchased in his son's name (as the rue Le Sueur house would be). He bought and sold small fortunes' worth of jewelry at the Paris auction house. Investigators even suspected that some of Maurice Petiot's large purchases were made with his brother's money. Whatever the total, the doctor's income clearly seemed greater even than F300,000–F500,000 per year. Where it came from, no one has ever found out, but Petiot was certainly not particular about his methods. A few years later he would resort to wholesale murder, and despite psychiatric and criminal records that strongly hinted at danger, no one managed to stop him until it was much too late.

Number 21 rue Le Sueur
(Photo Lapi-Viollet)

The stove at the
rue Le Sueur
(Photo Lapi-Viollet)

Number 66 rue Caumartin, residence of the Petiots, where thousands of curious Parisians milled in the street during a police search (Photo Lapi-Viollet)

Commissaire Georges Massu (right)
inspecting the lime pit at 21 rue Le Sueur
(Photo Lapi-Viollet)

*Gravediggers sift the
lime through sieves and
pack the remains in
plain wooden coffins
(Photo Lapi-Viollet)*

*Georgette Petiot with Maître René
Floriot (Photo Lapi-Viollet)*

The 1944 arrest of
Raoul Fourrier (center)
(Photo Lapi-Viollet)

Edmond Pintard
and his lawyer
(Photo Lapi-Viollet)

René Nézondet after
his arrest in connection
with the murders
(Photo Lapi-Viollet)

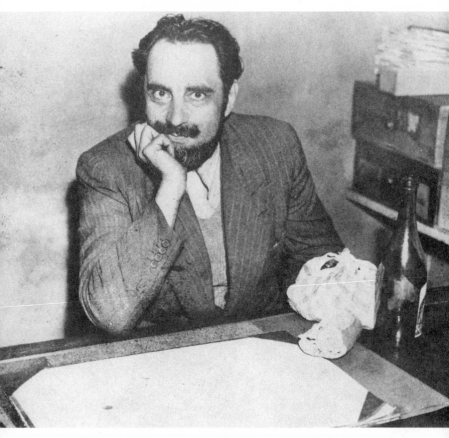

Dr. Marcel Petiot, alias Captain Henri Valéri, as he looked when arrested on October 31, 1944 (Wide World Photos)

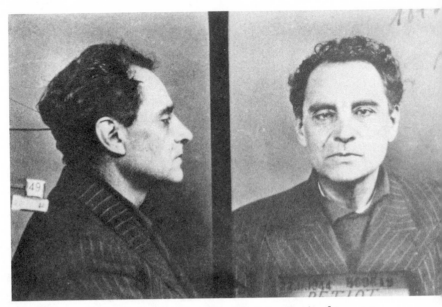

*Police Judiciaire mug shot of Petiot soon after his arrest
(Photo courtesy Archives de la Ville de Paris)*

Maître Pierre Véron (Wide World Photos)

Dr. Petiot on trial (Photo Keystone)

The president of the tribunal, Michel Leser (at center, holding documents)
(Photo AGIP — Robert Cohen)

Maurice Petiot (standing, at left) *and René Nézondet on the stand*
(Photo AGIP — Robert Cohen)

Paulette (Madame Yvan) Dreyfus
(Photo Keystone)

Eryane Kahan testifying
(Photo AGIP — Robert
Cohen)

Petiot and Floriot doze during the trial (Wide World Photos)

Maître Paul Cousin (holding femur) *and other lawyers pose with bones while the court inspects 21 rue Le Sueur (Wide World Photos)*

Petiot at the moment he was sentenced to death (Wide World Photos)

The guillotine after Petiot's execution. Bloodstains and water cover the pavement (Wide World Photos)

"Maître, my friend, if anyone publishes something on my case after my death, ask them to include photographs of the people I have been accused of killing. Then, perhaps, one day they will be found, and my innocence can be proved."

— DR. MARCEL PETIOT

Jean-Marc Van Bever

Marthe Khaït

Joachim Guschinov

(Photos of victims courtesy Archives de la Ville de Paris)

Joseph "Jo le Boxeur" Réocreux

Claudia "Lulu" Chamoux

Annette "la Poute" Basset

Adrien "le Basque" Estébétéguy

Gisèle Rossmy

Joséphine Grippay
"Paulette la Chinoise"

Joseph "Zé" Piereschi

Yvan Dreyfus

Lina Wolff

Gilbert Basch

Denise Hotin

Dr. Paul Braunberger

Kurt and young René Kneller

Margeret and René Kneller

10

THE ARREST

By April 1944, ten suspects in *l'affaire Petiot* were in prison: Maurice and Georgette Petiot, Fourrier, Pintard, Porchon, Nézondet, Malfet, Monsieur and Madame Albert Neuhausen, and Léone Arnoux. Charges against them ranged from murder and conspiracy for Maurice and Malfet down to receiving stolen goods. Curiously, while Maurice, Nézondet, and Neuhausen were held for over a year, Georgette, Fourrier, Pintard, and Malfet were released with the others after four or five months. Ultimately all charges against the "conspirators" were dropped. The prosecutor concluded that although Pintard, Fourrier, and the other procurors had played revolting roles and had accepted money under guise of patriotism, they appeared to have been ignorant of Petiot's real activities. He signed the release for Maurice and Georgette with mixed feelings, consoling himself with the thought that "even if Justice can do nothing against them, the name that they bear and whose sad reputation affects them personally, may serve as a constant source of shame unless Petiot's amoral numbness has conquered them as well." The decision to release Maurice, who quite obviously knew much more than he cared to admit, was probably partly due to the fact that he was found to have terminal cancer (he would die not long after his brother's trial). Above all, as the case against Petiot grew more complex, the prosecutor saw that trying to juggle ten incidental charges of complicity would only turn the trial into a circus and weaken his case against the one central figure.

Meanwhile, where was Dr. Petiot? As the weeks and months went by, the police gained fairly thorough knowledge of who Petiot was and just what he had done, but the man himself had vanished without a trace when he hopped on his bicycle and rode away from the rue Le Sueur. The reported sightings inevitable following any well-publicized crime began pouring in. An occultist wrote that Petiot had escaped to Morocco via Marseille; another insisted that he was alive and living in the Neuilly section of Paris, at either number 4 or 20 boulevard Jukermann or else 2 or 4 rue de Chartres. Still another occultist said he lay dead on a country road in the Yonne. The police checked all of these leads, not because they believed them, but out of fear of looking ridiculous should they prove correct. People reported seeing Petiot all over France. It was simultaneously reported that he had been arrested at the Spanish and the Belgian borders, and that he had been seen boarding a ship for South America. A tip from a town in northwestern France led police to a stock of contraband tobacco, but not to Petiot. Papers were found at Nantes with the name Marcel Petiot and a rue Le Sueur address, but these proved to concern another Marcel Petiot, a cinematographer who had briefly lived at number 18. Among the rue Le Sueur mail forwarded to Massu were a coded letter —

NE FINMXVCREI RSWV NI 15 PSXIOFTI C 14 LGYTIU – XKIPW – VSK TSIV

RAVILO

— which could have been a message from one of Petiot's Resistance comrades or a ruse by Petiot to make one believe that it was; and a morbidly humorous notice from a fire-insurance company warning the owner of 21 rue Le Sueur that a F1,063.50 premium had not yet been paid. Several more "missing persons" were also identified as victims, but most of them subsequently returned from vacation and were surprised to find themselves listed among the dead.

By the end of April 1944, Petiot was no longer front-page news. Every few days the newspapers published the results of Judge Berry's latest interrogation or an updated list of victims, but there was not much else to report. On June 6 the Allies landed in Normandy, and from then on the Nazi-controlled press spoke of little but the shattering Allied defeats. The Germans were victorious everywhere, they said, yet each day the Allies paradoxically retreated from a point a little bit closer to Paris. On August 19, with General Jacques Leclerc's French Second Armored Division still miles from the city, the Paris police went on strike and held the Préfecture against German tank attacks. The Resistance set up barricades and engaged in bloody street-fighting against the better-equipped but disorganized German troops. The city was surrendered to the French army on August 25.

As the war moved east toward Germany, the purge began in France. Pétain, Laval, and the Vichy government, French Gestapists and collaborators of all kinds were hunted down. The collaborationist press had disappeared on August 18, and the new newspapers, many of them former clandestine publications, printed lists of collaborators and announced imminent purges: next week begins the purge of factory workers; the week after, the purge of writers; police, the following week; and so forth. The French historian Robert Aron estimates that more than 125,000 civilians were legally tried for collaboration, 120,000 functionaries and officers purged, dozens of thousands arrested and held for weeks or months, then released without trial, and dozens of thousands more marked for life by accusations neither proved nor dismissed. At least 30,000–40,000 Frenchmen were summarily tried and executed by vigilance committees that sometimes broadened their criteria to include personal vendettas and business competition. Chaos reigned in a country with 500,000 dead, 1.5 million homes destroyed, and 3 million people returning from prison and labor camps. Finally, in 1945, the government decided that the unabated lust for vengeance was hurting the reconstruction of France; it disbanded the official anticollaborationist offices and sealed, until 1995, the records on collaborators who had not yet been tried.

In a sense, the spirit of the purge almost led to Petiot's capture. On June 24, a man named Charles Rolland reportedly presented himself at Massu's office and told the commissaire an incredible story. In November or December 1937, Rolland said, he had been in Marseille, where he met a prostitute who asked if, for F100, he would be willing to make love to her in front of one of her clients. Rolland did it, and he later talked with the voyeur, who identified himself as Dr. Marcel Petiot. Since Rolland was in difficult financial straits, his new friend the doctor helped him out by initiating him into the drug traffic. Petiot would meet Rolland at the Cintra-Bodega Bar and give him a packet of cocaine. Rolland would take it to the American Bar, hide it on top of the toilet tank in the men's room, and signal to a waiting customer. The customer, sidling out of the toilet, slipped the money to Petiot, who was sidling in. These dealings lasted three weeks, until Rolland reported to Tunisia for his military service. He returned in October 1939, chanced upon Petiot again, and briefly resumed his old job of pushing drugs in Marseille bars. Petiot was only passing through Marseille at the time, and when he left he gave Rolland his Paris address at, as the latter told Massu, 21 or 23 rue Le Sueur.

In early 1940, Rolland said, he went to Paris and decided to look up Petiot. He went to 23 rue Le Sueur, which he meticulously described to Massu. Petiot told Rolland never to come to his house again and promised to write to him care of general delivery at the rue Legendre post office if he required his services. Shortly afterward, Petiot did contact him, and Rolland recommenced the cocaine sales in a café on the place de l'Opéra. Subsequently Rolland was arrested for another crime; he did not see Petiot again until he returned to the rue Le Sueur in January 1943, at which time the doctor said he did not want to work with him anymore and ushered him out quickly. But Rolland ran across Petiot in Marseille in late February of that year. In the course of their conversation, Petiot claimed he possessed an infallible aphrodisiac, in suppository form, which he had successfully used on more than sixty women. Petiot also mentioned that he had joined the Parti Populaire Français, a French collaborationist political and military group known to work with the Germans to fight against Resistants. Rolland said he had later heard that Petiot, dressed in a German uniform, had left on March 7 for Pont-Saint-Esprit, near Avignon, to engage in "anti-terrorist" activities.

Neither Massu nor any other police officer took this extraordinary statement seriously. They could prove that Petiot had been in Paris on most of the dates when Rolland presumably saw him in Marseille, and he was preparing to liquidate Adrien le Basque and his friends when he supposedly marched off in uniform. Petiot had ostensibly given Rolland the rue Le Sueur address almost two years before he bought the house, and the building in which Rolland claimed to have met Petiot in 1940 (still a year before its purchase) differed from 21 rue Le Sueur in every possible detail. Among other errors, he said it was in the fifteenth arrondissement, that it was a corner building, that there was a concierge, and that Petiot lived in an apartment there. He even had the house number wrong. A real mythomaniac could have woven a more convincing tale by using facts from the newspapers. This, combined with the ludicrous extravagance of the story and the fact that Rolland was never called at the trial or confronted with Petiot, made some people suspect that Charles Rolland never existed at all, and that Commissaire Massu had composed the entire story himself in the hope that it would provoke the proud Dr. Petiot into doing something foolish. Not inconsistent with this theory is the additional fact that Massu took the strange step of turning over Rolland's complete deposition, and no other, to Jacques Yonnet, a journalist for *Résistance*, a major daily newspaper. Yonnet published it on September 19, 1944, under the heading "Petiot, Soldier of the Reich," and prefaced it with the remark that he assumed no responsibility for the truth of its contents.

The ruse, if such it was, succeeded. Several days later a letter was given to *Résistance* via Petiot's lawyer, René Floriot, which the newspaper published on October 18. The letter explained in detail Petiot's Resistance activity, claimed Rolland existed only in some policeman's sick imagination, and ended with these noble words:

The author of these lines, far from having committed dishonorable acts, far from having forgiven his torturers and even farther from having aided them, adopted a new pseudonym immediately after his release by the Germans [in January 1944] and asked for a more active role in the Resistance so that he could avenge the hundreds and thousands of Frenchmen killed and tortured by the Nazis. He remained in contact with his friends, and fought for the Liberation to the best of his abilities despite the constant fear of arrest. He is still doing all he can for the cause, and begs your pardon if he cannot take the time to get involved in polemics on this matter. Having lost everything but his life, he is selflessly risking even that under an assumed name, scarcely hoping that pens and tongues finally freed from their shackles will now tell a truth so easy to guess, and forget the filthy kraut lies that it takes about two grains of good French common sense to see through.

[signed] PETIOT

The police were elated. Certain oblique references and the rapidity of his reply made them suspect that he was still in Paris and probably serving in the French Forces of the Interior (FFI). In a mass effort, with the help of military security, they decided to compare the handwriting in the letter with samples from thousands of FFI officers in Paris. Meanwhile they asked several well-placed army officers to keep an eye out among their men for someone matching Petiot's description. Among those assigned to this task was Captain Henri Valéri, in charge of counterespionage and interrogations at the army base in the Reuilly section of Paris.

This tactic did not have the chance to succeed. On October 31, 1944, a Captain Simonin and three other military officers went to the métro station Saint-Mandé-Tourelles, just outside the eastern city limits, at 7:00 A.M. and loitered there inconspicuously for more than three hours. At 10:15, Dr. Petiot, alias Henri Valéri, entered the station and walked toward the platform. One of Captain Simonin's men asked him the time. As he raised his arm to look at the late Joseph Réocreux's watch, handcuffs were slapped on his wrist. A violent kick sent him to the ground, and the four men pounced on him and bound his feet, then carried him out to a waiting car. Simonin conducted the first interrogation before turning him over to military security, which in turn sent him to Police Judiciaire headquarters. It was only later that people began to wonder how Simonin had identified Petiot, why he had arrested him without telling any of his superiors, and why he had conducted the interrogation — something he had no reason or right to do. When they thought of this, it was too late. Simonin had disappeared and would never be found. Soon afterward police learned that his real name was Soutif, and that he was a notorious collaborator who had been responsible for hundreds of deportations and the execution of dozens of patriots.

11

CAPTAIN HENRI VALÉRI

THE PETIOT CASE had been the major news story for months
after it broke, and now that the manhunt had reached a conclusion, few people were interested. The fact that the Occupied
press had used it to boost circulation, and that the Germans had
apparently favored it as a harmless diversion for the French
people, was now a prime reason to shun it. At a time when self-
righteousness was the order of the day, when Resistants were
glorified, collaborators legally or illegally purged, and when
everyone who had simply "managed to get by" during the
Occupation dredged his memory for some small action he could
boast as an example of his Resistance activity, Petiot was not a
particularly popular topic, and the newspapers treated him
cursorily or with disdain. The former underground publication
Combat, which had become a daily paper after the Liberation,
scarcely mentioned Petiot's capture at all except to point out
that it did not intend to give it further coverage:

Doctor Petiot, whom the Occupation press, for its own reasons of strategic necessity, rendered inordinately famous, was arrested yesterday and turned over to the Police Judiciaire. His first declarations depict him, too, as a hero of the Resistance. . . . We believe we have fulfilled our journalistic obligations by relaying this news without commentary. We will do the same each day, but we refuse to glorify an affair which is repugnant from so many points of view. Too many tragic or urgent problems demand our attention for us to permit ourselves to go into the scandalous details of sensational news items.

After the first few days following Petiot's capture, neither *Combat* nor any other paper continued to "do the same each day" in reporting on his case. There were no stupendous new developments, and there was not much to report. For nearly a year and a half, until the opening of the trial, the Petiot case sank into the obscurity of the *juge d'instruction*'s chambers.

Captain Valéri was leaner than the photographs of Dr. Petiot, and a heavy beard concealed his features. In his pockets police found a loaded 6.35mm automatic, F31,700, and fifty documents, including a Communist-party card issued only eight days previously, identification papers in the names Valéri, Wetterwald, Gilbert, de Frutos, Bonnasseau, and Cacheux, and a set of orders indicating that he would be assigned to duty in Indochina. Another few weeks or months, and he might never have been found. The Valéri papers gave various addresses in Paris or the suburbs, and bore photographs of Petiot both with and without his beard. One ration card would prove particularly embarrassing to Petiot: it was in the name René, rather than Henri, Valéri, and stated that its bearer had been born on May 8, 1935, at Issy-les-Moulineaux. The entire surface of the card had been damaged by water, apparently to conceal the fact that the original name, Kneller, had been rubbed out and replaced. Petiot showed uncanny nerve in keeping this obvious clue;

what, then, was one to think of two other documents he was carrying — the original and carbon of a tract Petiot had written demanding that an official accusation of collaboration be drawn up against Commissaire Georges Massu.

Massu had, in fact, been suspended from his post and confined to his office on the quai des Orfèvres several days earlier for suspicion of collaboration under the Vichy government, and thus narrowly missed the long-awaited pleasure of seeing Petiot behind bars. No specific charges were made, and it appeared the case was the unfortunate result of ambitious officers who coveted his position and a rather natural suspicion of everyone who had held an important post during the Vichy government's reign. Massu was held in his office for days without being told why, and in a fit of humiliation and despair, the proud commissaire slit his wrists and was rushed to the Hôtel Dieu close to death. He recovered and his case finally came up before a commission that found him innocent of all charges. He was eventually given a new post on the force, which he held until 1949, when he retired to become security chief and an agent for the American embassy in France.

Petiot, in his tract, dredged up a case in which Massu had been inadvertently responsible for the arrest of a young Resistant who had hidden weapons and Communist-party propaganda in a café. The youth was later shot by the Germans. This was never held against Massu even during the official inquest on his case, and given the commissaire's initial caution in the Petiot investigation, one could hardly accuse him of wanton over-zealousness. Doubtless, unfortunately, he had thought he was going after a criminal and ended up catching a Resistant. But, referring to Massu's arrest, Petiot wrote:

One might think that Massu has been suspended — at the end of a rope. Not at all. Massu was simply suspended from duty and sent into retirement with all his rights and benefits intact, including that to be paid for information he sent to certain Resistance newspapers [that is, the Charles Rolland deposition] — information from dossiers he compiled while so faithfully serving the Gestapo.

Granted that part of Petiot's mission in the FFI had been to search out and denounce traitors, and considering the recent dates of the tract and of Massu's arrest, one is almost led to wonder whether the hunted had not blithely turned and captured the hunter. But whether or not Petiot had actually played a role in his pursuer's arrest, it was evident that the fugitive had not spent his nearly eight months at large fearfully concealed, but had placidly changed his name and life and carried on much as before.

Police found that for several days after the discovery of the bodies at the rue Le Sueur, Petiot had stayed with various friends whose names were never learned, then met a house-painter named Georges Redouté, age fifty-six, a casual acquaintance whom he had treated once or twice. The unfortunate Redouté, who would spend months in prison for harboring a criminal, told police that on March 27 he had met Petiot walking in the street with two suitcases. Petiot said he had nowhere to stay and claimed he was a Resistance member fleeing the Germans. Redouté took Petiot home to his apartment at 83 rue du Faubourg Saint-Denis, just a few blocks from the café where Pintard had found so many future victims. Redouté gave Petiot a mattress on the floor and shared his meager supply of rations. The painter had read the newspapers, and he asked his lodger if bodies had really been found at the rue Le Sueur. "Yes," replied Petiot, "but they were bodies of Germans and informers." That evening as they went to bed, still uneasy, Redouté asked him to swear on his son's head that he had not killed. "I cannot swear, because I have killed. But I assure you those were German corpses."

Petiot stayed at Redouté's home for months. He went out infrequently and then only at night. He let his beard grow. During the day he sat around doing puzzles or reading the newspapers, and talked to Redouté about his Resistance activities. In the past, he said, he had made regular trips to the provinces and to l'Isle-Adam, a town fifteen miles north of Paris, to fetch arms dropped by English planes and bring them back to Paris. He and his group had killed enemies of France and thrown them in the Canal de l'Ourcq (which runs through Paris and feeds into the Seine, where bodies linked to Petiot had been found) and the Bois de Boulogne. Petiot assured his host that the triangular room and viewer were stupid lies dreamed up by the collaborationist press to discredit him. Redouté's remaining doubts were quickly dispelled, and the housepainter firmly believed he was protecting a patriot who would be vindicated after the war's end.

In the days following the uprising against the Germans, Petiot was out all day long, and he returned in the evening with hand grenades and other objects he claimed his comrades and he had taken from Germans they killed. On August 20, he said he had taken part in the fierce battle that day at the place de la République, and he brought home a drum.* Three or four days after the Liberation, Petiot appeared at Redouté's wearing a tricolor armband; he told his host he had enlisted in the FFI at the Caserne de Reuilly to ferret out collaborators and carry on the work of purifying and rebuilding France. He was quickly promoted to captain and had an automobile at his disposal. One day Redouté suggested that, now that the Germans were gone, Petiot could go to the police and clear himself of the false charges leveled against him. Petiot replied he would not do

---

* Some time after Petiot's arrest, an army lieutenant who had fought at the République told police that during the fighting a bearded man who looked like Petiot had approached him and said: "I cannot tell you who I am. Nonetheless you know me. Everyone knows me. If I told you my name you would be terrified." The lieutenant had not noticed this man fighting.

this as long as his wife and brother were still in prison. Shortly afterward, Redouté returned home from work to find Petiot and all his possessions gone, and he had never seen the doctor again.

Petiot had not, as Redouté believed, simply gone to the barracks and enlisted under a false name. He went first, the investigators learned, to the army post on the quai de Valmy, where he picked up some useful information, including the fact that a Dr. Henri Gérard had been arrested and sent to Germany. Petiot needed identity papers, and he particularly wanted to be known as a doctor — one aspect of his old identity he did not care to relinquish. Wearing an armband and an official air, Petiot presented himself at the Gérard home as a representative of the International Red Cross charged with negotiating the return of prisoners from Germany. As he was unfolding his tale and explaining to Madame Gérard that the prisoner's identity papers would facilitate his task, Dr. Gérard himself walked into the room; he had not, in reality, been deported, but only held in a Paris prison for several weeks and released. Petiot did not lose his poise, and impressed the doctor with stories of his Resistance activity, his captivity, and his torture — he even exhibited his filed teeth. While the two medical men sat and drank together, Petiot casually inquired whether Gérard knew of other doctors who were still held by the Germans. Gérard gave him the name of Dr. François Wetterwald, who had been arrested by the Gestapo for Resistance activity on January 15, 1944, and deported to the concentration camp at Mauthausen, Austria, in April.

Petiot went to Wetterwald's home on the rue d'Alleray and told the same story to the doctor's mother, who was willing to do anything to obtain her son's release. To make the necessary arrangements, Petiot told her as well, he would require certain details from her son's identity papers. Madame Wetterwald brought them, and when she left Petiot alone for several minutes with the pile of documents, he removed the few he needed to prove he was François Wetterwald, a medical doctor and a member of the French army. Madame Wetterwald thanked Petiot as he left; her son remained at Mauthausen until the Allies liberated the camp in 1945. Thus, when Petiot arrived at the Caserne de Reuilly, it was as Dr. François Wetterwald, alias (for security reasons) Dr. Henri Valéri. He used this latter name, taken in slightly altered form from the brass plaque left by the previous owner of his office at 66 rue Caumartin, presumably so that Wetterwald's former associates would not recognize him as an impostor. Petiot dared use this name even though, several months earlier, every newspaper in the country had printed the opening lines of the 1933 prospectus he had distributed in Paris: "You are hereby notified that the medical offices previously occupied by the celebrated Dr. Valéry will henceforth be run by Dr. Marcel Petiot."

Police investigators learned that Petiot's service at the Caserne de Reuilly was, at first, exemplary. Valéri had been promoted to the rank of captain quickly, as was common in those turbulent times, but on his own obvious merits. His two secretaries, as had his patients, adored him; he was a tireless and dedicated patriot who had often spoken of his great deeds in the Resistance. He often complained that the purge was not moving quickly enough, and was so devoted to the task of tracking down France's enemies that once, they said, apparently without thinking it strange, he had spent three nights a week for several weeks in a cemetery at Ivry where he was convinced German soldiers and collaborators were hiding.

Outside his immediate circle, the reports on Petiot were more compromising. Madame Juliette Couchaux, the owner of a café on the rue du Faubourg Saint-Antoine, filed a complaint that on September 12, FFI Lieutenant Dubois, the concierge of a nearby building, came to search her house on some flimsy pretext. He took F3 million worth of jewelry and conducted Madame Couchaux to a detention cell at the Caserne de Reuilly.

Two or three days later she was led before a bearded officer she later identified as Petiot. She complained of the theft and her arrest. Petiot replied, "Madame, I have a bit of advice for you: withdraw your complaint, sell your café, and disappear." Madame Couchaux refused to follow this odd suggestion, whereupon she was thrown into La Petite Roquette prison. She was released two months later by the puzzled prison authorities, who could not understand why she was there. Madame Couchaux added that during her detention at Reuilly a cellmate, speaking of Petiot, had said: "It's really terrible. The officer who questioned us was wearing on his fingers the rings which were stolen from me and which I had come to complain about."

Even more compromising was an incident that apparently took place under Petiot's orders and may, indirectly, have led to his arrest. On September 16, Corporal Jean Salvage and Lieutenant Jean Duchesne, both FFI men from Petiot's sector at the Caserne de Reuilly, and a civilian with the Rabelaisian name of Victor Cabelguenne had gone to the home of Monsieur Lareugance, the elderly mayor of Tessancourt, at Versailles, ostensibly to make inquiries into Lareugance's alleged collaboration. They didn't do much of that. Instead they blew open a safe with hand grenades, stole F7 million in cash and a stamp collection valued at F5.5 million, then led the old man out to a country road, battered his head in, and finished him off with a revolver shot in the temple. Three youths witnessed the killing and reported it. They were referred to the killers' superior officer, Captain Henri Valéri, who called the witnesses hoodlums and threw them in prison. A lieutenant who was ordered to lock the youths up found the situation suspicious and planted a man in the cell with them. The plant soon learned the real state of affairs, and the lieutenant went to Captain Valéri who, he assumed, had misunderstood and was unaware of the accusation the youths had made against the FFI men. Valéri told the lieutenant to drop the case; Salvage, Duchesne, and Cabelguenne were in prison, he claimed, the stolen stamps had been given to a Captain Grey, and he, Captain Valéri, didn't know where the money was. Captain Grey later reported that the stamps had also disappeared, and Petiot's subordinates did not remain long in prison — if, indeed, they were ever sent there.

When this story came out in the days following Petiot's arrest, police picked up Cabelguenne and Duchesne just as they were preparing to flee Paris and learned some even more startling information. Valéri had befriended them and Salvage and had often spoken to them of his Resistance activity. He told them he had killed sixty-three collaborators, including a "boxer." What was more, both Cabelguenne and Duchesne (and presumably Salvage) had been told by a Captain Warnier on October 28 that Captain Valéri was really Dr. Marcel Petiot, and they assumed several other people at the army post knew this as well, though the question of identity was never discussed with Valéri himself. Captain Warnier had also told them he was going to the Police Judiciaire for a copy of Petiot's fingerprints; but he never did this, and police apparently never spoke with him to discover if he had really identified Petiot and if so, how. For several days before his arrest, Petiot had been staying in an apartment owned by the family of Jean Salvage on the rue Paul Bert in the suburb of Saint-Mandé. Few people other than Salvage himself knew of this arrangement, yet the Saint-Mandé-Tourelles station where Petiot was captured was where he caught the métro to work in the morning. In addition, just before he was assigned to Captain Valéri's sector, Salvage had served under Captain Simonin, Petiot's mysterious captor.

Police inspectors were eager to question Salvage on these points, but they ran into unexpected difficulties. The *juge d'instruction* was inordinately slow to issue a warrant, and the military authorities said Corporal Salvage had been sent on a mission; they would not specify where, and could not say when he might return. The police concluded he was protected by important people. At first they thought it was because he had played an important role in Petiot's arrest. Later they felt sure of this, but they no longer believed Salvage's actions had been oriented toward his duty to society, but rather toward personal interest, and they could not figure out who might be shielding him. It seemed as though Salvage and Simonin, and perhaps others, had conveniently disposed of Captain Valéri when he no longer fitted into their own particular plans. It was rumored that during the next year several people who offered to give information on Simonin met sudden deaths. This puzzling aspect would never be cleared up, even though the journalist Jacques Yonnet wrote increasingly virulent articles about it as late as 1946 and implied that the Petiot affair was but the tip of something much more important and widespread.

12

PETIOT: HERO OF THE RESISTANCE

PETIOT'S LINE OF DEFENSE was absurdly simple. He was innocent, he said, of any crime. Indeed he had killed, but as a soldier and a Resistant liquidating the enemies of France — a perfectly legitimate and even praiseworthy enterprise at the time. He challenged the judge and police to prove anything against him, and peacefully settled back into his new role of martyred hero. From his cell in the Santé prison he wrote to a Colonel Ruaux, his former commanding officer at the Caserne de Reuilly:

Mon Colonel,
    You are receiving the first letter I have been able to write from my cell.
    In it, you will find no protestations of innocence, for they would be utterly useless.
    Captain Valéri is, as you know, incapable of having committed acts which would make an honest man blush with shame.

His only regret is being no longer able to fight our enemies at your side.

His only hope is that you will not forget him, and that, later, he might resume his place among his friends and participate in the last battles in whatever capacity you may choose to assign him.

With deepest respect, sincerely yours

PETIOT
Captain Valéri
Sector 7 – Cell 7*

Juge d'instruction Ferdinand Goletty had taken the Petiot dossier from a Judge Mariotte, who had held it for about a week after the original magistrate, Georges Berry, was transferred to collaboration cases. Goletty was new on the case, but he had studied it carefully, and this attitude of innocent patriotism was the last posture he or anyone else expected Petiot to take. It was a good one: by calling himself a Resistant, Petiot was introducing a whole new set of complications, particularly at a time when passions ran high and sometimes obscured reason. Even a judge had to be extremely careful with such delicate material, and the main emphasis of the investigation suddenly veered from the murders to the question of whether or not Petiot had belonged to the Resistance. At times, this confusion seemed to turn the question upside down altogether, leading Petiot's lawyer, René Floriot, to complain that the prosecution had "left aside the question of his innocence or guilt, and seem[s] to say simply that if Petiot was not a Resistant, then he was a murderer and should be condemned, Q.E.D. What sort of justice is this? What sort of logic?"

Except under scrutiny, even Petiot's story itself was good. He

* This letter was never sent. The prison authorities screened Petiot's correspondence, and several letters, such as this one, were held and placed in his dossier.

had, it seems, made it up long before, since he had repeated the same tale to Dr. Gérard, Redouté, his comrades at the Caserne de Reuilly, and even to his cellmates at Fresnes back in 1943 — well before any defense was needed and at a time when this particular one would have earned him death at the hands of the Germans. Petiot had planned carefully. Either that or he was telling the truth. The story he told Goletty, and to which he held until the end of his life, is as follows.

Petiot's Resistance activity began shortly after the Germans arrived in Paris in 1940. Initially, he provided falsified medical certificates to Frenchmen eager to avoid forced labor in Germany, and later he came into contact with a group of anti-Franco Spaniards in the Parisian suburb of Levallois-Perret. "I did some very good things with these people, but I do not want to tell you about them since my case is a simple one and I have no desire to complicate matters." He did not know the names of these comrades, since they worked under pseudonyms such as Gómez and Alvarez, nor could he specify the exact dates of his work, though he pointed out that during this period his bicycle had been stolen and he had filed a complaint at the commissariat de Levallois-Perret.*

Another phase of his activity consisted of gathering information from wounded or sick workers returning from Germany. They were first sent to a German organization on the rue Cambon, and there a French sympathizer — an Alsatian, Petiot believed, though he had never met him — referred many of them to him. Through cautious questioning he was able to elicit details on German troop movements and weapons developments. Among others, he had learned of a new weapon formed

---

* Petiot reported the theft on December 12, 1941. He did not mention that, to replace the missing machine, he seems to have simply stolen another one. A bicycle license plate was found at the rue Le Sueur registered in the name Ginette Mielle. Mademoiselle Mielle's bicycle had been stolen from a shopping area in the nearby suburb of La Garenne-Colombes on December 17, 1941.

of a three-bladed propeller that operated on the boomerang principle and which was being tested on the banks of the Elbe about forty miles southwest of Berlin.

Petiot himself had invented a weapon, just as he had cured constipation and discovered perpetual motion in 1936 (discoveries he did not mention to Judge Goletty). His secret weapon was short-range, silent, and all wounds it inflicted were lethal. It was ideally suited for sniper operations, and had it been adopted, "a five-ton truck could have carried enough of the gadgets to liquidate the million Germans trampling France under their jackboots." He himself had tried the weapon on German motorcyclists twice, once on the rue Saint-Honoré, once on the rue La Fayette, both times in broad daylight. The wounds inflicted were so inconspicuous that no one ever suspected the men died of unnatural causes. Petiot had given plans for the weapon to a secretary named Thompson at the American consulate in Paris around 1941 (the American embassy had moved to Vichy), at the time when the United States broke off diplomatic relations with Germany. Thompson had passed them on to another consular secretary named Muller, who had spoken with Petiot on the telephone and assured him his invention would be studied closely, but nothing had been done. Petiot did not say why he had never offered his weapon to the Resistance, and now he stubbornly refused to give Judge Goletty even the vaguest description of it.

At a date he could no longer recall, Petiot received formal training from a man sent from London to organize the Maquis in Franche-Comté, on the Swiss border. He learned unarmed personal-defense techniques as well as the use of Resistance weapons such as the revolver, submachine gun, hand grenades, and plastic explosives. He did not remember the man's name.

His medical practice brought him in contact with more and more members of the Resistance, he made himself more and more useful, and he was eventually assigned to head a group

that would ferret out and liquidate informers who had infil-
trated the Resistance network led by Pierre Brossolette, a famous
Resistant who was killed in March 1944. This task in itself should
have been minimal, but Petiot and his comrades were so ardent,
and felt so strongly that collaborators did more to demoralize
the French than the uniformed occupying troops, that they
actively searched out and killed collaborators wherever they
found them. The slang name for an informer is *mouchard*, from
the French word for a fly, *mouche*. Petiot named his group Fly-
Tox after a well-known brand of liquid fly-killer, comparable
to Flit or Raid.

Some collaborators were discovered through common knowledge or were denounced by patriots, but generally Fly-Tox employed its own special methods to detect them. Members of the
group stationed themselves outside the Gestapo office on the rue
des Saussaies and observed those who came and went. Non-
uniformed employees had to show Gestapo identity cards to the
guard at the door. When Petiot's men observed such a person
leaving, they followed him to a secluded place, then identified
themselves as plainclothes German police officers and announced
he was under arrest. This was done to double-check their suspicions: if the suspect was a collaborator he would protest that
there was some mistake since he worked for the Germans himself. Thus condemned by his own words, the victim was shoved
into a truck and driven away. Sometimes he was questioned at
the rue Le Sueur, but few people had been killed there and the
bodies were always concealed elsewhere. More frequently the
prisoner was interrogated in the moving truck, then summarily
clubbed to death with a rubber hose filled with sand, lead, and
bicycle spokes, and buried in the woods near Marly-le-Roi, a
few miles west of Paris. Petiot estimated his group had killed
a total of sixty-three people — about half Germans, the other
half French — and every one had deserved his fate.

In the course of their Resistance work, Petiot and his comrades heard of escape routes to Spain and South America, and though they did not deal with this specialty themselves, they occasionally passed on the information to people who could use it. Petiot sometimes helped to the limit of his abilities. False identity papers were obtained by the Vichy minister of state, Lucien Romier, from a member of the Argentinian consulate known only by the code name Desaix or De C. A police commissioner in the seventh arrondissement of Lyon provided documents that facilitated the crossing of the Spanish border, and from Spain the travelers could easily go on to Portugal and board a ship for England or South America. A furrier named Guschinov, among others, had taken this route and had written to Petiot announcing his safe arrival in Argentina. The actual passage was effected by a group of specialists under the leadership of André le Corse, whom Petiot had never met. Petiot worked through an intermediary, one of his former patients known as Robert Martinetti. He did not know Martinetti's real name nor where he could be found. When necessary, they had met at the Paris Auction House on the rue Drouot, a secret contact point where Petiot had spent every afternoon from 3:00 to 6:00 o'clock during the time of the group's operation.

Petiot admitted he had been unwise in mentioning the escape organization to Fourrier and Pintard. He had originally cultivated them because he thought a barber and a makeup artist would come in handy when members of Fly-Tox required a disguise; but it turned out that Fourrier and Pintard had ideas of their own and set about finding clients only to make money. Unsavory as their motive was, the results were unexpectedly fruitful, since the milieu in which Pintard recruited at the rue de l'Echiquier café was riddled with informers, and a steady stream of victims marched willingly into the Fly-Tox execution den. Petiot proudly admitted the liquidation of François le Corse, Adrien le Basque, Jo le Boxeur, and their friends. They had come not to escape, he said, but to learn the Fly-Tox escape route and expose it to the Gestapo. Eryane Kahan was much the same. Petiot claimed her German lover had listened at the door during their conversations, and that the Jews she sent to him were all traitors in the pay of the Nazis.

In this delirious proliferation of noble acts, Petiot had also engaged in sabotage. Sometimes he used plastic explosives, sometimes another device he had invented, consisting of a bottle holding gasoline and sulfuric acid separated by a cork. A man would sneak into a boxcar that contained valuable German supplies and suspend two of these bottles from strings thumbtacked to the roof. During the voyage, the bottles would knock against each other or the walls, break, and start an inexplicable fire. The added advantage, Petiot remarked, was that "this very simple device did not cost over one hundred francs."

Though he willingly spoke about his own activities, Petiot was reluctant to identify his comrades; he did not wish to see other brave and innocent men put in the same sad position as himself. One of the few names he mentioned was Cumulo, the code name for the courageous leader of the Resistance group Rainbow, whom Petiot claimed as a close friend. Cumulo was by far the younger man, but Petiot said they had the same brown hair and silhouette and had been easily mistaken for one another. But Cumulo was dead, as were Pierre Brossolette, Lucien Romier, and several others Petiot mentioned. Cumulo, whose real name was Jean-Marie Charbonneaux, had been trapped by the Germans in October 1943. After a daring rooftop chase, rather than be captured and risk giving in under torture, he had grabbed at one of his pursuers and leaped to his death six stories below. For those of Petiot's colleagues who were not known to be dead, such as Martinetti, there was no proof that they had ever been alive. Petiot had astonishingly few witnesses to confirm his story: he had none at all.

Petiot said Yvan Dreyfus had been responsible for his arrest by the Germans in 1943, but that though he knew Dreyfus to be

a collaborator, he had not killed him. After Fourrier had turned
Dreyfus over to Petiot near the place de la Concorde, Petiot had
turned him over to Robert Martinetti on the Champs-Elysées
(this was, in fact, where the Gestapo shadows lost them). Martinetti took an evasive route to the rue Le Sueur, where "Albert"
or another Fly-Tox man was waiting. It seemed probable that
his group had killed Dreyfus, and with good reason, but Petiot
could not be sure since when the Germans arrested him "the
Jew" was still alive at the rue Le Sueur.

The Gestapo took "Dr. Eugène" to the rue des Mathurins
barbershop, where they expected to capture other members of
the group. En route, Petiot managed to lay his overcoat down
in a nearby café, and to conceal a note in it informing his group
that he had been arrested and that they should abandon operations at the rue Le Sueur. A bit later, Petiot almost managed
to elude his captors, but as he ran, he realized that his wife,
son, and comrades would only suffer if he escaped, so he
stopped.

I said to the officer [who was chasing him]: "You see, I could
have gotten away." He replied: "That would be utterly pointless.
You need only come to the rue des Saussaies and sign your deposition and you will be released immediately." As I hesitated and said
"But . . . ," he clicked his heels and said, "You have the word of a
German officer!" with which I went off to spend eight months in
prison.

He went on to describe his imprisonment, the torture, the
periodic threats of execution, Guélin's and Beretta's attempts to
fool him, and his own absolute refusal to compromise France
for his own personal safety. He knew that the Germans had
searched the rue Caumartin and his property on the rue de
Reuilly, and he assumed they were also familiar with the rue Le
Sueur. After all, there had been bills and documents concerning

it at the rue Caumartin, they had taken his key to the rue Le Sueur, and two of his former patients who were important buyers for a German agency and closely tied with the Gestapo had been to the building to purchase a chandelier Petiot had bought at auction and stored there. If the Germans had been to the rue Le Sueur — and even Petiot's questioners had to admit it seemed unlikely that they did not investigate there — they would surely have noticed anything unusual. Mountains of bodies, Petiot explained sarcastically, generally qualify as unusual when found in someone's home.

When he was released from Fresnes in January 1944, Fly-Tox had ceased to exist. Some members had disappeared after his arrest, others later; still others were disheartened as the months dragged on and the daily-awaited Allied invasion did not take place. Petiot knew most of them only under assumed names and had no way of contacting them. He was ill and exhausted and went to Auxerre to rest. It was not until February 8 that he summoned the courage to enter 21 rue Le Sueur and face the damage he was sure the Germans had wrought. In fact, the situation was worse than he expected. Valuable medical equipment and furniture had been stolen, the whole place was in complete disarray, and two heavy marble slabs he had cemented over an old manure pit had been shoved aside. When he looked into the pit, he found it was full of bodies poorly concealed under an electric iron, a drill, several boxes, and two large cushions. The odor of putrefying flesh was terrible. He immediately wrote to his brother, asking for 200 kilograms of quicklime to destroy cockroaches, but which he really wanted to disinfect and destroy these unknown corpses cluttering up his house. He pointed out to Judge Goletty that, if he had known the bodies were there, he would have brought the lime himself when he returned to Paris from Auxerre rather than risk implicating his brother in such a dangerous affair, as, unfortunately, he had done.

Where had the bodies come from? Petiot assumed at first that his Fly-Tox comrades had continued their work and foolishly used his house as a dumping group for dead collaborators and Germans. He angrily reproached the few remaining members for such unspeakable carelessness, but they denied all responsibility and said the Germans must have done it. Still, something had to be done. They had no automobile and their truck was in need of repair, so there was no question of transporting the corpses out of Paris as they had done before. Petiot suspected the Germans were following him, so two comrades offered to take care of the disposal themselves. They apparently hit upon the idea of burning the remains, which Petiot did not know at the time and would not have recommended, since the bodies were still relatively fresh and the lime had desiccated only the exteriors. But on Friday, March 10, the two comrades told Petiot they expected to finish the job by Saturday evening or Sunday morning. Instead, on Saturday evening, the fire was discovered. He arrived in twelve minutes — not the half hour mentioned by the police — "but I saw that the police and firemen, with typical impertinence, had broken open the doors, and there were the firemen, several policemen, and the crowd."

He had identified himself to one of the policemen (incorrectly, according to the police) and took the risk of mentioning his Resistance group. The policeman told him to flee and they would see what they could do to hush up the affair. The next day Petiot was to call a Monsieur William or Wilhelm to find out the results, and when he did he was told there was nothing to be done since the Germans already knew everything, and he should disappear. He went in search of Pierre Brossolette; he was told he was dead, and other Resistance members were hesitant to use Petiot since his notoriety would make it dangerous for him to undertake active missions. He was given the new code name of Special 21 and assigned minor administrative duties, which frustrated his eager mind, and he had rejoiced when he was finally able to resume an active role at the time of the Liberation. He admitted stealing Dr. Wetterwald's papers, but claimed the main reason was that he wished to go on active duty and he stood a better chance if he was thirty-three, as was Wetterwald, rather than forty-seven, as his Valéri papers stated.

Goletty asked why he had not turned himself in after the Liberation. If his case was so simple, surely he could have cleared it up quickly and gone on with his work?

I felt that the accusations against me were so manifestly false, I was so convinced that my innocence would be obvious to anyone who gave the least bit of thought to the matter, that I did not imagine I ran any risk of imprisonment. Nonetheless, I did not go to the police because the police had not yet been purged of collaborators, and because I was more useful to France continuing the fight than discussing my personal affairs.

Mysterious "political enemies" in Villeneuve-sur-Yonne had been responsible for every accusation brought against him; now he dismissed charges or refused to answer questions on the grounds that the purge was not over — "It is being done with eyebrow tweezers when what we need is a shovel!" — and hidden traitors were just waiting to use his information to the detriment of the French Republic. He snickered at the charges and said it was only at his lawyer's insistence that he had deigned to answer them at all.

13

"I WISH TO EXPLAIN MYSELF IN COURT"

PETIOT WAS PLACED in cell 7 of sector 7 at the Prison de la Santé — death row, despite the fact that he had not yet been convicted. His room measured nine feet by twelve feet, contained a bed, chair, and deal table, and the judas was always open and a guard stationed outside his door twenty-four hours a day. Petiot did not seem to mind at all. He took up smoking, and was almost never seen without a cigarette dangling from his lips. He wrote poetry, and also turned out a three-hundred-page manuscript called *Le Hasard vaincu* (Beating Chance, or Chance Defeated), which described methods for winning, or minimizing losses, at the races, roulette, lotteries, poker, and other gambling activities.

Le Hasard vaincu, which would be published at Petiot's expense in manuscript facsimile at the time of the trial, is a curious and virtually unreadable book filled with interminable digressions and irrelevant, if mildly amusing, anecdotes. The overall tone toward the reader is deprecating, and repeatedly cautions him to do the calculations for himself, since he is suspected of laziness. Those parts of the book that are coherent are generally neither original nor instructive. Petiot relates strange wartime anecdotes, bits of his own experience, and occasionally comments on the Resistance and collaboration or the rue Le Sueur affair. "Follow me well," he tells the reader on one page, "as the barber said, lathering the customer's face and preparing to tell the interesting story of the vampire of the rue . . ."; and as a footnote to a calculation he fears might give the reader misgivings about the author's mental state, he say: "To reassure you, I would like to let you know that 3 experts have found me perfectly sane. But since these gentlemen obstinately refused to be examined and have their own sanity gauged, I do not know whether one can have the slightest confidence in their conclusions. Nonetheless . . ." More often, one finds curious illustrative digressions such as the following, which occurs in Petiot's introductory explanation of the laws of probability.

At the end of that memorable battle between God the Father and Lucifer, they sent out diplomats, signed an armistice, and set up rules for eternal Peace based on an equal division of the mortal souls yet to come between "the two Major Powers."

Lucifer had the best of it, since he did not even have to bother manufacturing them: like the broom-maker who steals brooms ready made, while his competitor has to steal the bristles, handles and wire.

What I am telling you may clash with tradition, but if you think about it a bit you will see that Lucifer, who before the war had been Jehovah's right-hand man, his Chief of Staff, was perfectly familiar with strategy and armaments before he began his revolt.

He would not have risked the coup d'etat had he thought he would lose. The celestial phalanxes clothed in shining armor with their white and luminous wings — easy targets — with only the antiquated artillery depicted in Milton, were no match for the V-2's and atomic bombs Satan knew well before we did.

I like to believe that Jehovah, with Saint George at his side, fought as best he could, but could not conquer, could not master an adversary who balked at no method and would willingly have sunk all into Nothingness. The only hope was a compromised Peace with divided zones of power. We see today, alas, its unfortunate results.

A friend even assured me that God took one Hell of a thrashing in this battle, and that only a few atoms of infinite Goodness and divine Providence remain. He held these excessively pessimistic beliefs — which explains it — at Fresnes, after 5 months of Nazi torture.

My faith is more optimistic.

In their peace treaty, God and Satan (Lucifer had changed his nom de guerre) agreed to split fifty-fifty. But how could they *choose* the blessed and the damned?

There was, of course, the old method using the scales of divine justice, but you can be sure that well before the first Dreyfus Affair and others like it, Satan had invented the technique of the "thumb on the scale," and God knew it . . . So Satan suggested "Heads or Tails," played with a celestial orb.

The game went on and on, and would be going on still if, at the end of 4,000 years, as the Bible tells us, God had not happened to notice while balancing his accounts that Satan had populated his entire realm and had no lack of manpower, while eternal paradise remained rather empty, and the celestial choir was short on singers.

The Almighty had always watched the coin closely when Satan said "Heads I win, Tails you lose!" and noticed nothing amiss . . . but still the Creator, who knew his Laws as though he had made them, had the Revelation that Satan *had cheated*, because in the Laws of Probability, the Rule of large numbers would predict near perfect equality and, in a game of "Heads or Tails," perfect equality at the end of the World.

All this is to plant firmly in your mind the fact that this Law is absolute. You know the end of the story. God broke the treaty and parachuted a camouflaged envoy down to reconnoiter the terrain, and decided to brand members of his own flock at birth. But Satan had his own methods and, all things considered, still seems to do pretty well for himself. But that's another story.

Strangest of all was Petiot's dedication:

> To you
> who have given me this leisure . . .
> The research has been done
>   by "Doctor EUGENE," ex-Chief of the Resistance Group
>   FLY-TOX
> The columns of numbers were set up
>   under the direction of "Captain VALERI"
>   of the 1st Army, 1st Paris Regiment
> The errors in the operations were committed
>   by Doctor Marcel PETIOT . . .

The book, aside from helping the reader win at games of chance, was presented as amusement for the author and a guide on methods of "escaping boredom."

If Petiot was bored and required recreation, his accusers had more than enough puzzles to occupy their time. The evidence linking Petiot with the identified victims continued to build up slowly. But now there was another problem. No one had quite expected him to take the position he had; denial, yes — but not a plea of justifiable homicide. Two lieutenants from the Direction Générale des Etudes et Recherches (DGER, or Military Security) were appointed to investigate Petiot's Resistance stories — Albert Brouard and Jacques Ibarne; the latter had worked for *Résistance* under the pseudonym Jacques Yonnet and was the author of "Petiot, Soldier of the Reich," which had recounted the questionable testimony of Charles Rolland.

Brouard and Ibarne dissected Petiot's story, interviewed Resistance members, and attempted to verify even the vaguest among the few tangible details. It was unavoidably difficult to prove that something did *not* happen, and since Petiot's assertions were so general, and his justifications for silence legally, if not reasonably, worthy of consideration, their task was difficult and frustrating. Nonetheless, in their report dated May 3,

1945, Lieutenants Brouard and Ibarne felt confident they could reject Petiot's story as pure fantasy:

. . . Petiot's statements, his hesitations, his contradictions, his glaring ignorance of the structure of the Resistance and even of the nature and operation of those sectors for which he pretends to have worked, the numerous improbabilities in his declarations, his systematic habit of mentioning only Resistance comrades who are either dead (Cumulo, Brossolette) or who cannot be found (the members of Fly-Tox) lead one to believe that Petiot was not at any time in serious contact with any Resistance organization whatsoever. He has simply exploited information he possesses. . . . *We formally reject the hypothesis that the accused played even the remotest part in the Resistance.*

Among other objections, they found that no one in Lucien Romier's entourage had heard of Petiot or Dr. Eugène, there was no Desaix or De C at the Argentinian embassy, nor had a Lyon police commissioner ever been involved in clandestine passages. There was an Englishman who was sent to Besançon — Captain H. Ree — but when he arrived in late 1942 he had gone directly to Montbéliard for sabotage, and at no time had he instructed anyone in the use of Resistance weapons.

No German motorcyclists had been killed in mysterious ways, though one had died on the rue La Fayette — one of Petiot's specified locales — when he was hit by a truck. As for the secret-weapon plans, the American consular secretary Tyler Thompson had never heard of Petiot, Eugène, Valéri, or any secret weapon, and the other American with whom Petiot claimed to have spoken, Muller, simply did not exist. As for Thompson, his signature had been affixed to certain documents posted on American-owned properties in Paris, and Petiot might have learned his name from them.

Petiot had also mentioned early Resistance work with a group of anti-Franco Spaniards at Levallois-Perret. These people actually did exist and knew Petiot, but not quite in the capacity he claimed. Two illegal aliens, Miguel and his pregnant mistress Liberta, were in hiding at the Levallois home of Grégoire González, and the three of them comprised the Resistance group les Guerrilleros in its entirety. When Liberta's baby was born, Petiot certified the birth, and he returned two or three times to treat the infant; during one of the visits his bicycle was stolen. Given Petiot's statement about the bicycle and the fact that there was no other anti-Franco group in Levallois, there was no doubt that he was referring to les Guerrilleros. He had never at any time participated in any of their activities, though he once told González to contact him if he ever got into trouble. González was arrested and did appeal to Petiot, who sent along a false medical certificate with his apology that he could do nothing else for the moment. Petiot said that after González's release, however, he would be able to get him out of the country.

Ibarne and Brouard's report listed twenty-five points in Petiot's testimony that seemed to disprove his story. Petiot answered these charges with indignation and ridicule. When he annotated a copy of the Military Security report, Petiot discounted each point with one of three accusations: Ibarne and Brouard were lying, they were themselves ignorant of the Resistance, or they had altered his original statement and refuted one of their own making.

Petiot's knowledge of Resistance organization, procedure, and terminology, stated the report, was vague or incorrect, as when he called Rainbow a "group" rather than a "network." Petiot replied: "Term employed 36 times in 8 D.G.E.R. reports, and particularly in one: 19 times in 7 pages." Petiot's assigned code names and numbers were unlike any the Resistance had ever used. Furthermore, no one had ever heard of Fly-Tox, nor would Brossolette's organization have set up such an independent execution squad. ("The proof that they needed an autonomous group comprised of people unknown to the other members is that right after my disappearance, they were all raided at the same time.") Above all, his descriptions of Cumulo were totally incorrect (only their erroneous transcription of it, Petiot said), and it was impossible that he could have known him under that name, since Jean-Marie Charbonneaux had adopted that pseudonym only after Petiot was in prison, and he had been killed before Petiot's release. Among all the Resistance members questioned, only two thought they remembered hearing the names Petiot or Augène (sic); both were uncertain, one was a mythomaniac, and their stories implied that Petiot had been a Gestapo informer. Not even his accusers took this suggestion seriously.

The investigators pointed out that there were complete records of all official Resistance members, including names, addresses, and photographs, from which they had been able to reconstruct, for example, the entire membership of Rainbow. Petiot and his "group" were not to be found among them. They questioned Petiot's reluctance to name members of his group — an attitude they had never encountered in hundreds of previous interrogations. "Those who compile these dossiers [of Resistance groups]," Petiot replied, "are either lunatics or criminals. Surely they know that some D.G.E.R. officers are former Gestapo members. On the first day of the next war, the first people the spies will execute are the people on those lists, thanks to those lists." They promised Petiot that their investigation was being pursued with the utmost discretion and he need not worry about such things. Petiot merely laughed at the notion that Yonnet-Ibarne and Goletty could ever keep a promise or even knew the meaning of discretion.

Petiot almost created doubt with one point before it toppled back upon him. In the event that he lost contact with Brossolette's group, he said, he had been instructed to go see Brossolette's mistress, "Mademoiselle Claire," in an apartment whose address he could no longer recall but which was located near the Seine. No one in Brossolette's group had ever heard of this woman, and in their report Brouard and Ibarne dismissed this as another transparent fiction. It subsequently turned out that Mademoiselle Claire did exist. She was Madame Clémence Davinroy, formerly the code secretary for the Resistance group Parsifal and presently a member of the French provisional government. Madame Davinroy, however, testified that she had never been Brossolette's mistress (although she knew him well), had never owned an apartment near the Seine, and had never heard of Petiot under any name. She suggested that he might have heard of her through her friend Robert Lateulade, who had been at Fresnes when Petiot was there. Coincidentally, Petiot and Lateulade had actually shared the same cell for a time, and when Petiot was released Lateulade, who was deported and died in a German camp before the Liberation, sent him to see another Resistance member named Lazerges. It seemed likely that Petiot had learned some of his more plausible scraps of information from these two men and not through his own Resistance activity.

On May 3, 1945, when the report was completed, only four of the original ten suspected accomplices were still in prison: Maurice Petiot, Raoul Fourrier (who had been rearrested after six months of liberty), René Nézondet, and Albert Neuhausen — Nézondet would be released three days later, having completed his fourteen-month sentence for nondenunciation of a crime, and Neuhausen on May 18, after serving thirteen and a half months for hiding a bunch of suitcases. *Juge d'instruction* Ferdinand Goletty continued the task of building up background information on the victims, identifying clothing, verifying Petiot's statements, and trying desperately to master a dossier that had assumed gargantuan proportions. Petiot was brought to Goletty's chambers every few days and questioned, confronted with witnesses and accomplices, questioned again and again. The same stories were repeated and elaborated. Finally, on October 30, Petiot told Goletty: "I refuse to answer any more questions because I wish to explain myself in public, in court, as quickly as possible." He had been in prison for exactly one year now, he complained, and if the present questions had any significance they should have been asked long before.

Petiot's decision was firm, though occasionally his delight in sarcasm and argument got the better of him. On November 3, Goletty once more questioned him.

GOLETTY   When did you buy the house on the rue Le Sueur?

PETIOT   I have decided not to answer any questions except in public.

GOLETTY   For what purpose [did you buy the house]?

PETIOT   If you just put "ditto," things will move along more quickly.

GOLETTY   Did you ever live in this building or use it for some purpose, and if so, when?

PETIOT   Ditto.

GOLETTY   How did you furnish the building? Where did the furnishings come from?

PETIOT   Idem.

[Et cetera.]

On November 16 Goletty confronted Petiot with Guélin, who denied any collaboration and gave a perfectly innocent explanation of the Dreyfus affair. Petiot sat in silent fury while Guélin spoke, but was finally unable to control himself and broke his vow of silence. "I have decided not to answer any questions, but I do want to congratulate the witness on his wonderful imagination. I love the fairy tale he just told you." On December 10, perhaps out of sheer boredom, he answered several questions concerning Dr. Braunberger.

GOLETTY Didn't you meet him on June 20, 1942?

PETIOT This must be some sort of joke. Really, how can you expect me to remember the year in which I met someone?

GOLETTY Why were some of his clothes found in suitcases which came from the rue Le Sueur?

PETIOT I met Dr. Braunberger once in my life, and I am asking you one more time to at least show me these so-called clothes of his. You are certainly not unaware of the fact that all of these things which were stolen — because there was never any search warrant — spent over a year in the hands of the Franco-German police, and the Nazis could have removed or inserted anything they pleased. The least I can ask is to see them now.

GOLETTY The letters from Dr. Braunberger coincide strangely with those from the aforementioned Khaït, Van Bever, and Hotin.

PETIOT Could you give me the definition of this word "coincide"?

GOLETTY These letters are all from missing persons. Their handwriting is all distorted, and the phraseology is similar.

PETIOT I was not aware of this definition of "coincide," but since these deductions were made by people working for you, I consider them utterly devoid of significance.

Petiot's final pretrial interrogation took place on December 28. Goletty had prepared forty-eight pages of questions covering every aspect of the case. Petiot refused to answer a single one.

Hastened by Petiot's attitude, the State moved into the final preparatory stages for the trial. Goletty submitted his dossier — weighing thirty kilograms — to the Chamber of Accusations, a panel of three Appeals Court magistrates (roughly equivalent in function to a grand jury in the United States) that determines whether a case should go to trial. They decided that it should, and turned the dossier over to the procureur général's office for drafting of the formal act of accusation.

The procureur général is nominally involved in a French criminal case from the beginning. In theory, the Police Judiciaire's investigation and the *juge d'instruction's* interrogations are conducted under the procureur's supervision and authority, though unless there is misconduct, he rarely really intervenes in routine cases; the procureur's function is not usually apparent until he or members of his staff of avocats généraux and substitutes draw up the act of accusation and prosecute the case in court. But when a crime has political overtones or attracts significant public interest, the procureur's office frequently plays a more active role throughout the investigation, and for an extremely important matter, the procureur général may personally take charge.

In the immediate postwar years, however, the authorities shied away from cases that even remotely concerned the Resistance. It was a delicate topic to begin with, and since many officials had retained their posts under the Vichy régime, they feared that their own honor might become involved in the debate. The procureur général had decided not to touch the Petiot case, and had passed it on to one of his assistants, who gave it to another assistant, who gave it to another — until finally it had reached the newest, youngest, and most inexperienced member of the office, Avocat Général Elissalde.

Elissalde, age thirty, had already devoted months to the case, attending interrogations and poring over the huge dossier, which he knew almost as well as Goletty. When the time came to construct the case summary, he carpeted the entire floor of his apartment with the dossier. He would leap from place to place and room to room, reading out scraps from here and there and shouting them out to his new bride, who spent her honeymoon taking dictation on Dr. Petiot.

Petiot was accused of murdering twenty-seven people for plunder. His loot was estimated at F200 million worth of cash, gold, and jewelry — which was never found, though treasure hunters searched his properties and picked through the rubble of 21 rue Le Sueur when it was demolished in the 1950s. Elissalde recognized that evidence to back up the accusations was flimsy and that, taken individually, few if any of them were strong enough to earn a conviction. Since French law permits a charge based on "presumption of guilt" when circumstantial evidence is so overwhelming as to leave no normal doubt in the minds of a jury, Elissalde took the position that, taken as an ensemble, the remarkably similar disappearances of so many people, virtually all of whom were last seen with Petiot or known to be in contact with him, were sufficient cause for presumption of guilt. He restricted his official summary to a concise thirty-eight pages; by law, the case summary, as well as the rest of the dossier, had to be shown to Petiot's lawyer, and Elissalde did not wish him to know what the prosecution's strategy was going to be. For the prosecution's own use, he wrote out two hundred cramped pages of additional notes expanding on details.

In late January 1946, the procureur général ordered Petiot sent before the Assize Court of the Seine on March 18. It was only then, after setting the trial date, that he appointed Avocat Général Pierre Dupin to prosecute the case; Dupin, who was not noted for courtroom brilliance, had only six weeks to read the dossier and no hope of mastering it. For the defense was René Floriot, then recognized as the greatest living criminal attorney in France — a great innovator, who had helped replace the emotional oratorical technique popular in the early part of the century with a logical courtroom style. A recent French minister, Françoise Giroud, described him as "a lawyer the way another might be a surgeon. When a surgeon operates on a stomach, he does not ask whether the stomach's owner is an honest man and whether he likes him or not. He fights against death, trying to save the man who has confided his life to him."

A practicing lawyer since 1923, the forty-four-year-old Floriot had handled a number of major criminal cases. In 1936 he defended two youths accused of stealing F20 million in a train robbery and won their acquittal. A week later, evidence appeared proving them guilty. He had defended Mussolini's mistress, Magda Fontanges, who shot and wounded the French ambassador in Rome, and he got her off with a one-year sentence. After the war he represented the Nazi ambassador to occupied France, Otto Abetz, who was sentenced to twenty years at hard labor rather than a death sentence, and Jean Luchaire, a prominent journalist and collaborator who was ultimately executed. Most recently, he had unsuccessfully defended Henri Lafont, leader of the French Gestapo, basing his case on the dubious contention that Lafont, having been granted honorary German citizenship during the war, was simply an enemy soldier and could not be shot as a traitor. Public sentiment being what it was, no argument could have saved Lafont, who was shot with his aide Pierre Bonny and seven others in December 1944.

Floriot, a powerful, leonine man with horn-rimmed spectacles, was not married, did not smoke, and drank only before his final oration at a trial, when he had a single glass of champagne to give him the appropriate uplift. His only hobby was pheasant shooting, and he was reputedly one of the best marksmen in Europe. His life was the law, and his law was a logical genius and a calculated dramatic effect untempered by moral considerations. Whenever he received a new dossier, he picked it apart, memorized it, and rebuilt it as best suited his needs. He based his case entirely on the facts, and though he juxtaposed and interpreted them according to his own plan, the facts were always at his command to counter any attack. When the case had been built into a thing of beauty and the trial reached its end, Floriot showed no more interest. He never seemed to care particularly about the outcome.

Floriot had begun working on the Petiot murder case in March 1944 when Georgette and Maurice retained him as their lawyer. It seemed certain that he had spoken with Petiot at some point during his eight months of flight, and he had subsequently attended his every interrogation. Every morning for several months before the trial, Floriot wheeled out a cart with coffee and the Petiot dossier, which he discussed from every angle with three of his assistants: Paul Cousin, Pierre Jacquet, and Eugène Ayache. Each was assigned a third of the file and spent his full time studying it, pursuing investigations and discussing the results with Floriot. Cousin had recently married, and after a brief honeymoon he told his wife to go stay with her parents, since otherwise she risked being alone until the following April.

For both prosecution and defense, the task of collecting information was not always easy. The prosecution found it highly suspicious that Petiot so readily forgot some things and just as readily recalled others in detail. He in fact did have a fine but abnormal memory that often forgot names, faces, and places, yet held reams of extraneous information. When Floriot asked about a certain building important in preparing their case, Petiot could not remember anything about its location. But he described its proximity to an elevated métro line, a locksmith on one side, a bakery on the other, the wood molding around the door, and the tile floor of the vestibule. With the help of a map of the métro and several days of walking, the assistant Ayache was able to find it.

When the day of the trial arrived, Floriot was ready. Elissalde was lumping all twenty-seven cases together; Floriot was taking them one by one. Petiot was in an excellent mood and could hardly wait. He told guards and fellow prisoners at the Santé that this was going to be a wonderful trial, an amusing trial, and that he would make everybody laugh.

PART THREE

14

PETIOT ON TRIAL

THE TRIAL opened at the Palais de Justice on Monday, March
18, 1946.* The evidence, a teetering mountain of trunks, hat-
boxes, and suitcases weighing several tons, occupied an entire
wall of the wood-paneled courtroom and lent it the atmosphere
of a railroad-station baggage office — a decor, as it turned out,
not altogether inappropriate for the tone the proceedings would
take. At the center of a long desk sat the president of the tribunal, Michel Leser, who would conduct the proceedings and,
at least theoretically, maintain order and channel questions from
lawyers to witnesses. On either side of him were two magistrates, who, pursuant to the French system, played little part in
the trial itself but who, along with the president and the jurors,
would ultimately deliberate on the evidence and determine guilt

* Since no official court transcript was made, the trial sequence that
follows has been reconstructed entirely from contemporary journalistic
accounts, supplemented by material from interviews with some of the
participants.

and the penalty. Flanking the scarlet-robed magistrates on each side sat the jurors. Beyond them, to the judges' far left sat the clerk of the court, and situated to the panel's far right were Avocats Généraux Elissalde and Dupin. This single long line of people, typical of a French criminal trial, constituted the State.

In front of and below the official prosecution and jury sat the civil-suit lawyers. In France, victims of a crime or their relatives are entitled to have their own lawyer present their case and, in the case of conviction, to request damages and negotiate their amount. In some situations the civil-suit lawyers are more effective than the State's attorney, and in the Petiot affair one suspected from the start that this might be true, since they outnumbered Dupin by a dozen to one. There was Maître Jacques Bernays for the Wolffs' family, Maître Jacques Archevêque for Madame Guschinov, Maître Claude Perlès for Madame Braun-berger, Maître Dominique Stéfanaggi for the Piereschi family, Maître Charles Henry for Paulette Grippay's relatives, Maître André Dunant for those of Adrien le Basque's mistress Gisèle Rossmy, a Maître Gachkel for the Basch and Anspach families, a Maître Léon-Lévy for the Knellers', and Maître Pierre Véron for the survivors of Madame Khaït and Yvan Dreyfus. Véron was assisted by Dreyfus's brother-in-law, Maître Pierre Rein; and several others had brought associates to swell the ranks crammed into chairs behind glass cases filled with umbrellas, canes, hardware, and mysterious packages that completed the assortment of evidence.

Next to the court clerk and at a right angle to the prosecution bench in the French courtroom is the defense: the prisoner's box, to the clerk's immediate left, is on a level with the judge and jurors; the defense attorney and his assistants are below it, level with the civil-suit lawyers. Whether by design or curious coincidence, the press is seated immediately to the left of the accused, thus assuring journalists the best seats in the house.

Witnesses must stand, or lean, at a small curved railing situated at a focal point between the opposing sides — in front of and facing the president.

On this first day there were fifty visiting attorneys and magistrates, the eighty witnesses, a hundred journalists and photographers, hordes of police, and more than four hundred spectators. Yellow passes signed by Leser were required for admission, but as the Petiot trial was billed as the second-greatest theatrical event of the year after *The Madwoman of Chaillot*, enterprising black marketeers, trained under the Occupation, sold counterfeit passes, and sensation seekers packed every available space.

The trial opened at 1:20 P.M. with the selection of all seven jurors and three alternates out of a larger pool drawn by lot from the voter-registration lists. Until 1941, the French criminal justice system had used twelve jurors (and since 1958 there have been nine). In all cases the jurors deliberate together with the three magistrates and decisions are reached on the basis of a two-thirds majority rather than unanimity. During the Occupation, the number of jurors used had been reduced to six, and a simple majority, even by a one-vote margin, was sufficient for condemnation. During a thirteen-year postwar transition period, an additional juror was added and a six-to-four majority was required for conviction. The alternates, today as then, sit through the entire proceeding, but play an active part only if a juror falls ill or is disqualified, at which point one of the alternates steps in and the trial continues without a break. Only five challenges were permitted, so the selection and swearing-in of the jurors — all men, it turned out — was soon finished.

At 1:50 Petiot was ushered into the courtroom. He had asked that his handcuffs be removed outside, which was done. He wore a blue-gray suit, purple bow tie, and a gray overcoat, and carried a small sheaf of papers. Photographers began taking pictures. Petiot at first modestly hid his face, then struck several dramatic poses before politely saying, "I think that's enough for now, gentlemen." He took off his overcoat, folded it carefully, looked at it, unfolded it, folded it again, and placed it carefully on the seat behind him. The court watched in silence. He turned to give everyone a pleasant smile, then glanced at President Leser to indicate he was ready.

The clerk of the court read the lengthy indictment, terminating with twenty-seven repetitions of the accusation that there existed sufficient evidence against Petiot, Marcel André Henri Félix, of having, either in Paris or any other place "on such a day 194[x], in any case within the statute of limitations [ten years for first-degree murder] willfully put to death [X], born at [such and such a place] on [such and such a date], and that this willful homicide was committed with premeditation and malice aforethought, for the purpose of preparing, facilitating, or effecting the fraudulent appropriation of clothing, personal items, identity papers, and a portion of the fortune of the above-mentioned victim."

Petiot looked bored and drew caricatures of the prosecution on the back of his notes. The clerk read out the names of the eighty witnesses to make sure everyone was present. Colonel André Dewavrin, de Gaulle's chief of intelligence, who was supposed to testify on Petiot's Resistance activity, was found to be away on a mission.

FLORIOT   I wonder how long he'll be gone?
DUPIN   So do I.
FLORIOT   You have means I lack for finding out.
DUPIN   So I do.

At 3:15 the preliminaries were over and Leser began to read the summary of Petiot's past life that the police had pieced together. Petiot listened with bored amusement; from time to time he leaped up to correct a detail while Leser timidly, futilely, tried to maintain some semblance of order. His presentation was intended to be an introduction to the personality of the man they were there to judge, and, indeed, it was.

LESER [reading]   He was a mediocre student —

PETIOT   I only got "very good" on my thesis. I should be modest about these things.

LESER   You were involved in politics in the Yonne, but contrary to your statements you were never in opposition with Flandin.°

PETIOT   I was the Socialist candidate. Do I have to draw you a diagram to show you my position with respect to Flandin?

LESER   You were well thought of as a doctor. Your patients found you quite seductive.

PETIOT   Why, thank you.

LESER   Nonetheless, a woman in the town, Madame Mongin, had several complaints about you, among them that you stole items from her house and replaced an antique stove with a copy.

PETIOT   If that's how we're going to begin, this is not going to go very well.

LESER   I'll begin however I please.

PETIOT   Madame Mongin wanted to sleep with me. I declined this honor. She lied.

LESER   Next you're going to tell me the whole dossier is false.

PETIOT   No, I wouldn't say that. Only eight-tenths of it is false.

Leser mentioned the theft of the cemetery cross.

PETIOT   Why don't we stop this farce right now? This story was made up by all the bigots and idiots in the country. In fact, this cross disappeared two hundred years ago. There must be a statute of limitations, isn't there, Monsieur le Président?

As Petiot launched into a long explanation, Dupin interrupted him.

PETIOT [shouting]   Would you please let me finish my story?

LESER   I forbid you to speak in that tone. Speak softly.

PETIOT   All right. But I don't care to be treated like a criminal.

° Pierre Etienne Flandin, former prime minister, originally from the Yonne. During the war he was a collaborator by sympathy and briefly served as Vichy foreign minister. At the time of Petiot's trial, Flandin was in prison, charged with treason. He was acquitted in July 1946. Though a good person for Petiot to have the reputation of attacking, he had, in fact, left the Yonne before Petiot became involved in politics there.

And I beg the gentlemen of the jury, who will be the final arbiters of this fight, to carefully note all the lies in the dossier.

The theft of electricity started Petiot on another windy tale, and this time it was Leser who interrupted.

PETIOT   Will you *please* let me continue? I do think I have some rights here. This is *my* trial.

Leser threw his arms in the air. "I've never seen anything like this."

PETIOT   Don't throw your arms in the air, Monsieur le Président.

LESER [impotent with rage]   I'll throw my arms in the air if I want to.

PETIOT   Oh well, if it pleases you. In another minute you'll have reason to throw them even higher.

Leser turned to the doctor's life in Paris and the leaflet he sent out upon his arrival. "This is the prospectus of a quack!" he remarked without thinking.

PETIOT   Thanks for the advertising, but I would appreciate it if you kept your opinions to yourself.

FLORIOT   A court is supposed to be impartial. I demand that you withdraw this characterization of "quack."

LESER   Forget I ever said anything. You claim to have earned an astronomical salary, yet you declared only twenty-five thousand francs on your tax return.

PETIOT   I earned three hundred thousand to five hundred thousand francs yer year, which is hardly astronomical. When a surgeon earns eight or ten million, he declares a hundred thousand; it's a medical tradition. I didn't want to seem like some kind of dope. Besides, it proves that I'm a patriot: the French are notorious for tax evasion.

Leser asked about the death of his patient Raymonde Hanss.

PETIOT   The autopsy proved that my injection had nothing to do with her death. I even telephoned Dr. Paul at the time to find out the results of his inquest. He told me, "If you start asking questions about everyone who dies, you're going to be a very busy man." Dr. Paul loves to joke, you know.

The subject turned to the theft at the Joseph Gibert bookstore.

PETIOT   I didn't steal anything. I put the book under my arm by mistake while preoccupied with my invention.

Leser tried in vain to stop him from going into a complete description of the machine with full anatomical details of its application. "All inventors are thought to be crazy." Petiot added.

LESER   It was you who pretended to be crazy every time you had troubles with the law.

PETIOT   On the contrary, I always maintained I was quite sane. No one ever knows whether he is crazy or not. One can only be crazy by comparison.

Leser described the rue Le Sueur house and placed a sinister interpretation on the triangular room.

PETIOT   Look, I planned to put a radiotherapy machine in that room. I installed the false door because I found it decorative and be-cause I ran out of wallpaper. As for the viewer, it was under the wallpaper. Does that suggest anything to you? You can't see through wallpaper very well, can you? These are all lies told by the German press, so let's just stop talking about them. Or else, rather than ask-ing me what I did, why don't you ask me what I didn't do. Things would move along much more quickly.

LESER   Your arrival at the house was rather strange.

PETIOT   When the police telephoned, I came at once. That proves I was innocent. They say it took me half an hour to arrive. That annoys me. It took me twelve minutes to go from the rue Caumartin to the rue Le Sueur and ten minutes to return. They made up the story of my lateness to justify the fact that they had forced open the door, which I find astonishingly presumptuous.* A heater which is operating scarcely constitutes the beginning of a fire.

LESER   But you said, "I am risking my head."

PETIOT   I was. And I'm still risking my head here today, even though I am innocent.

LESER   You refused to answer Judge Goletty's questions.

PETIOT   That's not altogether true. I told Monsieur Goletty, "Perhaps I will answer you with a pair of slaps."

Petiot repeated his story of finding bodies in his house when he returned from Fresnes and told how his Resistance comrades had helped dispose of them.

DUPIN   What comrades? Give us names.

PETIOT   I will not give you my comrades' names because they are not guilty — no more than I am. Several of them offered to come and testify on my behalf, but I didn't want them to. They deserve the Liberation Cross for liquidating thirty krauts, and you would decorate them with handcuffs.

DUPIN   Let them come and I will give them the Cross. You have my word.

PETIOT   No, I will not tell you their names until the purge is complete. Not as long as men who pledged allegiance to Pétain are still free.

Leser was troubled by Petiot's assertion that he had joined the Resistance as soon as the Germans arrived. "But there was no Resistance at that time," the president stated. The audience shouted in protest at the suggestion that France had peacefully let itself be conquered. "No organized Resistance, I mean." Leser apologized, and hastily went on to ask about Petiot's secret weapon. It was evident that Leser had already lost control of the trial and would have difficulty wresting it back from the glib and confident Dr. Petiot.

---

* Several neighbors had, in fact, told the *juge d'instruction* that the firemen had entered the building before the policeman Teyssier went to call Petiot. Petiot was quite possibly right.

PETIOT   I'm not going to tell you anything. This is certainly not the place to discuss it. It is a short-range weapon, useful primarily for defensive purposes. The only people who would use it now are the Germans, who would love to get rid of the Allied occupying forces and prepare for another war.

He went on to tell how he had killed a German on horseback in the Bois de Boulogne. Someone in the audience shouted, "Call the horse to the stand!" Petiot spoke vaguely of Rainbow, Fly-Tox, Cumulo, and the Englishman who had taught him Resistance tactics. He mentioned for the first time that his group had blown up German trains in the Chevreuse Valley near Versailles.

Pierre Véron really was a Resistant, and his credentials as such were so impeccable that he had been asked, for strategic reasons, to codefend Maréchal Pétain (he refused). During the Occupation he was part of a group that helped downed Allied pilots escape from France, concealing them in his apartment for days while carrying on his practice. After the D-Day invasion, he left Paris and blew up, if not trains, bridges all over France, as his group covered the flanks of the two Allied forces converging on Paris from the west and south. Véron began firing questions at Petiot.

VÉRON   What are plastic explosives?
PETIOT   . . .
VÉRON   How do you transport plastic explosives?
PETIOT   Wait a minute, it's coming back to me. Several comrades filled a suitcase with plastic explosives and detonated them with a bomb with a timer, and then came to hide at my house.
VÉRON   What is this "bomb with a timer?"
PETIOT   A German grenade . . . you know . . . the ones with the handle. We heard the explosion thirty minutes later —
VÉRON   German fragmentation grenades have a seven-second fuse!

Petiot mumbled something and fell silent, glaring sullenly.

FLORIOT   Is this a trial or an entrance exam for the Polytechnic Institute?

VÉRON   This is an examination on the Resistance, and it didn't take long to show that your client is an impostor.

Petiot hastened to say: "You didn't let me finish. I wasn't going to say that it exploded half an hour later, but that half an hour later the Germans came to my house." But he knew he had erred seriously, and Véron listened with an indulgent smile. "What right do you have to talk," Petiot shouted, "You defender of traitors and Jews!"

Leser ended the day's proceedings at 6:30. Petiot, having regained his composure, said: "I hope you're not stopping on my account. I'm not in the least bit tired." He smiled pleasantly.

THE THEATRICS of the first day drew an even larger crowd the second. Leser opened with the Resistance again.

LESER   How did you go about detecting and liquidating these alleged German informers?

PETIOT   It was very simple. My comrades and I observed the civilians who came out of the rue des Saussaies. We followed them in a truck. In a secluded place, we stopped them and said we were the German police. Their reactions gave them away. We shoved them in the truck and buried them in the forest near Marly.

DUPIN   Give us some names.

Floriot whispered, "Adrien Estébétéguy."

PETIOT   Adrien Estébétéguy."

DUPIN   Did you kill them yourself?

PETIOT   I killed two German motorcyclists with my secret weapon.

VÉRON   Where? How? This is not the sort of thing that passes unnoticed. We could check up on your statement.

PETIOT   You're just searching for dramatic effect!

VÉRON   No, but I won't tolerate having you dirty the name of the Resistance for your own ends!

The audience applauded.

PETIOT   Shut up, you defender of Jews. You're working for the traitor Dreyfus and you're a double agent yourself!

Véron raised his fist and took a step toward Petiot. "Take that back or I'll knock your teeth in!"
The audience laughed, and this interchange furnished headlines for all the newspapers. Even before Véron returned home that evening, his wife had read exaggerated accounts of the accused and the lawyer almost leaping at one another's throat. Leser placated the two men and restored order. Floriot had slept through most of the interchange, sprawled across his desk.

VÉRON   Tell us about your secret weapon.
PETIOT   I've told you a hundred times, and I'll tell you a thousand more until you finally understand: I'm not going to reveal information which could only be used against France.

Floriot woke up and laughed.

LESER   Give us the names of your comrades.
PETIOT   Where have you been? I already told you I'm not giving them to you.
LESER   It would certainly help your case if you gave us the names.
PETIOT   All right. I'll give them to you.
LESER   When?
PETIOT   As soon as I'm acquitted.

"I rather doubt that you will be," Leser said, with a surprising lack of impartiality that no one seemed to notice.

PETIOT   I'm sure of it.
DUPIN   Why don't your men come forward of their own accord when they know their chief's head is at stake?
PETIOT   You're the one who says my head is at stake. Fortunately, you're not the one who's judging me, but the jurors. I have more confidence in them than in you.
DUPIN   I have given you my guarantee they will not be arrested.

PETIOT   Yes, of course, we all know that tune. You make the promises and it's your little buddies who make the arrests.

He was asked about the escape route and the people who had been killed when they presented themselves for escape.

PETIOT   The first victim was Jo le Boxeur. He was easy to spot as a collaborator; he had a head like a pimp — you know, like a police inspector.

He spoke of Lucien Romier, of the employee at the Argentinian embassy, and of the police commissioner in Lyon.

PETIOT   I'm sorry, I have a poor memory for names. I only remember initials.

A LAWYER   What are the names of the people who actually helped escapees across the border?

PETIOT   Oh, you know, they changed names frequently.

LAWYER   How convenient.

VÉRON   How about just a few names?

PETIOT   There was Robert in the Saône-et-Loire. At Nevers, a German who committed suicide. At Orléans you met someone at the train station café.

He was asked about his arrest.

PETIOT   They took me to the rue des Saussaies. "Oh, so you're Dr. Eugène!" said the infamous Jodkum. He had my head crushed, suspended me by my jaw, filed my teeth. We don't need to go into it. I saw one of my comrades lying on a stretcher, bleeding, foaming at the mouth.

He put his head in his arms and began to sob. "Excuse me."

LESER   Why were you released?

PETIOT   My brother paid a hundred thousand francs. My comrades were astonished to see me out, and I had great difficulty getting back into an active role.

LESER   How about the bodies at the rue Le Sueur?

PETIOT   I found a large pointed heap of them when I went there. I was very annoyed. I didn't want that sort of thing about my house.

LESER   Is that why you asked your brother for quicklime?

PETIOT   Oh, no! The lime was for exterminating roaches, but since my comrades couldn't haul the bodies away I had the idea of putting them in the lime. That didn't work very well, so my two comrades thought of burning them in the stove. I had already lit it to destroy a rug infested with mites.

Petiot had told several stories about the lime: it was to white-wash the building, to kill bugs, to destroy bodies. All the versions were in the dossier, and Dupin could have caught him in a dozen contradictions. He never did.

Petiot was asked about his activities during the eight months he was sought. He described the battle at the place de la Ré-publique and an assault on a blockhouse at the boulevard Saint-Martin.

PETIOT   It was there that I received a bullet — I mean, a bullet struck a store window just behind me.

LESER   What nature of work did you do at the Caserne de Reuilly?

PETIOT   I uncovered collaborators and interrogated them. I arrested a Duke de la Rochefoucauld, Count of la Roche-Guyon, who fought for the Germans; a woman named Bonnasseau; Fox, the director of Phillips; Muller, Cornu —

A LAWYER   Strange how his memory for names has returned.

DUPIN   You enrolled under a false name.

PETIOT   Yes, I borrowed the papers of Dr. Wetterwald. I was almost fifty years old, and he was only thirty-three.

DUPIN   You didn't borrow them, you stole them. And every time you were called as a doctor to write a death certificate you stole the dead man's papers.

PETIOT   That's a lie. I only took a dead man's papers once — Harry Baur's, the well-known actor.

DUPIN   You don't look anything like Harry Baur. Don't tell me you hoped to pass for him?

PETIOT   He was tortured to death by the Nazis, and I wanted to avenge his death. I did what I did out of sportsmanship. I'm not asking for your thanks.

LESER   What did the other officers at the Caserne think of you?

PETIOT   Let them tell you. But they knew who I was.

LESER   They knew and said nothing?

PETIOT   I was finally denounced by a comrade, if you can call him that. Among the twelve disciples, Jesus found one Judas. Fifty men trusted me. The fifty-first was a traitor.

DUPIN   What about all the other stolen papers found on you when you were arrested?

PETIOT   There's plenty of false information about me in the dossier. There's thirty kilos of it.

Dupin continued to press Petiot, but the prosecutor's command of the facts was unsteady. Floriot advised him to learn the difference between "always" and "sometimes," "everyone" and "a few people," and "yes" and "no." The two began to shout, the audience broke into hysterics, and Leser frantically tried to make himself heard.

PETIOT [during a brief lull]   Don't I have the right to say anything? I'm involved in this, too, you know.

VÉRON   Poor fellow. Are you bored?

Court was recessed at 4:30. When it reconvened, there were even more people packed in than before, and Petiot noted there was no place to lay his coat. The discussion turned to Denise Hotin and Madame Khaït. Petiot's response to the Hotin accusation was simple.

PETIOT   I have news for you. I have never even heard that name before. Monsieur le Président, you may continue.

LESER   How gracious of you to permit me.

Véron began firing questions about the Khaït disappearance.

VÉRON   Just answer yes or no, did you give Madame Khaït saline injections?

PETIOT   You are a very talented lawyer. I shall have to send you some clients.

Floriot smiled. Véron spoke of Raymonde Baudet. Petiot gazed dreamily into space. "She was a very lovely girl."

VÉRON   She was not. She was quite plain.
PETIOT   You met her when she was past her prime.
VÉRON   You sound like something out of a bad novel.

This idle banter continued for some time before the president of the tribunal interrupted.

LESER   Maître Véron, please ask specific questions. This is truly extraordinary — one of them won't ask questions and the other refuses to answer them!
PETIOT [complaining to Véron] This is ridiculous. I sent Mademoiselle Baudet to you and it was I who paid your fees.

This was true. Petiot had been most solicitous at the time and insisted Raymonde Baudet should have the best lawyer. He had asked Floriot for a reference, and Floriot had recommended Véron.

VÉRON   It is less dangerous for you to send me clients than for me to send them to you.

The day closed at 5:45. Petiot learned quickly and had recognized his errors from the previous day; the newspapers showed grudging admiration for his wit and confidence. He had contradicted himself and the evidence on several points and had glossed over or ignored several others. No one believed he was telling the truth, but the prosecution lacked the skill and force needed to nail down his lies. Reporters began to keep score of the trial: Petiot had won on points the second day.

Humor could not change the facts, though. David Perlman, a correspondent for the *New York Herald Tribune*, interviewed Leser and two jurors as they left the courtroom. Leser told him: "Petiot is a demon, an unbelievable demon. He is a terrifying monster. He is an appalling murderer." One juror said: "He is mad. But of course he is mad. He is intelligent, though. He has a terrible intelligence. He is guilty, and the guillotine is too swift for such a monster." The other remarked, "We are only hearing about the bodies that were found, but how many more he killed, and how many bodies he hid, we shall never know."

This was an incredible breach of court procedure, and Floriot leaped at the opportunity for a mistrial. The appellate court replaced the two jurors with alternates and reprimanded Perlman, but maintained that the trial could continue. From then on, Leser scrupulously observed every procedural propriety. In retrospect, it seems remarkable that more serious measures were not taken, given that not only two jurors but the chief magistrate himself had manifested a predisposition in the case. Possibly the feeling was that the Petiot case had one ineluctable outcome, and the sooner reached, the better.

ON THE THIRD DAY, the trial continued with the victims. Albert Palle, writing in the former underground newspaper *Combat*, complained that the victims flashed by so quickly that one never had a chance to feel the tragedy in its full dimensions or perceive the victims as real human beings at all. And, as well, the horror of the war had "normalized" murder and emptied it of meaning. "Human life is sacred!" Dupin shouted, and the audience laughed. "There's nothing to laugh about," Leser roared indignantly. "Those of you who wish to amuse yourselves should get out and go to the theater." Petiot's callous dexterity had turned the trial into an entertaining duel of wits, and despite the horror of the crimes, the third day would end with the score "Prosecution 1, Petiot 2."

It was pointed out that Van Bever had disappeared after difficulties with Petiot, that he had written strange letters, and that some of his identity papers had been found in Petiot's possession.

PETIOT Big deal.

Floriot mentioned that Van Bever had enemies in Troyes. There were questions as to whether or not he had been an addict.

PETIOT   *She* was certainly an addict. You only need to look at her photograph. Her whole body was covered with pimples.

He went on to describe the sex life of Jeannette Gaul and Van Bever in minute detail. The audience burst into laughter, and Leser's face turned purple as he tried to silence Petiot. Finally he moved on to the Guschinov case.

PETIOT   Guschinov was taken across the Spanish border by André le Corse and Robert Martinetti.
DUPIN   How did you meet Robert Martinetti?
PETIOT   He was one of my patients. I was treating him for an affliction I don't care to name.
DUPIN   Where is Guschinov now?
PETIOT   In South America.
DUPIN   We haven't been able to find him.
PETIOT   South America is a big place.
FLORIOT   Have you looked? I don't see anything in the dossier about investigators being sent to South America.
DUPIN   Inquiries were made.
FLORIOT   Yes, I have copies of your inquiries here. Madame Guschinov wrote to two people asking if, by some chance, they had seen her husband. Of course they hadn't seen him, any more than you have seen ninety-nine percent of the people in Paris. This is ridiculous.
PETIOT   I received three letters from Guschinov on the stationery of the Alvear Palace Hotel in Buenos Aires. Light blue paper, it was. By the way, did you know that in South America they slit envelopes on the side rather than at the top the way we do? Isn't that odd?
LESER   Were you paid for this passage?
PETIOT   No . . . Well, yes, in a way. Guschinov was a furrier. I asked him if he had any ermine for my wife. I love ermine because of the color. Instead of ermine, Guschinov brought me five sable skins. I don't know anything about furs. I thought they were worth

about ten thousand francs. But these five skins were all exactly the same color, and it seems that's very rare. [His voice breaking with emotion] They were worth a hundred thousand francs.

DUPIN   You told Guschinov to remove all the marks from his clothes.

PETIOT   An elementary precaution when one changes identity. If you knew anything about the Resistance —

DUPIN   I know more about the Resistance than you do.

Petiot shrugged. "Perhaps, but not from the same side."

ARCHEVÊQUE   Tell us the names of the members of your group.

PETIOT   What? Again? Is this going to happen every day? Are you trying to turn it into a comedy? Look, I explained this all yesterday, and you seem to be the only person who didn't understand anything that was going on. You're making us look like idiots. I'm ashamed of you. There are foreign journalists here covering this trial. What is the rest of the world going to think of French justice?

The court hurried on to Dr. Braunberger.

PETIOT   I saw him for ten minutes in my life; at a luncheon following a first communion.

PERLÈS   His hat and shirt ended up in your house.

PETIOT   We'll see about that when the time comes.

PERLÈS   You are mentioned in one of the letters he wrote to his wife after his disappearance.

Floriot jumped up, but Petiot motioned for him to resume his place. "Let it go."

PERLÈS   The gentlemen of the jury will please note that the accused refuses to answer.

This time it was Petiot who jumped up, and Floriot turned to soothe him: "Don't answer. It's too ridiculous."

Perlès droned on. Petiot scribbled or rested his head on his arms.

LESER   Listen when you're being questioned.

PETIOT   I am listening, but it doesn't really interest me very much.

PERLÈS   My questions interest the jurors.

PETIOT   That's all you ask of life, isn't it?

PERLÈS   You're anti-Semitic.

PETIOT   No, I wasn't before the war. I wasn't during the Occupation. But after everything I went through in Fresnes at the hands of the Gestapo . . . [his voice breaking] After all that I endured and did for Jews . . . and now, when I see so many Jews against me, I am beginning to become anti-Semitic.

The proceeding turned to the nine criminals and prostitutes.

PETIOT   Réocreux wanted to go to Argentina with his mistress and a friend. He paid Fourrier twenty-five thousand francs per person. François le Corse came first with a woman. Ten of my men accosted him behind the Madeleine and played the police trick. François said he was from the rue Lauriston [French Gestapo headquarters] and that Lafont would vouch for him. That was the end of François.

LESER   Describe the execution.

Petiot pretended to be scandalized. "Goodness, you have sadistic tastes! I was not there myself, so all I can tell you is that he was hit over the head with a rubber tube filled with sand, lead, and bicycle spokes for flexibility."

LESER   Were you present at any of the executions?

PETIOT   Yes, about a third of them.

LESER   Details?

PETIOT   Oh! There was Jo le Boxeur. He told us he was a poor bastard gone astray because of an unhappy childhood. His real name was Grosjean or Granjean [this was false]. He offered to betray Lafont. He wanted to be part of our group, and offered us four hundred thousand francs. But we knew that he just wanted to discover the escape route like the others. We were a bit scared of him because he was huge and mean, but when his time came, he fell on his knees and begged. The woman with him pulled out a revolver. She was one hell of a woman.

Adrien le Basque was easy to spot. You only needed to look at his face to see what he was. Monsieur le Président, if you wouldn't mind passing around his photograph, the people can see for themselves. He was tough, and he caught on right away. We had to shove a gun in his ribs to get him into the truck. He was taken to the rue Le Sueur, and he pulled out a knife. One of my men was wounded near the liver before we killed him. It was a real butchery.

DUPIN It's true that the men worked for the Gestapo, but why did you kill the women?

Petiot shrugged. "What did you want me to do with them?"

DUPIN That sort of reasoning could take you far.

PETIOT They whored for the Germans. They would have denounced us.

DUPIN Have you no respect for human life?

PETIOT For the lives of Gestapo members? No. Have you?

DUPIN What gave you the right to judge and execute people?

PETIOT If there had been a procureur de la République at the time, we would gladly have let him take the job. It was not a very pleasant one.

DUPIN How much money did you get?

PETIOT We didn't work for money. We didn't get a penny.

DUPIN What about the four million Estébétéguy sewed into the shoulder pads of his suit?

PETIOT Why ask me? You've got his suitcase right there. Why don't you have a look?

The clerk tried to extricate an ivory-colored suitcase with black leather corners. The pile teetered and threatened to fall, and Leser hurriedly called a recess until things were safe.

PETIOT You'd better post guards in the room; we don't want anybody stealing anything! [Turning to Floriot] Say, if they do find some money, do I get ten percent?

After the recess, the clerk pulled out several suits. Petiot snatched them, waved them in the air, and threw them back at the clerk.

PETIOT   You see? The shoulders are intact. Why should they have hidden money anyway, since they had no intention of leaving?

FLORIOT   Look, Petiot, why don't you give me a chance to do my job? Maître Dupin, why should they have wanted to escape, anyway?

DUPIN   They were criminals. The police were after them.

FLORIOT   You're not serious. You don't honestly believe members of the Gestapo were afraid of French policemen?

Petiot was asked about the groups of Jews sent to him by Eryane Kahan.

PETIOT   Yes, I killed the Basches and the Wolffs. I didn't know they were Jews, but I knew they were German spies sent by Eryane Kahan.

DUPIN   What about the Schonkers — the parents of the Basch couple?

PETIOT   I don't know anything about them, but if it makes you happy, you can put them on my account. They came from the same bunch, and if I had met them I would have killed them.

DUPIN   Why didn't you kill Eryane Kahan if you knew she was collaborating with the Germans?

PETIOT   I hoped she would send me more traitors. If she had sent me a hundred I would have killed a hundred. And she would have been the hundred-and-first.

DUPIN   I don't see how you can call the Wolffs traitors. They were Jews fleeing the Nazis. They were one hundred percent Resistants.

PETIOT   They were Germans.

BERNAYS   They fled Holland on July 12, 1942, and were in constant fear of arrest.

PETIOT   They came from Berlin.

FLORIOT   I have here a report written by Inspector Batut. It says that the Wolffs entered France with a passport issued in Berlin and which is perfectly in order.* Frightened refugees do not apply to

* Floriot's facts were correct, but he neglected to mention one important point: the Wolffs entered France with a German passport in 1933; they did not have German passports in 1942.

their government for a passport. When they arrived in Paris they "hid" in a hotel requisitioned by the Germans.

PETIOT   They hid the way I did on my honeymoon. I pulled the sheets over my head and said to my wife, "Try to find me."

As THE COURT settled into place on the fourth day, Petiot was heard addressing the audience.

PETIOT   A certain General V — Victor, I believe — had been parachuted into the countryside near Lyon. To capture him, the Germans mobilized four hundred prostitutes! Another —

LESER   We are not here to listen to war stories, Petiot, but to discuss the case of Yvan Dreyfus.

PETIOT   Very well. Dreyfus was sent to me through Guélin and Chantin — sad individuals, those two. Guélin got in touch with Fourrier, the barber. It was in Fourrier's apartment that I met Dreyfus. Fourrier had told me that Dreyfus had just been released from the camp at Compiègne and had to get out of the country as quickly as possible. At the time I didn't have very many men; most of them had gone to Lyon for a bit of mopping up. It was obvious that Dreyfus was a Jew. He told me he worked in the radio business, and by questioning him, I could see that he knew what he was talking about. Guélin was a lawyer. I was completely taken in. I said to myself, "This is something different from Jo le Boxeur and his kind. We're going to get this man out of the country."

LESER   Did you ask him for money?

PETIOT   I never asked for money. It was Fourrier who did. I took Dreyfus toward the Concorde, and on the way Robert Martinetti met us and led Dreyfus in the direction of the Naval Ministry and the Champs-Elysées. I went home.

LESER   What happened to Dreyfus?

PETIOT   I don't know. Maybe he went to South America, maybe my group killed him — I never had the chance to ask. It was because of that traitor that I was arrested the next day. The Germans tried to pretend that Guélin and a certain Beretta had been arrested as well, but they gave themselves away and I knew it was a trap. They asked me what had happened to Dreyfus. I told them, "If he's a Jew, what difference does it make to you that he's disappeared? And if he's an informer, don't worry, you'll find another." I was risking my neck, Monsieur le Président, but it was fun.

LESER We're not asking whether you had fun.

FLORIOT I would like to point out that there is a Gestapo file, dated 1943, furnishing incontrovertible proof that Dreyfus agreed to act as an informer. There is no cause to be sentimental over the fate of Yvan Dreyfus.

VÉRON What reason do we have to believe a file of which there is only one copy, and no original?

DUPIN If Dreyfus were still alive, no one would dream of prosecuting him.

PETIOT Dreyfus was a traitor four times over: a traitor to his race, a traitor to his religion, a traitor to his country, and a traitor —

LESER Don't moralize, Petiot, it doesn't become you.

The cases had been presented in the chronological order of their discovery. The Knellers came last, and everyone anticipated a dramatic turnabout. How could Petiot accuse a German Jew of collaborating when the victim was only seven years old?

PETIOT Kneller was one of my patients. I can't tell you what I was treating him for. It was an embarrassing affliction and professional secrecy prevents me from revealing it.

Petiot had said this before. He seemed to think that by hinting that Guschinov, Cumulo, and Kneller had socially shameful diseases he would halt questions about them or possibly discredit them.

PETIOT Kneller told me he wanted to escape to the free zone. He didn't have very much money. He already owed me two thousand francs for his treatment. I paid for his false papers out of my own pocket and asked him to leave me his furniture as collateral.

DUPIN And you took it to the rue Le Sueur.

PETIOT Look, I'm not really very proud of this. They were Germans.

LESER Germans who fled their country when the Nazis came to power.

PETIOT   They've probably already returned and are getting ready for the next war.

LESER   Oh, leave us alone with your "next war."

PETIOT   At the rate things are going, we won't have long to wait. Anyway, the Knellers spent the night at the rue Le Sueur. I told them to take two bottles of cognac as a present for the man who would lead them across the border.

DUPIN   There was a child.

PETIOT   Yes, he was a delightful boy.

DUPIN   "Was" is the operative word. His pajamas were found in your house. So was a shirt with Kurt Kneller's initials.

PETIOT   Those must be the pajamas in which he slept that last night. Why would they want to take dirty laundry with them — particularly with their initials on them? And what earthly reason would I have to keep such things?

DUPIN   This is where your system of defense falls apart. During the *instruction* you didn't even dare answer the questions you were asked about the Knellers.

PETIOT   That's not true. I answered plenty of questions. I stopped answering them when I was told to sign a list of three hundred sixty-two questions no one ever asked me.

DUPIN   Judge Goletty showed you the clothing inventory and you refused to comment.

Floriot woke from apparent slumber. "You just say anything that comes into your head," he said to Dupin. "Petiot never saw that inventory. Show me the interrogation in the dossier that proves he did. You've never even read the dossier. Show me the proof and I'll stop practicing law right now."

Elissalde tried to whisper to Dupin, but the latter charged ahead in righteous indignation.

DUPIN   Judge Goletty repeated it to me just this morning.

FLORIOT   Then call him to the stand and we'll see.

PETIOT   No one showed me the list or the suitcase. Who knows what has been put in those suitcases?

Leser adjourned the court for fifteen minutes. When they reconvened, there was no further mention of the inventory. Dupin had seen Goletty in the hall and learned that Floriot was right. Dupin would never listen to Elissalde, did not know the details himself, and grew tired of looking foolish. Finally he stopped challenging Floriot on questions of fact altogether, and thus weakened the prosecution even further. The defense walked all over him.

The presentation was over, and the first witness was called. Commissaire Lucien Pinault took the stand. He had worked on the case from the beginning and it was he who had taken over from Massu and led the investigation following Petiot's arrest. He stepped up with confidence, but even before he could begin, Petiot caught him off guard and elicited a testimonial.

PETIOT   Was I known to frequent unsavory places or to associate with criminals or loose women?

PINAULT   No.

PETIOT   Did people think of me as a greedy man who valued money above all else?

PINAULT   No, you seem to have left rather the opposite impression.

PETIOT   [choking with emotion]   Thank you.

Pinault recovered himself and gave evidence showing that Petiot and Cumulo looked nothing alike.

PINAULT   And among all the people I interviewed, none had ever heard of Dr. Petiot or Dr. Eugène.

PETIOT   You just made a mistake, that's all. But don't worry, it's not your fault.

FLORIOT   Didn't your investigations show that Guélin was working for the Germans?

PINAULT   He was an informer, yes.

FLORIOT   Haven't two bodies found near Marly been identified?

PINAULT   Well, it's not within my jurisdiction, but I have heard that two Gestapo agents were found buried near the woods at Marly.

An inspector Poirier took the stand. He had spoken with several hundred of Petiot's patients, he testified, and many of them were frightened by the doctor's eyes.

PETIOT   Here we go. They're going to start saying I'm crazy again.

Floriot forced Poirier to admit that Eryane Kahan was an adventuress and that Lafont, before his execution, had acknowledged the participation of Réocreux and Estébétéguy in his group. Floriot then read a 1942 police report stating that Dr. Braunberger had returned home several days after his wife reported him missing, and he gently chided Poirier for making unproved assertions. The report had been only a means of closing a seemingly pointless investigation, and had no basis in fact. But fact quickly seemed to be losing its importance in the trial. The press chalked up another round for Petiot and ridiculed the incompetence of Dupin and Leser.

ON THE FIFTH DAY, the court was scheduled to go to the rue Le Sueur. Petiot had demanded that the jurors see the building about which so many lies had been written and discover for themselves just how innocent it really was. Professor Charles Sannié, the director of the Identité Judiciaire, took the stand. He had conducted the inspection of the building, and now gave the court a long and tedious description of what they were about to see. Long before he finished, the journalists went to their cars and raced madly across Paris, running red lights and shouting to startled policemen and pedestrians: "Get the hell out of the way! Petiot is coming!"

At 2:00 P.M. the official proceedings moved from the Palais de Justice. Leser daintily lifted the hem of his scarlet robes as he descended the steps. Petiot turned his coat collar up against the rain and smiled at the onlookers. The streets around the court building had been barricaded, and fifteen cars and a swarm of motorcycle police waited to effect the move with, as one person claimed, the maximum amount of chaos and discomfort.

The rue Le Sueur was closed to traffic, and three hundred policemen were stationed along the block to maintain order. Spectators crowded every window and shop, and repeatedly

burst through police lines to get a closer look at Petiot. Flanked
by two inspectors and surrounded by gendarmes, the handcuffed
Petiot was led into his house. "Peculiar homecoming reception,
don't you think?" he asked one of Floriot's assistants.

Leser did his best to retain some semblance of dignity. Dupin
looked irritable and sulked throughout the visit. A fine rain continued to fall, and the long judicial robes dragged in the mud
and sodden lime. The journalists, audience, and neighbors tried
to fight their way past the police. One reporter was thrown to
the ground, the sleeve of a gendarme's uniform was ripped off,
and Maurice Petiot's wife Monique was seen kicking another
policeman. Someone tried to close the front door. Leser shouted:
"My God, don't do that! Court is in session and it must be a
public audience! Isn't that so, Maître Floriot?" Floriot grinned.
Leaving the courtroom had been an unusual step, and there were
a thousand opportunities for a mistrial.

The crowd forced its way in and set off in all directions. The
library was ransacked. Someone threw a bale of papers out of
a window to those waiting in the street. Mothers, with the
newspapers' maps of the building in their hands, showed their
children the stove and the pit. Leser frantically tried to collect
the members of his court. One group of lawyers posed in the
courtyard, smiling, with human thighbones in their hands, while
photographers took pictures.

The court moved into the doctor's consultation room. No one
had thought to have the electricity turned on. Candles were
brought, and the whole visit was punctuated by the striking of
matches as they blew out.

PETIOT   Truly this is enlightened justice!

The avocat général, his robes covered with plaster dust and
cobwebs, moodily explained the layout of the building.

DUPIN   From here, the victim followed that corridor, which leads
to the triangular room, where he thought there was an exit. He

entered, and tried to open the door on the far wall. Before he discovered that it was false, the door behind him closed. It was locked with a chain and had no knob on the inside.

Leser, Dupin, Petiot, Floriot, Sannié, and three jurors managed to pack themselves into the triangular room. Their candle blew out; no one could find a match, nor did they dare move in the utter darkness. A cry went up, and a few moments later a policeman pushed through with a flashlight, like Diogenes gone astray. They noticed that the viewer was not in the wall.

FLORIOT Where is the viewer? It was supposed to be under seals.

SANNIÉ I don't know.

FLORIOT You don't know! You had better find it or you should lose your job.

SANNIÉ I think it was left in the courtroom.

PETIOT Despite Monsieur Dupin's macabre description, I had intended to install a radiation therapy machine in this room.

SANNIÉ Don't be ridiculous. You couldn't even get an examination table in here, much less the machinery.

DUPIN This is where you killed your victims after locking them in.

PETIOT If you know anything about construction, you can see that the walls are only thin plaster. That wouldn't hold anyone. Besides, it's impossible to kill anybody in this little hole. Monsieur le Président, how would you go about killing someone in here?

A JUROR Petiot told us the executions took place in a truck.

PETIOT [nonchalantly] Oh, well, of course you can kill anywhere. [Suddenly losing his temper] If I had told you I had never killed anyone, I could understand your obstinacy. But I admit that I executed several people, so what difference does it make whether they were killed here or there? Why do you keep harping on such silly things? The rest of the world really is going to think we're a bunch of imbeciles in France!

Dupin kept trying to speak, but no one paid much attention. He finally pouted: "Will you let me say something? If things are going to continue like this, I'm leaving." As the conversation went on around him, Dupin left and wandered aimlessly from room to room. The rest of the jurors and lawyers were ushered into the triangular room in three shifts. Outside, the people wandered about, and Leser rushed around trying desperately to keep order: "No smoking in the courtroom!" "Silence in the court!" The strangely informal circumstances promoted a certain camaraderie, and one lawyer who had vehemently attacked Petiot was heard chatting with him: "Listen, my dear fellow . . ." "Yes, of course, old chap . . ."

The court arrived at the stables and found Dupin there, but he dashed off. "Wait a minute and I'll get out of your way," he said. "You'll have more room like that." As they stood in front of the pit, Petiot turned pale, tottered, and almost fell in. When they descended the stairs to look at the stove, he stumbled again. Journalists wrote that at last his crimes had proved too much for him. It turned out that Petiot was taken from prison in the morning before breakfast and returned after dinner: he had eaten only a slice of bread and a bowl of thin soup each evening for the past four days, and was merely faint from hunger. Leser made sure he was better fed from then on.

SANNIÉ   Human remains were found here and here. On the landing over there was a sack with half of a corpse in it.

PETIOT   It was a German army mail sack, wasn't it?

SANNIÉ   I believe it was a cement bag.

FLORIOT   I assume you know where this sack is. You do have it under seals, don't you?

Sannié flushed and mumbled incoherently.

FLORIOT   This is really incredible!

The court forced its way back to the waiting cars. The crowd shouted: "Death to the assassin!" Despite Petiot's confidence, the rue Le Sueur had seemed more horrifying than most people had previously imagined, and several jurors reported having nightmares about it for days afterward.

Back at the Palais de Justice, Sannié returned to the stand and described the house again. Floriot forced him to admit that Petiot's fingerprints had not been found anywhere. No one really listened. Most of the crowd would not even have come back except that Massu was scheduled to speak.

When Massu took the stand, Petiot returned to the question of the German army mail sack on the steps at the rue Le Sueur.

MASSU   I think it looked more like a potato sack.
PETIOT   Where is it now? Did you keep it?
MASSU   I think the Identité Judiciaire has it.
FLORIOT   That's what they think, too, but nobody around here seems to be sure of anything.

Floriot questioned Massu on minute details of the dossier. Massu could only reply that "Inspector Batut handled that, you would have to ask him." Or Inspector Poirier had covered another point, or Pascaud, Hernis, Renonciat, · X, Y, Z . . .

FLORIOT   Tell me then, commissaire, just what did *you* do as chief of the Criminal Brigade?
MASSU   I directed criminal investigations.
FLORIOT   I see.

The court was left with the impression that the entire investigation had been conducted in the most careless fashion imaginable.

THE TRIAL reopened at 1:00 P.M. on the sixth day, and the hall was so crowded that a foreign journalist was squeezed into the prisoner's box with Petiot, who smiled amiably and edged over to make room. In the audience were Prince Rainier of Monaco and the wife of Félix Gouin, the provisional president of the Republic.

The first witness was Marius Batut, Massu's competent assistant. If Floriot expected more easy victories, he was disappointed by the inspector with a face like a friendly prizefighter and a firm command of the facts. Batut described parts of the investigation, the discovery of the suitcases, and the identification of several victims. Floriot tried to trip him up on procedural details, but Batut always had the right answer and had always conducted his investigation strictly according to law. Petiot remained silent, digging his pencil point into the wood of his box.

BATUT   I would like to add that the Germans took a great interest in the affair. They followed the investigation, asked us questions, and required us to file a daily report.

LESER   What do you think of the Kahan woman?

BATUT   I do not believe that she worked for the Gestapo. The Germans said we could arrest her if we liked. They weren't interested in her. Her friend Dr. Saint-Pierre asked me not to turn her over to the Germans if we caught her.

VÉRON   Collaborators were not usually afraid of the Germans.

BATUT   No. Nor of us. Whenever we arrested them, they were generally released two or three days later. They came back to see us afterward; they were all very polite.

VÉRON   After his arrest, did Petiot make any accusations against Madame Kahan?

BATUT   No, he did not.

VÉRON   Do you think that the Wolffs and the Basches were Gestapo informers?

BATUT   I can swear under oath that they were not.

VÉRON   What do you know about Yvan Dreyfus?

BATUT   Not much. Just what I've read in the reports.

VÉRON   What was Guélin accused of?

BATUT   Intelligence with the enemy.

VÉRON   Do you think, then, that his testimony about Dreyfus's work for the Germans can be believed?

FLORIOT [interrupting]   Didn't Dreyfus work for the Germans?

BATUT   I don't think so.

FLORIOT   To regain his freedom, didn't he agree to do a certain job for the Germans?

BATUT   I would have to say yes. He was a poor unfortunate like the rest of them. To get out of prison he agreed to furnish some information, the importance of which he had no way of knowing.

FLORIOT Then why did you say he didn't work for the Germans?

BATUT You're trying to confuse me. I warn you, you won't succeed.

DUPIN Maître Floriot, you have already spent fifteen minutes picking at this witness for no purpose.

FLORIOT If you had spent even five minutes reading the dossier, you would see the purpose. For two days the police have been trying to confuse the issue. Their testimony goes on forever and they never say anything. I am just trying to pin down some precise facts. Inspector Batut, were the suitcases shown to the victims' families during the Occupation?

BATUT Not as far as I know.

FLORIOT Why not?

BATUT Maître, you seem to be forgetting that we *were* under the Occupation.

FLORIOT You were in contact with the German police. Lafont came to see Monsieur Massu about Estébétéguy.

BATUT I wasn't there. I know that Lafont was interested in some Gestapo members who had committed a robbery at Hautefort. All of them had disappeared, except for a man named Lombard, who didn't disappear.

PETIOT Are you sure?

The spectators turned and stared at him in stupefaction.

PETIOT You just said that Lombard is alive. Can you give us his address? Don't ask *me* where he is.

No one did. Floriot, at least, already knew perfectly well. Lombard had been a codefendant in the trial of the rue Lauriston Gestapo three months earlier — the trial at which Floriot himself defended Lafont. Lafont's last words as he went off to be shot had been: "Maître Floriot, you have been admirable. I hope, in the future, you will have better causes to defend." That future had apparently not yet arrived.

FLORIOT   Your investigation seems to have been conducted very hastily.

Batut glanced at Floriot's assistants — seven of them today.

BATUT   I don't have a dozen secretaries working for me, Maître.

PETIOT   How many patriots did you arrest and turn over to the Germans to be shot?

Batut was speechless with rage.

PETIOT   Yes, of course, you didn't count them. There were too many.

VÉRON   Remember, Petiot, you're the murderer here.

PETIOT   To conclude with this witness, I —

LESER   If anyone is going to do any concluding around here it will be me.

An Inspector Pascaud came next. He looked like a scholar fallen on hard times and was terrified of Floriot. He had questioned the Spaniards at Levallois-Perret and found that Petiot had never worked with them.

PETIOT   I think someone is confused. My group of Spaniards didn't live at Levallois.

Floriot brought up the Braunberger case. It was found that a set of detachable cuffs had disappeared, and an hour was spent trying to find out when they had been misplaced.

FLORIOT   Are you policemen or magicians? Everything seems to vanish around here. Inspector Pascaud, who broke the seals on the suitcase?

PASCAUD   I didn't.

FLORIOT   Who *did* break the seals on the suitcase?

PASCAUD   I'm the only one who would have opened it for Madame Braunberger.

FLORIOT   How strange. If you didn't open the suitcase, and if no one else opened the suitcase, how did the suitcase get open?

PASCAUD   I don't know.

An Inspector Casanova was more confident, though his voice tended to come and go like a weak radio broadcast. The first part of his testimony was lost completely when all eyes turned to the actress Paulette Dubost, who entered the courtroom and sat on the steps. The Petiot trial was turning into something of a social event.

CASANOVA The two people found dead near the forest at Marly could not possibly have been killed by Petiot. They were buried there in July 1944, and were not even dead before March 11. We know who executed them. There were eleven men, and one of them has made a complete confession. They judged the men at the rue de la Pompe Gestapo office and machine-gunned them. There is a complete dossier which gives all the facts.

Floriot sat leafing through his papers and taking notes.

Captain Henri Boris was called by Véron. During the war he had directed aerial operations for de Gaulle. He had been arrested by the Germans and imprisoned at Compiègne, where he shared a cell with Dreyfus. He testified that Dreyfus had supplied the Resistance with radios, and claimed the man would never have betrayed his country.

FLORIOT What about the agreement he signed?

BORIS He was compelled to sign those letters. I would have done the same thing if I had been in his place and the Germans had offered me a way out of prison — so would anyone. And I would have forgotten about the letters as soon as I was out. While we were in prison, I gave Dreyfus all sorts of names and information. If he had been a collaborator he could have turned them over to the Germans. I never had any reason to regret these confidences. . . .

VÉRON Petiot, how did you obtain your plastic explosives?

PETIOT We got sheets of it from —

VÉRON Plastic explosives don't come in sheets.

PETIOT I knew about detonators when you were still breast-feeding. You've never even seen plastic explosives.

VÉRON No, I've only driven around with one hundred fifty kilos of them in the trunk of my car.

BORIS   There were no plastic explosives in France at the time Petiot says he used them.*

PETIOT   A man parachuted in from London brought them.

BORIS   I was in charge of all parachute operations. What was his name? I'm sure I must know him.

PETIOT   I don't know his name. I didn't ask questions. I think the Germans found out about him and he fled to Corsica, where he committed suicide.

The audience broke into laughter. Yet another possible witness had conveniently disappeared.

VÉRON   How did you detonate your plastic explosives?

PETIOT   I put them between two German grenades and set them off.

BORIS   You couldn't detonate plastic explosives like that.

PETIOT   They didn't go off.

VÉRON   Captain Boris, have you ever heard of a Resistance group called Fly-Tox?

BORIS   Neither I nor anyone else has ever heard of it.

PETIOT   Captain Boris, since you know everyone in the Resistance, do you know the student who killed a German named Ritter?

Boris smiled. "No, I don't."

PETIOT   Well I do.

LESER   Petiot, can't you try to control yourself a bit?

PETIOT   We've know each other for six days now. Do you really think I can control myself?

Jean Hotin, the former husband of Denise, managed to amuse everyone. He described the search for his wife that he had undertaken six months after her disappearance.

HOTIN   It was four-thirty. I went to the doctor's office and saw a sign on the door saying his hours were from five until seven. I

---

* After reading about this debate in the newspapers, a man wrote to Leser to say that he had regularly obtained and employed plastic explosives during the period Petiot mentioned.

didn't dare ring. Besides, I had a train to catch, and there was work to be done at home. So I left.

PETIOT   I never had such a sign on my door.

The audience laughed throughout Hotin's testimony. The newspapers all agreed that he must have escaped from a novel. "It is Zola," Floriot said, "it is Balzac, but it is not Petiot." The lawyer questioned the farmer with barely restrained amusement.

FLORIOT   When did your wife discover she was pregnant?
HOTIN   I don't know.
FLORIOT   Well, when was her last period?

Hotin blushed.

FLORIOT   Surely you know about these things. You must know when she became pregnant?
HOTIN   No.
LESER   Look, man, when were you married?
HOTIN   Um . . .
LESER   Forget it.

The final witness of the day was Captain Mourrot of the Villeneuve-sur-Yonne constabulary. He raked up every old crime, and juxtaposed the murder of Louisette Delaveau with the accusation that Petiot had been driving without headlights. The original dossiers from Villeneuve were all in the record, and Floriot was able to show that the captain had almost invariably forgotten or distorted the facts. It was Mourrot who had testified, years earlier, before a judge, that Petiot's headlights had been lit but were invisible.

MOURROT [concluding proudly]   And I gave him seven traffic tickets. And besides that, he murdered Madame Debauve — I knew he was the killer all along.
FLORIOT [laughing]   There's only one problem, gentlemen of the jury. Before he accused Petiot, do you know how many other people

he "knew" were guilty and interrogated? Nine, gentlemen, nine. If they hadn't closed the case, he would have accused the entire town.

Mourrot remained oblivious of the fact that his vituperation and petty charges were only whitewashing Petiot's past. Having completed his list, he prepared to sum up with a flourish.

MOURROT And yet, Petiot was not a sorceror, he —
FLORIOT Yes, I think we can see that.

THE NEXT DAY was Sunday. A day's rest seemed to do Petiot good, and he returned on Monday appearing much more relaxed than the previous week. So relaxed, in fact, that at one point he almost fell asleep; he lay across the front of the box, his fingers against his temples, his eyes staring dreamily into space, his back hunched in a caricature of boredom.

LESER Come, come, Petiot, sit up straight.
PETIOT Ummm?

The audience laughed again.
The first witness was Madame Guschinov, pale, feeble, "thin as an umbrella," as one newspaper described her, with profuse blond hair.

GUSCHINOV Petiot advised my husband to flee. On January 2, 1942, my husband left home. He told me Petiot was going to get him to Argentina, and that he had to have some injections because of health regulations.
PETIOT That's idiotic. You just read about injections in the newspapers. Besides, there weren't any health regulations in Argentina. She's lying.
GUSCHINOV My husband said he was worried about these injections.
PETIOT Why should he have been worried? He was my patient. I had been giving him injections for the past year. Why should he suddenly start worrying? You're lying.
LESER The witness is testifying under oath!

PETIOT   No she isn't.

LESER   What! You dare —

FLORIOT   The witness did not take an oath. She volunteered to testify as a witness in a civil suit and, as such, she did not have to take an oath.

ARCHEVÊQUE   If Guschinov was a regular patient of yours at the rue Caumartin, why did you have to take him to the rue Le Sueur?

PETIOT   We had to discuss the details of the trip. We needed privacy. I had a wife, a nurse, a housekeeper.

ARCHEVÊQUE   I still don't see why you couldn't talk at the rue Caumartin.

PETIOT   You don't know the rue Caumartin. But I will not invite you all over. I saw the mess you made of the rue Le Sueur the other day, and I don't care to have the same thing happen again.

ARCHEVÊQUE   A suitcase belonging to Guschinov was found at the rue Le Sueur.

PETIOT   I'm the one who told you it was his suitcase, and now you're using it against me! Look, you don't cross three borders carrying a big heavy suitcase like that. I told Guschinov, "You're not traveling first class," and gave him a bag. He had a lot of suits, and I said, "They'll get wrinkled, but you can always have them pressed when you arrive."

GUSCHINOV   Every month, I returned to Paris to ask for news of my husband. Petiot told me all sorts of stories about the passage, and said that my husband's business was going very well in Buenos Aires and that I should join him there. Petiot said he couldn't show me the letters, because they were too compromising and he had destroyed them. I cabled to some friends of ours there, and they said they hadn't seen my husband.

PETIOT   She's lying. I showed her the letters. She had found a young lover and didn't want to join her husband.

FLORIOT   She's lying! Everyone is lying!

DUPIN   Calm yourself, Maître.

Archevêque began speaking again, but Petiot cut him off.

PETIOT   Wait, Maître, let me speak. I haven't finished.

ARCHEVÊQUE   You're very intelligent, Petiot.

Petiot bowed. "Intelligence is only relative, Maître."

ARCHEVÊQUE Madame Guschinov, your husband told you, did he not, that it was through the intermediary Lucien Romier, who was then a minister at Vichy, that Petiot had obtained the false papers?

GUSCHINOV Certainly.

PETIOT That's another lie. It was only much later that Lucien Romier or people associated with him began supplying me with false papers. Madame Guschinov, would you be so kind as to tell me —

LESER If you wish to ask questions, will you kindly do it through me?

Petiot bowed again, excused himself, and clapped both hands to his mouth. He looked as though he were blowing kisses to the crowd.

FLORIOT Madame, when your husband wrote asking you to join him in Argentina, why didn't you go?

GUSCHINOV My health, business —

PETIOT She had found a younger lover.

FLORIOT But you had faith in Dr. Petiot?

GUSCHINOV Yes, I had faith in him.

FLORIOT During the investigation you said you didn't leave because you didn't have faith in Dr. Petiot.

LESER We still have a lot of witnesses to hear. At this rate, we'll still be here in July.

Joachim Guschinov's business associate, Jean Gouedo, took the stand. He told of his partner's preparations for the trip, and mentioned that the five skins Petiot claimed were a gift to his wife had been intended for sale in South America.

GOUEDO Petiot was going to send the money separately. My associate did not want to part with everything, and sewed some of it into the shoulders of a jacket.

PETIOT If I had wanted to kill Monsieur Guschinov, I wouldn't have had any reason to ask him for his money ahead of time. I could have just taken it afterward.

They returned to the subject of the Alvear Palace Hotel. Petiot gave the name of the desk clerk.

FLORIOT   Was a court-appointed commission sent to Buenos Aires to search for Guschinov?

DUPIN   Madame Guschinov telegraphed.

FLORIOT   How about the *juge d'instruction*? Did he send a photograph to identify this allegedly missing man?

DUPIN   It's all in the dossier. You know it as well as I do.

FLORIOT   There's nothing on it in the dossier, is there?

DUPIN   You know perfectly well there isn't.

FLORIOT   Yet you've had plenty of time since October 1944. Don't you think this was an oversight?

DUPIN   You're just looking for dramatic effects.

FLORIOT   I'm just asking whether you have made a certain very simple and very important verification.

DUPIN   I don't have to answer your questions.

FLORIOT   I can answer for you. You haven't done a damn thing.

LESER   Let's send a telegram.

FLORIOT   No one is missing or dead —

He was cut off by laughter on all sides.

FLORIOT   No one is missing or dead in the Guschinov affair. How can you say he's been murdered when you haven't even looked for him? Send the telegram and we'll see.

Denise Hotin had stayed with Madame Mallard when in Paris. Madame Mallard had since died, and was represented by her daughter, Gilberte Mouron, who testified that Denise had been sent to Dr. Petiot.

MOURON   Madame Hotin stayed with my mother while being treated for pneumonia.

PETIOT   Some of the treatments you say she received are hardly consistent with pneumonia. It sounds more like an abortion.

MOURON   Oh, no, of course not. But I don't know anything about things like that.

She became so confused that she called Leser "doctor" and Petiot "Maître," and left the court with the impression that she was trying to blame Petiot in order to conceal her mother's illegal activities.

A Monsieur Masseur was an eighty-three-year-old teacher from Neuville-Garnier. He had a gray handlebar mustache, wore a velvet-collared coat, and was somewhat senile. He looked at Leser as he began to speak.

LESER   Address the court.

MASSEUR   What court?

LESER [pointing]   That court.

MASSEUR   Oh. I know everything that goes on in Neuville-Garnier. I have lived there for twenty-three years. I was there when little Lily was born —

LESER   You mean Denise?

MASSEUR   We called her Lily. She was so cute . . .

LESER   Let's start with the marriage.

PETIOT [standing up]   Let me tell you a story about a young man —

LESER   Oh, no. We don't want to hear any stories.

Petiot sat down.

Masseur went on at length, repeated himself, digressed. He did not like the Hotin family and related all the scandalous stories available. He believed that Jean's parents had chased her out, and that perhaps her husband had killed her. He began to tell the whole story over again.

MASSEUR   Yes, I remember it well. She was bareheaded when she left, and she didn't take anything with her. Not so much as a small traveling bag. If you heard all the rumors in the town —

LESER   It must be a very noisy town. Do you have anything else to say?

MASSEUR   Oh, yes. I can tell you anything you like. Twenty-three years I've lived in that town, and —

LESER   Remove the witness.

Michel Cadoret de l'Epinguen was the man who had defaulted on his escape plans and whom Véron had chanced to meet in a restaurant.

PETIOT Ah, how do you do, Monsieur? I hope we shall have the pleasure of seeing Madame Cadoret this afternoon?

CADORET It was through Robert Malfet and Eryane Kahan that we were put in contact with Petiot. He told us we would have to spend three days hidden in a house near the Etoile before leaving, and that we would be furnished with false identity papers. There was something very suspicious about the whole arrangement. Petiot told us we would need vaccinations to get into Argentina. He said, "These injections will render you invisible to the eyes of the world."

PETIOT I see it all now. The mad doctor with his syringe. It was a dark and rainy night. The wind howled under the eaves and rattled the windowpanes of the oak-paneled library —

LESER Petiot, please.

CADORET He had dirty hands, which we found unusual for a medical doctor.

Petiot laughed.

CADORET He asked us for money. A real Resistance member does not work for gain.

PETIOT Weren't you asked for ninety thousand francs at first?

CADORET I don't recall.

PETIOT Think. It's very important. That's what saved your life.

The audience gasped.

PETIOT No one would have paid such an absurd sum except an informer who was getting his money free from the Gestapo. When you balked, I knew that you were not an informer like the others Eryane sent, and I gave your money back and refused to take you.

FLORIOT Did you refuse to go, or did Petiot refuse to take you?

CADORET I must admit we contacted him, prepared to tell him that we had changed our minds. But before we could say anything he announced that he could not help us after all, and gave us our money back.

Joseph Scarella was a restaurant chef who had met Petiot when Scarella was about to be sent to Germany for forced labor. When he took the stand, he asked Leser whether he should not be disqualified as a witness. Several days before the trial opened, he had gone to see Floriot and asked how he should act on the stand. Floriot had told him, "Follow the dictates of your conscience."

LESER I hardly think that disqualifies you. Thank you for your candor.

SCARELLA Petiot gave me a certificate saying I had syphilis so that I didn't have to go work in Germany.

PETIOT It was a false certificate.

SCARELLA I should certainly hope so! Petiot asked if I didn't want to leave the country altogether. I was very eager to go; there wasn't much work for a master chef under the Occupation unless you wanted to cook for the Germans. I do not cook for the enemy. Petiot said I would need to take about a hundred thousand francs with me, because it might be some time before I found work abroad. He asked if I had a wife or family. I told him I had a wife. He said I should take her along, because he didn't want her to come pestering him all the time asking for news of me the way some people did. My wife didn't want to go. I was lucky to escape.

It was 5:15 P.M. The next several scheduled witnesses had gone for a walk and could not be found.

DUPIN What are we going to do this evening, then?

LESER I, for one, am going to rest.

TUESDAY, MARCH 26, was the day of the experts. Dr. Albert Paul took the stand. He rolled up his shirtsleeves and smilingly rocked back and forth throughout his testimony. He appeared to know all five hundred pages of the coroner's report by heart, and recited a litany of human remains: shoulder blades, collarbones, vertebrae, two "voluminous and globular skulls," feet, thigh bones, pelves, fingers, two peritoneal walls, five kilograms of hair — some long, some short — several skillfully detached scalps. The guard next to Petiot recoiled in horror when Dr. Paul described how the faces and scalps had been peeled away from the skulls in a single piece. Petiot didn't listen, but whispered to Floriot.

DUPIN   How many bodies were there?

PAUL   Who knows? We were able to reconstruct ten bodies, but if one takes into consideration the fifteen kilograms of charred bones, the vast quantities of small fragments, and the large amount of hair, it is obvious that there were many, many more.

DUPIN   Were you able to determine the ages and sexes of the victims?

PAUL   Half were men, half women. They were between twenty-five and fifty.

DUPIN   When did they die?

PAUL   The fire and lime had so badly damaged the corpses that it was impossible to determine the time of death.

DUPIN   Could you determine the cause of death?

PAUL   No, I'm afraid not. No bullet wounds. No skull fractures. Of course they could have been stabbed, strangled, asphyxiated, or poisoned, but there's no way to tell. There are so many ways to kill people. Or an injection, if you like, but I'm not one to hypothesize. One curious thing that I did notice was that many of the bodies had scalpel marks in the thigh. When I'm performing an autopsy, I don't put my scalpel down on the table, but I stick it into the thigh, the way you stick a pin in a pincushion.

DUPIN   Weren't similar bodies found in the Seine in 1942?

PAUL   Yes, indeed. Between May 1942 and January 1943, thirteen bodies were fished out of the river. Since then, things have returned to normal — three or four a week. [Laughing] At the time, I was afraid it was one of my students. They were all carved up in the same way, and it was very well done.

FLORIOT   I would like to point out that Dr. Petiot never took a dissection course when he was in medical school.

PAUL   That's a shame, because he dissects very well.

FLORIOT   I beg your pardon. You should say, "The dissector dissects very well."

Dr. Piédelièvre presented another portion of the coroner's report. Petiot feigned passionate interest, sitting with one hand jammed in his pocket while he feverishly took notes with the other. Floriot laid his head on his arm and went to sleep.

PIÉDELIÈVRE I'm afraid the bodies were so putrefied and damaged by the quicklime that it was impossible to make any estimation of the time of death.

PETIOT Isn't there a method using insect larvae?

PIÉDELIÈVRE Yes. The diptera and coleoptera lay eggs on corpses. By measuring the size of the larvae and examining their tracks as they burrow through the flesh, one can arrive at a fairly accurate estimation. In this case, the lime and fire had destroyed the traces of the insects.

PETIOT Yes, of course, you're a coroner and know these things much better than I. Diptera and coleoptera . . . hmm. This is fascinating, could you tell me more about it?

PIÉDELIÈVRE It doesn't really have anything to do with the case at hand.

PETIOT No, perhaps not. But if you will permit me, I would like to drop by and discuss it a bit further after the trial is over.

Professor Henri Griffon of the police toxicology lab had examined the viscera for traces of toxic substances. He had found nothing. He suggested that the triangular room had been used as a gas chamber. Floriot woke up, yawned, polished his glasses.

FLORIOT It would have made a very poor gas chamber. There was a large gap under the door.

GRIFFON It could have been stopped up with a rug.

FLORIOT That's only an hypothesis. Can you produce this rug?

A JUROR What kind of gas would have been used?

GRIFFON Just about any kind, except perhaps lighting gas, since there was no jet in the room. I should also mention that I found five-hundred-and-four ampoules of morphine at the rue Caumartin. That's a huge amount.

PETIOT I used it for painless childbirths.

FLORIOT   Did you find any poisons at the rue Caumartin?
GRIFFON   Only the morphine.
FLORIOT   Morphine is not a poison.
GRIFFON   That depends upon the dose administered.
FLORIOT   Was there any morphine at the rue Le Sueur?
GRIFFON   No.
FLORIOT   I see. No poison at the rue Le Sueur. No way to block the opening in this famous gas chamber of yours. Nothing at all? Thank you very much.

Three psychiatrists had examined Petiot before the trial to determine his legal responsibility for his acts. One of them, Dr. Génil-Perrin, had also examined Petiot in 1937 and had commented at that time on his attempt to feign insanity.

GÉNIL-PERRIN   I have examined Petiot and found him to be remarkably intelligent, and endowed with an extraordinary gift for repartee . . .

The audience laughed and Dupin assured the doctor that they had already noticed this even without the benefit of his professional eye.

GÉNIL-PERRIN   . . . but a stunted moral development. He is entirely responsible for his acts.
A DR. GOURIOU   Petiot is perverse, amoral, and a simulator. Throughout his life he has pretended insanity whenever it suited his convenience. I do not consider him to be a monster, but insufficient moral education has permitted him to acquire a taste for evil.
FLORIOT   His patients found him extremely competent and utterly devoted.
GOURIOU   In some doctors I have treated, mental disorders manifest themselves through an exaggerated devotion to their patients.
FLORIOT   Did Petiot ever try to feign insanity with you?
GOURIOU   No. He lied to us about any number of things, but not about that.
FLORIOT   In your report, you say that Petiot completed his medical studies in a "mysterious" fashion. Do you know the grades he received on his examinations?

GOURIOU I saw his grades. I recall that he got "medicore" in dissection. He managed to avoid taking certain courses generally considered essential. His thesis was received with the notation "very good," but that's not difficult. One can buy a thesis if one wants to. At any rate, a thesis is based on book learning, and gives no evaluation of the true personal integrity of the physician.

FLORIOT You seem to be insinuating a lot of things for which you have no proof. Tell me, you examined Petiot's family as well. How did you find his sister?

Gouriou hesitated. "She is quite normal."

FLORIOT Are you certain?
GOURIOU As certain as I can be after a brief psychiatric examination.
FLORIOT Psychiatry moves in strange ways. Petiot does not have a sister.

Gouriou fled the box amid peals of laughter.

Dr. Georges Heuyer complained that Petiot had been difficult to examine, since he had wanted to ask all the questions himself. The audience laughed, Petiot rolled his eyes, Floriot settled down to go to sleep, Leser felt he was losing his grip and recessed the court.

Edouard de Rougemont, a pompous graphologist with a flowing white beard, had examined the Van Bever, Khaït, Hotin, and Braunberger letters. His reports had been written by hand, in Gothic script, with important words illuminated in red, the whole sewn together with gold braid. With an affection bordering on lasciviousness, he discussed the curves of certain letters and the hand's movement while making certain sweeps.

ROUGEMONT In conclusion, all of the things I have told you lead one to believe that these letters were written in a state of agitation. Either they were dictated to the author or the author was under constraint. It is not impossible that he or she was drugged at the time.

FLORIOT [in awe] You can tell all these things just from the handwriting?

ROUGEMONT Yes, Maître. Why, a skillful graphologist can plumb the depths of a man's soul through his handwriting. He can even tell whether the writer is lying or telling the truth.

Floriot quickly scribbled on a sheet of paper.

FLORIOT None can be more skillful than you. Here. Could you tell me whether I truly believe what I have just written?

ROUGEMONT Yes, of course. "Monsieur de Rougemont is a great scholar who never makes a mistake."

He blushed deeply.

FLORIOT If we had asked Petiot to write out his story and Monsieur de Rougemont to read it, we could have dispensed with this whole trial.

Colonel André Dewavrin was called to the stand. He was a mysterious figure, de Gaulle's right-hand man during the war, and an important leader in the Resistance. Many people had come to the trial today merely to glimpse him. Rather than Dewavrin, a Monsieur Vandeuille appeared in his stead.

LESER One does not send substitutes to court.

Vandeuille departed with dignity.

Jacques Ibarne (aka Yonnet), the journalist for *Résistance* and Military Security officer who had conducted part of the investigation of Petiot's Resistance activity, came next.

IBARNE The article "Petiot, Soldier of the Reich" was based on a police interrogation of a man named Charles Rolland. I subsequently discovered that its contents were entirely false, but I had published it with the caution that I took no responsibility for the information given.

FLORIOT After writing an article like that, Monsieur, a journalist should not have undertaken the military investigation you performed. You were hardly the most objective judge of the facts.

Ibarne mentioned that after publication of the article he had been summoned to Floriot's office and given Petiot's reply. A discussion arose as to whether a lawyer had the right to communicate correspondence he had received from a murderer being sought by the police. The lawyers asked each other, Dupin asked Leser, Leser asked the court clerk. No one seemed to know.

Ibarne described the results of his investigation. Petiot had never known Cumulo, Brossolette, or any members of Rainbow. No one had ever heard of Dr. Eugène or Fly-Tox, and the formation of an autonomous extermination group such as Petiot described would never have been permitted in the organized Resistance. Petiot had shared a cell at Fresnes for some time with a man named Lateulade, since dead in deportation, who had known Cumulo and Rainbow and could have discussed them with his cellmate. Petiot fired hateful glances at Yonnet-Ibarne throughout his testimony.

VÉRON Petiot, you say that you killed thirty-three collaborators and thirty German soldiers. You have told us how you liquidated two soldiers in June 1940. Tell us about the twenty-eight others.

PETIOT I had more respect for them than I did for your client.

VÉRON How did you trap them? How did you kill them?

PETIOT They were my patients.

VÉRON But you were not allowed to treat Germans. You were even required by law to post a sign to that effect on your door.

PETIOT I won't answer your questions. I didn't work for decorations or praise. When there are oppressors, there will always be avengers.

VÉRON How did you kill them?

PETIOT That's none of your damn business!

VÉRON What did you do with the bodies?

PETIOT I don't have to justify myself for murders I'm not accused of committing.

VÉRON You said earlier that you dumped the bodies outside of buildings occupied by the Wehrmacht. Where? Give us details.

PETIOT Go to hell. I'll talk about it after I'm acquitted, which is already a certainty.

VÉRON   Why didn't the Gestapo react? And why did the Gestapo let you out of prison when you had admitted smuggling people out of the country?

IBARNE   The Germans would have shot him instantly. As far as I'm concerned, he's a collabo.

PETIOT   Monsieur Ibarne, I saw you somewhere that you wouldn't care to have me mention here.

IBARNE   On the contrary, I insist that you mention it, because I'm certain I never saw you anywhere.

Petiot was silent, smiling.

IBARNE   Explain yourself!

PETIOT   [with hidden meaning]   Didn't you play tennis at the Racing Club?

IBARNE   I don't play tennis and I've never been to the Racing Club.

Petiot's bluff had failed, and he contented himself with a weak attempt at a knowing smirk.

FOURRIER, PINTARD, Maurice Petiot, Nézondet, and Porchon undoubtedly knew more than anyone except Petiot himself, and when they all appeared on March 27, the audience expected some shattering revelations. They were sadly disappointed. After more than a year in prison, none of the accomplices had any desire to compromise himself, and they were more intent on showing how truthful they were than on providing facts.

Raoul Fourrier scarcely spoke at all. The answers had to be dragged from him one by one, and he usually stopped after furnishing a minimal reply. The civil-suit attorneys battled for the right to question him, and above all others could be heard the shrill voice of a lawyer with a strong Marseille accent, whose questions were senseless to the point of incoherence. The subject turned to the pimps and prostitutes.

LESER   You introduced them to Petiot out of the goodness of your heart?

FOURRIER   Yes, of course. We only asked twenty-five thousand francs.

LESER   Do you call that the goodness of your heart?

FOURRIER   I didn't know they would bring their women.

LESER   How did they leave?

FOURRIER   On foot. I watched them go from my window.

LESER   Didn't you ever wonder how the organization worked?

FOURRIER   The doctor told me it was a secret.

"Francinet" repeated the same story.

PINTARD   I'm sorry now that I sent those people to Petiot.

LESER   I should hope so. Didn't you ever worry about them after they left?

PINTARD   No. Fourrier showed me a note from Jo le Boxeur saying he had safely arrived in Buenos Aires.

PETIOT   It would never have fooled Monsieur de Rougemont. I wrote it.

Nézondet recounted his arrest and his conversation with Maurice.

NÉZONDET   They sent me to Fresnes, you know. Then, a little while later, you know, they sent me back to the rue des Saussaies. An inspector said to me, you know, "Tell us the truth or you'll stay at Fresnes." I told him, "Okay, then I guess I'll just stay there for the rest of my life, because I don't know anything," you know. So they let me out. Before I left, you know, I asked Petiot what it was all about, and he said he smuggled people out of the country, you know, and they were going to fill him full of bullets. He said to tell his wife he loved her more than anything and that she should go where she knew to go, you know, and dig up what she knew. A little later, you know, I met Maurice. He was white like a sheet. He said, "There's enough to get us all shot there. The journeys begin and end at the rue Le Sueur." He had been to the house, you know, and found suitcases, postdated letters, syringes, a formula for poison, and some bodies. I said, "Your brother must be a monster," and he said, "No, but he's a very sick man and we have to take care of him." I know that Maurice has denied it all since, you know, but I never asked him to tell me these things.

Maurice was pale and shuffled slowly to the stand. His throat cancer had spread and he had only a few months to live. He gave Marcel a long look filled with affection and sorrow. He spoke slowly and with difficulty, but was perfectly calm, confident, and even politely defiant.

LESER   Speak up.

MAURICE   I'm sorry, I can't.

PETIOT   [whispering to Floriot]   I may not be doing very well, but he, poor fellow . . .

LESER   The last witness has just told us about certain revelations you made to him in 1943.

MAURICE   Monsieur Nézondet is a good fellow and means well, but he never really recovered after his arrest by the Germans. He imagines things.

Maître Charles Henry, the Marseille lawyer representing the family of Paulette Grippay, jumped in.

HENRY   Didn't it seem strange to you to discover all of these clothes, particularly German army uniforms, as you maintain?

MAURICE   No. I concluded that my brother had killed German army officers.

HENRY   And what conclusion did you draw from the presence of civilian clothes?

MAURICE   None.

Maître Henry's questions followed fast and furious, losing themselves in passionately irrelevant detail. He seemed like a clockwork barrister wound too tight.

PETIOT   The further we go, the worse it gets.

LESER   [apparently thinking of something else]   Voilà!

Roland Porchon could not be sworn in; since his release, he had been convicted of fraud and stripped of his rights as a citizen, including the right to bear witness. He was asked about Monsieur and Madame Marie, the couple he had sent to Petiot but who had been too frightened to leave. Porchon contradicted everyone and blamed everything on his wife. His wife had since divorced him, and blamed everything on him.

PERLÈS   Petiot, did you intend to help the Maries escape or to execute them?
PETIOT   I don't remember them. The whole story is completely uninteresting.

ERYANE KAHAN, the first witness on the tenth day, stepped up to the witness box with her strawberry hair, huge tinted glasses, a brown suit, and a round, veiled fur hat that constantly threatened to fall off her head as she trembled with emotion. Despite the warm weather, she wore gloves and carried a fur muff, and her handbag seemed to be filled with multicolored handkerchiefs, which she nervously pulled out to wipe her face or clean her glasses. She appeared to be in her mid-twenties, but was, in fact, fifty. She had a strong Rumanian accent. Petiot stared at the ceiling as she described the families she had sent to him.

KAHAN   Not only weren't they collaborators, they were in deathly fear of the Germans. They were so happy about the possibility of escaping that they considered Petiot their benefactor — almost a god.

She directly quoted the Wolffs in German, and Petiot winced as though the sound of that language pained him.

KAHAN   I wanted to leave as well, but Petiot said I would be more useful to him if I stayed for a while. I see now what a useful patsy I was.

She was asked about her disappearance after the discovery of the rue Le Sueur. She had first maintained she had fled in February because the Gestapo was after her. The evidence proved she had left her rue Pasquier apartment the day the newspapers printed Petiot's photograph, so she obligingly changed her story.

KAHAN I had worshiped him too. I knew him only as Dr. Eugène. When the Petiot affair hit the newspapers I had no way of knowing that he was the same person . . . until I saw a photograph. [She dramatically laid a handkerchief on the suitcases behind her.] I am a Jew, and I felt like a hunted animal, so I hid. I thought of sending my story to the police, but Maître Floriot advised me against it.

Floriot smiled menacingly. Eryane insisted that she had consulted him while she was in hiding. Floriot explained, more persuasively, that she had not contacted him until she was virtually under arrest and had little choice.

KAHAN People have portrayed me as an accomplice, as a procurer. Worse, as an agent of the Gestapo! [Emotion overcame her and her hat teetered dangerously.] They've called me a loose woman! I've been called everything! They've ruined me, and now they want to destroy me altogether!

Her reputation was, at best, uncertain. During interrogations she had spoken at length about her Resistance activity, but this activity had fallen into two categories: that preceding March 1944, and that following the rue Le Sueur discovery, when she was hiding from the police and needed a good story. In the earlier period, Eryane claimed to have done impressive things, but when the police asked about them, she couldn't remember the name of a single person who could support her statements — they were all as elusive as Petiot's Fly-Tox comrades. After March 1944, she really had furnished a few unimportant bits of information to peripheral Resistance members; she remembered not only the names of these people, but their exact addresses. This seemed suspiciously convenient. Moreover, shortly before his execution Henri Lafont identified a photograph of Eryane Kahan, gave accurate details about her life, and said she had given information to the Gestapo and had even denounced Jews. Lafont had no reason to lie; in fact he seemed intent on cleansing his conscience before he died and had become scrupulous about telling the truth.

DUPIN [to Kahan] All the information concerning you in the dossier is quite favorable.

FLORIOT Monsieur l'Avocat Général, you said a little while ago that she had papers identifying her as a member of the Resistance. It says here in the dossier that she is an adventuress who lies easily and consistently.

DUPIN You will have your chance to summarize the case later, Maître.

FLORIOT Madame Kahan, were you paid for sending people to Petiot?

KAHAN No, never.

FLORIOT Several other witnesses, and a number of your friends, have said you told them you had been.

KAHAN I never said that.

FLORIOT Then they are all liars?

KAHAN I don't know anything about it.

FLORIOT The honesty of this witness, as Dr. Paul might say, floats by in bits and pieces. Madame Kahan, didn't you have a German lover?

KAHAN He wasn't German. He was Austrian.

FLORIOT That's what Hitler said.

KAHAN It's not the same thing.

She went on to explain that her Austrian lover had given her information she passed on to the Resistance.

FLORIOT It seems that four Germans regularly visited your building, and that one of them was your landlady's lover.

KAHAN He was only her friend.

During that interchange, Floriot and Eryane Kahan alternately removed and polished their glasses in what seemed like a comedy routine. Dupin was not pleased with the way Floriot was discrediting a prize witness, and he changed the subject.

DUPIN   I should mention that Inspector Poirier came to see me in my chambers and told me that some of the things he said on the witness stand were not altogether exact.

FLORIOT   There is a dossier that gives us all the facts we need. I don't understand why you want to make an issue out of minor details. They don't change the facts.

DUPIN   I don't allow myself to speak to you that way. Don't force me to answer you. You play quite a different role from mine.

FLORIOT   Obviously. I am your adversary.

DUPIN   Your position is an ignoble one. I won't tell you what I think of your attitude.

FLORIOT   I —

LESER   Why don't you just ask another question, Maître?

FLORIOT   I would like to reply to Monsieur l'Avocat Général's attack.

DUPIN   I demand a recess!

FLORIOT   That's too easy.

LESER   Court is recessed. Madame Kahan, we will take up where we left off.

They returned a few minutes later with tempers cooled.

DUPIN   I would like to apologize for the harsh words I said a few minutes ago, and which may have offended the defense.

FLORIOT   Madame Kahan, did you ever go to a Gestapo office in a German truck?

KAHAN   It's possible.

FLORIOT   With a German officer?

KAHAN   Never.

FLORIOT   Did you greet a group of German soldiers in the street?

KAHAN   My Austrian friend was with them.

FLORIOT   Could you tell us what happened to the dossier indicting you for intelligence with the enemy?

KAHAN   I have never heard of such a dossier.

DUPIN   If there were charges against Madame Kahan, she would not be here.

FLORIOT   It is dossier number one-six-five-eight-two.

Dupin copied down the number with bad grace. Presumably he never found the dossier since, despite strong suspicions about her, it does not appear she ever had been indicted, but for the moment the court, spectators, and press had the distinct impression that the prosecution was protecting Eryane Kahan.

PETIOT   Did I ever have dirty hands, as Monsieur Cadoret has said?

Eryane Kahan did not answer.

PETIOT   Perhaps I did. I didn't feel very safe in the rue Pasquier, as you can well understand. My bicycle had a manual gearshift, and before I came I moved the chain by hand to the larger gear so that I could go more quickly if I needed to escape.

The audience laughed.

PETIOT   At least my hands weren't dirty because I raised them in allegiance to Pétain!
LESER   Don't be insolent.
PETIOT   Toward whom? Toward Pétain?
LESER   You know very well that magistrates had to swear allegiance. There were unusual circumstances.
PETIOT   I know a magistrate who didn't.
LESER   Madame Kahan, you may step down.

Charles Beretta was brought from Fresnes to testify. Floriot described the role he had played and the various Resistance groups he had denounced. Beretta was terrified by this image of himself — one which would shortly be presented at his own trial.

BERETTA   But I couldn't do anything else!
FLORIOT   Don't tire yourself, old man, we understand perfectly well.

Jean Guélin was also brought from Fresnes, where he was being held for collaboration. The only charge against him stemmed from his activity in the Dreyfus case, and his only interest now was to defend himself.*

GUÉLIN   I have been in prison for eighteen months and have been questioned only twice. Each day, I dreamed of this moment when I could explain myself before you. Monsieur le Président, you have the advantage of still being on the other side of the stand. I beg you to hear me out.

Guélin told them of the difficulties he had experienced in negotiating Dreyfus's release. He had done it all out of sheer patriotism and respect for Yvan Dreyfus, whom he praised endlessly as a Resistant and a handsome man. Never had he dealt with the Germans, whom he loathed and despised, except when it helped the noble cause of France. He wept.

GUÉLIN   I, who was such a patriot, who did everything I could for the Jews, look what has become of me. After all that I went through, it wasn't the Germans who prosecuted me, but the French. And now that, for once, they have a man of the world in prison, they don't want to let him go! Petiot, dare to look at me!
PETIOT   You little bastard.

But Guélin's fury was mainly directed toward Floriot, who effectively destroyed the former lawyer's defense.

GUÉLIN   Even if you are still on the right side of the stand, you can't stop me from telling you that I — I never received exorbitant fees from collaborators, and if there is someone here who has earned millions from traitors, collaborators, and members of the Gestapo, it is not I, Maître Floriot. You are the collaborators' lawyer!
FLORIOT   Is that why you asked me to defend you?
GUÉLIN   [bursting into tears]   I'm *not* a collaborator!

---

* He was, strangely, found guilty only of fraud. This was based on the fact that he had obtained money from Madame Dreyfus for her husband's freedom, knowing full well that her husband would not be unconditionally released. Guélin was forced to repay the entire sum he and Dequeker had gotten from her.

FLORIOT   Article eleven fifty-four of the dossier shows that you had a Gestapo identity card and a license to bear arms, and that the Germans protected you. I don't think we need hear any more from you. Thank you.

PIERRE PÉHU, the friend and employee of Guélin who had helped negotiate with Dreyfus, was the first witness on the eleventh day of the trial. He, too, was brought from the Fresnes prison to appear.

PÉHU   Guélin asked me to help him out. As a service to a country-man, I went to Compiègne to see what was going on. Dreyfus was so conspicuously a patriot that I didn't hesitate. He signed a certain paper I had been instructed to bring. Guélin took me to the rue des Saussaies, where he concluded the transaction. A month later, Guélin told me that Dreyfus was going to be liberated that evening. And, in fact, I did see him that evening, and I never saw him afterward. But a month later I was called to the rue des Saussaies, and they asked me what I had done with Dreyfus. Guélin had just told me that he was in South America, but, as we had agreed, I told them that Dreyfus had not left Paris yet and was still in hiding. The Germans asked Guélin to swear that this was true. He gave them a paper accepting full responsibility for Dreyfus's disappearance, and the Germans never bothered me again.

VÉRON   You were able to talk to Dreyfus at Compiègne. That proves you had connections somewhere.

PÉHU   I had a little piece of paper.

FLORIOT   Didn't you make a report to the German police?

PÉHU   Me? I used to be a police commissaire and was thrown out of my job by Vichy! I was a Resistant! I, make a report to the German police?

PETIOT   This is the man who fractured my sternum at the rue des Saussaies.

PÉHU   I am a Resistant!

FLORIOT   This is very serious. If one can believe the last few witnesses, we have mistakenly locked up nothing but Resistants at Fresnes.

Three witnesses who had known Yvan Dreyfus testified that he had been utterly dedicated to the Resistance. Véron read a telegram from Pierre Mendès-France, one of de Gaulle's ministers: I LEARN WITH STUPEFACTION PETIOT DARES SULLY MEMORY YVAN DREYFUS.

Of all the witnesses, Madame Dreyfus was the most pathetic. She seemed a broken woman and never glanced at Petiot, who, for once, remained silent throughout a witness's entire testimony. Painfully, she told of her long negotiations with Guélin and Dequeker and the repeated demands for more money.

DREYFUS   When I learned that Yvan had signed two letters, I was horrified.

FLORIOT   One of them promised that he would help expose a certain escape organization?

DREYFUS   Yes, that was the condition. Yvan never would have done such a thing, and I begged Guélin not to use the letter. He told me it was purely a formality, and that Yvan could tear the letters up himself.

VÉRON   You felt yourself at the mercy of Guélin and Dequeker?

DREYFUS   They profited from my inexperience.

FLORIOT   How much did it all cost you?

DREYFUS   Over four million francs. My husband returned, and we were going to leave Paris together, but then Guélin told me that there was one last formality that had to be taken care of at the rue des Saussaies. Yvan went the next day, and I never saw him again.

FLORIOT   Did he take any luggage?

DREYFUS   No, Guélin loaned it to him.

Fernand Lavie, Madame Khaït's son, explained the circumstances of his mother's disappearance. He told about the bizarre letters that reported she had fled to the free zone.

LAVIE   My mother never mentioned wanting to leave.

VÉRON   The night that your mother left, she was coming to see me. Do you know where else she may have gone?

LAVIE   My mother had seen her doctor recently and told him

that Petiot had given her false injections. I believe that her doctor advised her to go to the police. The evening she left, she did not take any money or luggage.

FLORIOT   Your father-in-law [David Khaït] is deceased?

LAVIE   I don't know.

FLORIOT   He was deported in June 1944 and never returned. When he first spoke with the police he said that it could only have been your mother who delivered the letter to the house on the day after her "disappearance," and he gave very good reasons for believing this. And do you know that three people, including a railroad employee, believe they saw your mother in the free zone in June 1943 — that is to say, over a year after her disappearance?

LAVIE   No, I didn't know that.

DUPIN   Those three people had never met Madame Khaït. They identified her from a photograph.

FLORIOT   Which is more than I can say for some people. Monsieur Lavie, didn't your mother also deliver a letter to your family's lawyer the day after her disappearance? The lawyer in question has said: "It was certainly Madame Khaït who came, my maid recognized her."

VÉRON   Let's call the maid to the stand!

FLORIOT   Surely you do not doubt the word of this lawyer!

VÉRON   Let's hear my maid.

FLORIOT   Where is Raymonde Baudet, who is one of the most important witnesses in this case?

DUPIN   Isn't she in Poitiers?

LAVIE   I haven't heard from her. I only know that she is in the country.

DUPIN   She must be aware that we are discussing her at the Assize Court of the Seine and that her presence would be quite welcome.

PETIOT   How many witnesses does that make whom you haven't been able to produce? Are we to conclude that they are dead? Did you murder them?

VÉRON   Monsieur Lavie, have you seen another letter, which Jean-Marc Van Bever allegedly delivered to a lawyer at about the same time as your mother's disappearance?

LAVIE Yes, an inspector showed it to me. He covered the signature. I thought the handwriting was the same as that in the letters we received.

FLORIOT Our friend Monsieur de Rougemont does not agree with you.

VÉRON Maître, if you manage to explain this away, you will, perhaps, eliminate one reason for condemning your client to death. There will still be twenty-six more!

Leser recessed the court. After the break, they discovered that there were no more witnesses in the room, and court was adjourned.

MADAME BRAUNBERGER related the story of her husband's disappearance one day in 1942, and told how she had identified him among Petiot's victims by his hat and shirt. The court clerk produced these two items, and she identified them again.

PERLÈS Perhaps the moment has come to ask Petiot how these articles came to be in his house?

PETIOT Perhaps the moment has come to ask, but the moment has not come for me to answer.

LESER Petiot, I would suggest that you answer.

PETIOT I will answer after the other witnesses in this affair have been heard.

DUPIN Your silence proves your guilt.

LESER I order you to answer.

PETIOT I told you that I will answer in half an hour. I'm not about to go anywhere, am I?

Raymond Vallée testified about the letters he had received. Petiot was contemptuous and spoke in barely concealed insults.

VALLÉE I wonder how Dr. Braunberger, who had met Petiot only once, several years earlier, could have known about a house Petiot did not buy until 1941?

Petiot leaped up and began shouting. The guard next to him grabbed him by the shoulder and tried to push him back into his seat. Using the familiar *tu* verb form in addressing him, he ordered Petiot to sit down.

PETIOT   I forbid you to use *tu* to me!
GUARD   *Assieds-toi.*
PETIOT   Fuck you!
LESER   Behave yourselves, gentlemen. Monsieur Vallée, you may step down.

Floriot grinned. Petiot had been on the verge of asking the witness a question and the witness had been dismissed. The court clerk whispered to Leser that he was running another risk of a mistrial. Leser sent a guard to find Vallée, who had already left the room. Five minutes later, Vallée returned to the stand. Petiot's question was perfectly trivial.

Dr. Braunberger's housemaid, nurse, and cook told the story of the doctor's disappearance over again. When they finished, Petiot stood up.

PETIOT   Now, may I see this hat and shirt? I had no earthly reason for killing that old Jew. I scarcely knew him. He had no money with him when he went, so I couldn't hope to gain anything. His hat and his shirt . . . The hat has the right initials on it, but it just happens to be two sizes larger than Dr. Braunberger's head. You say that the shirt is his. You say it has his initials on it. Even someone with my poor eyesight can see that there are no initials on this shirt. No hat, no shirt, no Braunberger case, it's finished!

He threw the two items at the clerk's head and sat down. There was stunned silence.

Christiane Roart, Clara Noé, and Michel Czobor, all friends of the Knellers, testified about the strange postcards they had received. No one seemed terribly interested in details anymore, and by the end of the questioning even Leser was glancing anxiously at the clock.

STÉFANAGGI   Petiot, perhaps you should tell us under exactly what circumstances the Germans released you from Fresnes.

LESER   Good grief.

PETIOT   Ask the Germans.

As if this had been a secret signal, several civil-suit lawyers jumped in at once and began to shout accusations.

HENRY   No one has understood anything here. The real question at hand is whether or not Petiot worked for the Gestapo!

PETIOT   I was tortured and I never admitted anything. You, lawyers of so-called innocent victims, you are treading on dangerous ground when you open up this last-minute offensive. In one word, you are all bastards!

THE LAWYERS [in chorus]   Thank you.

PETIOT   You're welcome. Anytime.

HENRY   This trial is before the wrong court —

LESER   Don't say that! Do you want this to go on forever?

HENRY   Petiot should not be here, but before the Special Court, to try him for intelligence with the enemy.

STÉFANAGGI   Yes, we are wasting our time here, trying to find out whether Petiot was really a Resistant. What we have to establish is whether he belonged to the Gestapo, and not he alone, but . . .

As Stéfanaggi reeled off a list that included many of the witnesses who had already been heard, Petiot shouted, Floriot beamed, and Leser shrieked. Everyone was talking at once, and above them all was heard the high-pitched Marseille accent of Charles Henry.

HENRY   Yes, Petiot should appear before the Special Court. All the obscurities which up to now have allowed Floriot to make a fool out of everyone would disappear . . .

Leser finally stood up and walked out, followed by the rest of the court. Henry continued to shout for several minutes before he realized that no one was listening.

APRIL 1 — All Fools' Day — the thirteenth day of the trial, was to be devoted to defense witnesses. The rumor spread that

Justice Robert H. Jackson and his colleagues from the Nurem-
berg trials, which were going on simultaneously and receiving
second billing in the Paris newspapers, were planning to attend.
Indeed, there was a new row of empty chairs behind Leser.
Journalists regretted that they were never filled, and that the
American judges never had the chance to witness the gay
abandon with which the Petiot trial was being conducted, unlike the depressingly serious international war-crimes trials. It
was a fairly calm day, with few outbursts from Petiot, but one
guard strolled about oblivious of an April Fools' joke pinned to
the back of his uniform, and a couple of foreign journalists em-
braced passionately during much of the afternoon.

Charles Henry stood up to explain what he had meant the
previous day. He was not, he said, saying that this trial should
be transferred to a special court, but that Petiot's accomplices,
and not Petiot himself, should be tried for complicity and collaboration. The lawyer's intentions were good, but it was impossible to tell where his meandering enthusiasm might lead
him, and Leser hurriedly silenced him.

The defense witnesses filed past in rapid succession.

A MONSIEUR COMTE   Petiot was the doctor of the poor. His devotion was legendary. Do you know Villeneuve-sur-Yonne, Monsieur
le Président? There are good people and bad people there. All good
Republicans are considered undesirable there. The affair Petiot? It's
nothing but a political move to slur Petiot.

A MONSIEUR PATHIER   Dr. Petiot did astonishing things at Villeneuve-sur-Yonne. He built the sewer system. The school was like a
leper colony, and he turned it into a model school.

A MUNICIPAL OFFICIAL   Don't be mistaken, Monsieur le Président,
Villeneuve-sur-Yonne may be small, but it is a veritable hotbed of
political turmoil. All you needed was to have good intentions and
someone was sure to slander you. There was a murder in the vicinity,
a theft, someone stole the cemetery cross; Petiot's political adversaries
blamed it all on him!

A MONSIEUR MUR   There are always fatheads who tell lies. Petiot was a Frenchman one hundred percent — no, two hundred percent!

A MONSIEUR OLIVIER I've known Petiot since 1920. He saved my son's life, and I'll always be grateful to him. And later he gave me an injection that made me sick for a few days so I wouldn't have to go to Germany.

Another defense witness, not too sure of his words, said that "what Petiot did at Villeneuve was incomprehensible." When the audience laughed, he turned toward the gallery with great dignity. "That may make you laugh, but we still miss Dr. Petiot at Villeneuve. He is a good man, and we will never forget all that he has done for us."

A deaf witness couldn't hear Leser's instructions for the swearing in.

LESER Say, "I swear."
WITNESS I can't hear you.
LESER No, "I swear."
WITNESS You will have to speak up.

Leser went over and shouted in the man's face.

WITNESS You don't have to shout. I'm not completely deaf.

Nor, it seemed, could he say much.

WITNESS I really can't contribute anything to your trial. I knew Petiot slightly before he left Villeneuve, but I haven't heard anything about him since.
LESER I'm not surprised.

Another witness told of a man who had fallen from a poplar tree. Petiot had treated him every day for forty-five months and had saved his life. Still another, a Monsieur Arent, said Petiot's motto should be Simplicity, Devotion, Altruism.

ARENT At that time I was absolutely certain that there was not a man on earth more honest than Petiot, nor more patriotic.
FLORIOT Are you less sure today?
ARENT Check.

FLORIOT   What makes you uncertain now?
ARENT   Reading the newspapers.

Inspector Gignoux, who had conducted the Van Bever and
Khaït investigations under, or in spite of, Judge Olmi, put in an
unexpected appearance and interrupted the stream of defense
witnesses. Véron was pleased by his presence and asked several
detailed questions, but Gignoux really had little to say and could
only confirm the fact that the two people were missing.

GIGNOUX   I'm sorry that I never found them.
FLORIOT   So am I.
PETIOT   In keeping with the prosecution's tradition, Inspector
Gignoux has related nothing but inexactitudes, but that hardly sur-
prises anyone. Let's move on.

Defense witnesses from Paris followed those from Villeneuve-
sur-Yonne. One had needed a rest, and Petiot had paid for his
vacation. He had cured another's daughter of constipation with
a strange machine. In 1942 he had obtained false identity
papers for a Madame Harant and two English officers who had
been shot down in France. Many of the witnesses were very
moving, but the audience had become so used to the absurd that
they laughed in a manner that offended even the prosecution.
And even though these statements unexpectedly confirmed less
plausible aspects of Petiot's position, they were too late and too
few.

A star witness was Lieutenant Richard Lhéritier, who entered
in the black uniform of the French paratroopers. He had been
dropped behind enemy lines in 1942, arrested at Lyon on May 4,
1943, and transferred to Fresnes on June 10, where he shared
cell number 440 for five months with Marcel Petiot. It was impossible to doubt his integrity, and his presence commanded
respect. Petiot had never spoken to him about Cumulo or Pierre
Brossolette. On the other hand, Petiot had spoken at great
length about Fly-Tox and his escape organization. He had given

Lhéritier useful advice on how to bear up under torture and on how to answer questions during an interrogation without surrendering any useful information. Petiot had been able to smuggle messages out of prison and had furnished his cellmate with names and addresses of Resistance members to look up if he were released or escaped. Lhéritier had never been able to use them, since he was sent straight from Fresnes to Ravensbrück. Petiot had treated his jailers with such sarcastic contempt that he had been an inspiration to his fellow prisoners. The court had not heard this side before and was impressed.

FLORIOT Do you think it strange that the Germans released Petiot?

LHÉRITIER Not at all. They were unable to get any information out of him, so they let him go in hopes of following him and discovering his secrets. I know a number of similar cases.

FLORIOT You spent five months in a cell with Petiot, Lieutenant. Do you think that a man can hide his true nature for that long?

LHÉRITIER No, sir. I do not believe one can be mistaken after five months together — particularly in a prison cell.

FLORIOT How can you explain his present situation?

LHÉRITIER First of all, I do not believe that Petiot acted alone. I cannot see that as being possible. Secondly, he was involved in politics. His party was heavily involved in the Resistance, but not in the official Resistance controlled by the Allies. I believe that his party gave him orders, which he carried out in his own fashion. Later, after the press created such a sensation around him, his party found him an embarrassment. They wouldn't have had a chance in the elections if they had recognized him, so they dropped him.* I know that Petiot is quite capable of sacrificing himself for a cause. I saw how he acted with the Germans. He risked his life every day just to say what he believed in.

* Lhéritier was referring to the Communist Resistance, which had functioned independently of and often in competition with de Gaulle's forces during much of the war. Following the Liberation, there were bitter disputes as to who would control the new government, and some accused the Communists of unscrupulous and illegal actions both during and after the war. Petiot was carrying a recently issued Communist-party card when he was arrested. A few, but only a few, lend credence to Lhéritier's theory.

PETIOT Can a reasonable man accuse me of having worked for the Gestapo?

LHÉRITIER I don't believe it. Whatever the outcome of this trial may be, I will always be proud to have shared a cell with Dr. Petiot.

Roger Courtot had also shared a cell with Petiot. He had been nineteen years old at the time. Petiot had told him about Fly-Tox, the escape route, and Dr. Eugène.

COURTOT No one can lie for seventy-eight days and seventy-eight nights. Besides, he had no reason to tell me these things. I could very easily have been an informer planted by the Germans, and he was risking a great deal. But he never worried about his personal safety. It's not possible that he worked for money.

Petiot wept silently during Courtot's testimony.

Mademoiselle Germaine Barré had asked to be allowed to testify. She was a young seamstress and, during the war, had worked for the Allied intelligence service. She had been captured and sentenced to death, and was reprieved only because she was pregnant. She was awaiting torture in Jodkum's office at the rue des Saussaies when preparations were made for Petiot's release.

BARRÉ I have read in certain newspapers that Petiot has been accused of collaborating with the Gestapo. I wanted to tell you that this is not possible. I was in Jodkum's office when he spoke to Petiot. When Jodkum asked him if he would pay a hundred thousand francs for his liberation, Petiot did not jump at the chance. Quite the contrary. He said: "I don't give a shit whether you condemn me or not. I have stomach cancer and I'm not going to live very long whatever you do. Don't do me any favors." Jodkum telephoned Petiot's home, and then to his brother for the money.

PETIOT Do you remember if he asked me to promise to do nothing against Germany?

BARRÉ I remember very well, Doctor. You refused to sign anything of the sort. Petiot was insolent and condescending, and made it very clear just what he thought of them.

THE WITNESSES had all been heard. The fourteenth day of the trial would consist of the civil-suit-lawyers' summaries of their clients' cases. The same facts would be repeated again with grandiloquence and rattling of swords. Spring had come to Paris, and the audience had more pleasant places to be.

Maître Archevêque reiterated the Guschinov case. He did not believe Guschinov was in South America, but had been basely murdered at the rue Le Sueur. Floriot lazily asked whether they had received an answer to their telegram. It had never been sent. Floriot lay down across his desk and went to sleep. Petiot had been dozing in exactly the same position all along.

Véron painted Petiot as a psychopath who eliminated Madame Khaït because she was a minor problem in a trivial lawsuit. He was a Cartesian who plotted his killings and line of defense well in advance.

VÉRON   When someone got in this man's way, he killed him. That is reason enough to have his head.

While Perlès spoke of Braunberger's hat and shirt, Petiot awoke and laughed, then went back to sleep.

Stéfanaggi did not need to prove that Petiot had killed Piereschi, since he admitted it, but the lawyer leaned heavily on the sterling merits of an unsavory victim to prove that said victim had not been a collaborator.

Charles Henry was to present the case of Paulette Grippay, but in the heat of his passion he never mentioned her name, nor her case, once during his hour-long plea.

HENRY   I am here today to shed light. No one has understood the Petiot trial — neither the court nor the prosecution. Petiot is even more guilty than you think.

He retold the whole story despite Leser's efforts to stop him, and emphasized the role of what he called "the Nazified bestiary haunting the outskirts of the Gestapo."

HENRY [Petiot] worked for an anti-French organism operating on the fringe of the Gestapo to defend the interests opposed to this latter entity. Seen in this light, of course, the whole trial becomes perfectly clear.

Elissalde buried his face in a handkerchief, the audience broke into hysterics, and Leser turned bright red trying not to laugh.

PETIOT [shouting] I would like to point out that it was not I who hired this man.

Henry took Floriot to task for apparently enjoying the trial.

LESER Oh, leave Maître Floriot alone.

HENRY [in conclusion] I have tried, amid general incomprehension, to explain that which no one, up until now, has explained. I hope that the gentlemen of the jury will condemn Petiot with full understanding. This is much better than to condemn without understanding.

He sat down.

LESER What about your client?

HENRY I have finished. I won't labor the issue.

André Dunant could scarcely hope to draw serious attention after Henry's speech; he briefly stated that Gisèle Rossmy could be reproached with no justifiable cause for her murder.

THE FOLLOWING DAY the summaries continued. The newspapers complained that most of the lawyers began with "I shall be brief," "I do not want to repeat what you have already heard," or "I do not wish to waste the court's time," and then charged right off repeating and wasting for hours on end. Bernays spoke for the Wolffs; Petiot stayed awake for an hour, finally dropping his head on his arms when the lawyer said, "You know my reputation for brevity." Gachkel spoke for the Basches and their relatives, and Léon-Lévy for the Knellers. Almost everyone joined Petiot and Floriot in an afternoon nap. Véron woke them up.

With lucidity, force, and considerable oratorical skill, Véron went back, point by point, picking apart the defense, showing all the improbabilities, hesitations, and contradictions. He briefly summarized the Dreyfus affair, and proved once again that Petiot knew nothing of the Resistance.

VÉRON   I don't know whether or not some of Petiot's victims worked for the Gestapo, but if they did, he never knew it, and their ashes will join those of the dead from Auschwitz and Dachau.

There is a legend that you all know well: the story of the ship-wreckers. Cruel men placed lanterns on the cliffs to lure ashore ships in distress. The sailors, confident, never suspecting that such evil deceit could exist, sailed onto the reefs and died, and those who had pretended to lead them to safety filled their coffers with the spoils of their foul deeds. Petiot is just that: the false savior, the false refuge. He lured the desperate, the frightened, the hunted, and he killed them by turning their instincts for self-preservation against them.

The Resistance has a duty to defend its dead, who gave their lives that France and freedom might live. If three hundred fifty thousand of our men and women made the supreme sacrifice, it was not so that a depraved criminal like Petiot could conceal his shame beneath the flag of the Resistance. Your verdict must make it clear that his imposture is not sanctioned by you. You must condemn him to death.

PETIOT   Punk.

VÉRON   Say what you like. I'll go to your execution.

It was Pierre Dupin's task to summarize the prosecution's case and formally call for the death sentence. Since he still scarcely knew the facts, he was forced to rely on style.

DUPIN   Never in a hundred years, gentlemen of the jury, has such a monster appeared before a court. Petiot has outdone Landru: twenty-seven crimes instead of eleven. You see before you the Bluebeard of our century, a modern Gilles de Rais. It was with horror that I undertook this case. Petiot indiscriminately murdered men, women, and children simply to rob them of their few earthly goods.

Petiot yawned and began to draw caricatures of Dupin.

DUPIN Petiot's perversity is equaled only by his skill as an actor in a self-created role. The man you see before you is the star performer in a fictional drama of the Resistance. It is a play that has grown within his imagination, and which contains not a single shred of real life. It will take me five minutes to show that everything he has said is a web of lies.

Petiot glanced at the clock and returned to his artwork.

Dupin spoke for two hours. At 7:00 P.M. Leser asked him to continue the next day and adjourned the court.

APRIL 4, the sixteenth and last day of the trial, drew by far the largest crowd. Extra chairs were placed around Leser for guests, political figures, and visiting magistrates. The spectators, armed with field binoculars and opera glasses to watch Petiot's face when he was condemned, burst through the police barriers and stood packed in the aisles and at the back of the courtroom. Several people fainted in the oppressive heat, but there was no room to extricate them, nor even for them to fall down. At one point during Dupin's summary when the audience proved particularly unruly, Leser asked the guards to remove the disturbing element, but no one would move and the guards felt unequal to the task. During recesses, people crowded around Petiot, who gave autographs and signed copies of *Le Hasard vaincu* with such blasé satisfaction that it seemed he regarded the trial as a reception organized for his own particular pleasure.

Dupin spoke for another hour and a half, and finally he reached his conclusion.

DUPIN No, we will not let Petiot soil the sacred memory of the French Resistance. The imposture is over, Petiot, the hour of judgment rings.

PETIOT   Signed, the Procureur of the Vichy régime.

DUPIN   The role of judge does not suit you.

PETIOT   Nor you.

Journalists had speculated over the words Dupin would employ in requesting the death penalty. He was notoriously squeamish about using the phrase "sentenced to death," and generally found some strange and elliptical substitute.

DUPIN   I have often hesitated before demanding the death penalty. Today I have no scruples about it. May Petiot soon go to join his victims.

The journalists did not think the phrase well chosen.

PETIOT   Thank God that's over.

René Floriot stood up at 3:00 P.M. He had drunk his one glass of champagne. For the first time in his career, he would drink a second glass halfway through his plea — a plea that lasted six-and-a-half hours. The courtroom was silent, and no one posed a single question as Floriot thundered on.

FLORIOT   After such a long trial, so many days of interrogations and testimonies, my adversaries have just spent fifteen hours by the clock trying to convince you of Petiot's guilt. Fifteen hours! The case cannot be very clear or simple.

Rest assured; I will not plead for fifteen hours — I will spare you that suffering. I will be as brief as possible, but I, I will not spin you a tale. I will not take liberties with facts and dates. I will plead my dossier, and nothing but my dossier; nothing I am about to say is not confirmed by an element of this dossier, and should you doubt me, I can tell you where to find it. When I have finished, I am confident that nothing will remain, amidst an affair which sad events and the malice of men have complicated seemingly beyond all reason, which might permit you to return the guilty verdict Monsieur l'Avocat Général demanded just a moment ago.

Everything in this case has been falsified. I accuse no one except the horrifying times we have so recently lived through, and which have left their mark on the preparation of this case. Petiot came before you to be fairly judged, but he was preceded by a monstrous reputation; the reputation of a low assassin who killed for plunder, a sadist who enjoyed the spectacle of death. Under the Occupation, the press mentioned that Petiot had been previously arrested, but they could not, of course, say that the charge had been fighting for his country. He had been arrested, period. Imaginations ran wild. The papers went on about bodies burning in a stove. When the Germans were defeated and we discovered the horror of the crematoria, a simple mental association sufficed to turn Petiot into a collaborator, a torturer, a Gestapist. But the case is not so simple, and we have allowed ourselves to fall into one confusion after another.

Petiot, Floriot said, would never have been accused at all if not for the bodies at the rue Le Sueur. Having found them, the police went back, trying to find identities to match with these unidentified corpses. To show how flimsy their evidence was, Floriot stated there had been a hundred original, tentative victims, but most had been dropped because (1) the real murderer was found, (2) it was learned that the "victim" had been deported, (3) the victims were killed while Petiot was at Fresnes. By a process of elimination, then, anyone the police could not prove Petiot had not killed, they assumed had been killed by Petiot. On the other hand, Floriot continued, almost two years after the Liberation, there remained sixty thousand unsolved missing-persons cases in Paris alone — excluding Jews — and these represented only cases where family or friends remained and were willing to file a report. (No one knew where Floriot found this figure, but in using it he presumably hoped his listeners would see that out of sixty thousand cases, a determined police force could, by pure coincidence, find circumstantial connections between twenty-seven of them and Petiot, or anyone else. It was an ill-advised line of reasoning: one could easily turn it upside down and wonder how many more of these unsolved sixty thousand cases could have been Petiot's work.)

FLORIOT Again, one imagines — and I owe this invention to the great talent of my learned colleague, Maître Véron — that one can make the following, very simplistic, rational construction: "Petiot has killed a certain number of people. He admits it. Either he killed them out of patriotism, in which case he is a Resistant, or else he killed them through cupidity, in which case he is a low criminal and a murderer." There is no other possibility, there is no other hypothesis, there is no third choice. "Thus," Maître Véron says to himself, "if I prove that Petiot is not a Resistant, I will automatically have proven that he is a murderer, and the jury will condemn him." He believes that he accomplished this by asking a few questions. Yesterday Monsieur l'Avocat Général, during two hours of summation, spent one hour and forty minutes — I timed it by my watch — calling Petiot a quack doctor, a false Resistant, and showing you his own horror at the rue Le Sueur. He, like Maître Véron, and like all the rest of my colleagues here, based his case on emotion and not on fact. But the facts can speak for themselves, and you shall hear them.

And Floriot returned to the beginning.

FLORIOT They have searched in Petiot's past for everything that can be used against him. But it truly seems that they only looked for the bad and ignored the good. One example: Inspector Poirier told us that the Police Judiciaire had interviewed two thousand of Petiot's clients. All two thousand had good things to say about him. There was not a single unfavorable report.

At Villeneuve-sur-Yonne the police questioned his political adversaries and the two doctors whose clienteles he had taken away. They did not speak with the vast majority of the population, which was very much in his favor. The simple fact that, despite it all, a number of people courageously presented themselves here in court only proves the investigation's bias.

Floriot recited Petiot's career, then, in an "unbiased" way. Infantryman in the First World War, seriously wounded, honorably discharged with 100 percent disability; studied medicine, received good grades, established his practice in Villeneuve-sur-Yonne. Devoted to his patients and the people, Petiot was elected to public office and reelected several times with crushing majorities. His enthusiasm, energy, and dislike of red tape provoked jealousy, and petty political enmities had cost him his position. He moved to Paris, and again there was the litany of devoted patients: Petiot riding his bicycle ten miles to treat a child for free; Petiot saving an infant's life; Petiot who almost went broke because he cared so little about money he forgot to bill his patients. Floriot neatly explained away the narcotics charges and the arrangement of the rue Le Sueur. The war came, and the same noble sentiments pushed Petiot into the Resistance. Perhaps his name did not appear on some official list, but that was not a necessary license for fighting to defend France. The evidence proved he hated the Germans. There was irrefutable evidence that he had furnished false medical certificates to help Frenchmen avoid forced labor, that he had obtained false identity papers for English parachutists, that he had saved a woman on the verge of being arrested by the Germans, that he had warned Jews about to be raided, that he had offered to hide people in flight from the Gestapo. There was the testimony of Lhéritier, Courtot and Barré. The contradictory statements about Cumulo, Brossolette, and Fly-Tox were misunderstandings, easily explained . . . . Floriot's choice of facts and rhetoric were overwhelming and sowed doubts in the minds of his audience. He came to the victims.

FLORIOT   Petiot is accused of twenty-seven murders. He admits nineteen of them and denies eight. He admits having killed the people sent by Eryane Kahan, the pimps and prostitutes, and Yvan Dreyfus.* If the prosecution can prove that he killed even one of the eight people he denies, then he should be condemned. For the others, the prosecution does not have to prove anything. It is up to Petiot to prove that he killed members of the Gestapo or Gestapo

---

* Actually, Petiot never had admitted killing Dreyfus, but apparently it seemed easier to prove that Dreyfus was a collaborator than that he had not been killed.

informers. If he fails to prove this for even one case, again, he should be condemned. Let us begin with the cases that he denies: Hotin, Van Bever, Khaït, the Knellers, Guschinov, and Braunberger.

Floriot quoted Jean Hotin's testimony: "I was married on June 5, 1941. On June 26 my wife had her period. At the beginning of July she told me she was pregnant." What nonsense! He showed a photograph of the plaque outside Petiot's office, which did not give the hours Hotin claimed, and he pointed out that Denise's identity card was found at Jean's house eighteen months after her disappearance, although no one would have dreamed of going anywhere during the Occupation without identification papers.

Floriot similarly disposed of the charges involving Van Bever, Guschinov, and the Knellers. In the dossier he found a number of statements from people who thought they had seen Madame Khaït, but no serious search had been made. Why not? Article 687 stated that Robert Martinetti existed and had been imprisoned. Where was he then?* The prosecution had not really proved many of the disappearances or disproved Petiot's statements at all.

Floriot's presentation was thorough and logical, and if it contained occasional contradictions, the jury did not notice at the time. Typical of his methods was his lengthy attack on the Braunberger charge, the main evidence for which consisted of a hat and a shirt.

FLORIOT   For me there remains the task of proving that these two objects could not possibly have belonged to Dr. Braunberger. I don't think it will be difficult.

First of all, a small detail you will find significant. You remember, when I interrogated Commissaire Massu, I asked him, "Tell me how you opened the suitcases." There is something you should know:

* Floriot distorted some of the facts slightly, as here. Article 687 was the interrogation of someone who had worked as an undercover agent at the rue des Saussaies and *thought he had heard* that Martinetti existed and had been arrested. In reality, Martinetti was never found.

forty-six [*sic*] of these suitcases were packed by the police at Courson, one at the rue Le Sueur, and one at the rue Caumartin, and they were all packed in the absence of Dr. Petiot. I'm not blaming anyone — Petiot was in flight at the time. But when they opened these suitcases again, particularly since they had been closed in the presence of witnesses who were themselves under indictment at the time [that is, the Neuhausens and Georgette Petiot], Petiot should have been asked to be present.

I can still see the notaries pleasantly saying, every time they opened a suitcase, "The defense can ascertain that the seals are intact." Of course they were intact. It had been opened fifteen times in my absence and closed again fifteen times in my absence. The seals may have been intact, but since they had been affixed there in the absence of both my client and myself, that did not guarantee much of anything.

Still, let us take the suitcases as they are. Note this fact — one which, I believe, no one has pointed out previously: the shirt was found in a suitcase packed at Courson, and, as you know, the suitcases at Courson had come from the rue Le Sueur. The hat marked *P.B.* was not found in a suitcase from Courson, but in a suitcase packed at the rue Le Sueur. This is what the police report says, at any rate, but unfortunately it is not true. In fact, the bag with the hat was packed at the rue Caumartin. It is a strange suitcase; whoever packed it threw in anything that came to hand, including a hat marked *P.B.* Judge for yourselves — one almost has the impression that a special suitcase was made up just for this hat. Other than the hat, it contains a pipe (Dr. Petiot's pipe), a blotter (his blotter, which was sitting on his desk), a camera (his camera), a flashlight (the sort doctors use to examine a patient's throat), and a notebook (it is his agenda, containing his medical appointments).

This is all rather curious. Thus one must say that Dr. Braunberger was killed at the rue Le Sueur; his shirt was in a suitcase from the rue Le Sueur that was sent to Courson. His shirt alone. None of his other clothing was found; no jacket, no vest, no trousers, nothing. All of them had markings which Madame Braunberger would have recognized just as easily. His shirt was found at the rue Le Sueur and his hat at the rue Caumartin! . . .

Now, we are told that this shirt bears the initials *P.B.*, but that they have been removed. Ah! gentlemen of the jury, I beg you to examine this shirt carefully during your deliberations. It could have been *B.P.*, it could have been *P.F.*, it could have been *F.R.* — it could have been just about anything you like, but no one can assert that it was *P.B.*, because you can see nothing at all!

We looked at this shirt together, Monsieur le Président and I. I will not ask for your testimony, Monsieur le Président, because I know you would not give it. Still, this is a material fact: you can look at this shirt, and you cannot make out the letters that have been removed from it.

We can put another of Dr. Braunberger's shirts at your disposal. I am sure that Madame Braunberger would willingly do the experiment, but I would rather it be you, gentlemen of the jury, so that you can see it with your own eyes. Try to remove the initials from another of Dr. Braunberger's shirts, and you will find that what remains is very clearly visible.

In the suitcases there are some shirts which have initials and some which do not, but on which the trace of initials is still visible. In his inventory, Monsieur Sannié never erred, and always wrote down what he saw. Remember this detail. Even with his microscopes, Monsieur Sannié could not say that this shirt was marked *P.B.*, and when he described the shirt he wrote simply: "Seal number 44. A man's shirt, blue cloth, made by David, avenue de l'Opéra." Period. That's it. Why? Because he could not read any initials. When he can read them, he says so. Look at seal number thirty-five. There are two other shirts from which embroidered initials were removed. Monsieur Sannié writes: "The initials which were on the left side, at the level of the belt, have been removed. It is probable that they were *A.E.*" Consequently, when he was certain, he wrote: "The letters are . . . ," and when he was less certain, he wrote: "It is probable that . . ." But since nothing can be seen on the Braunberger shirt, he said nothing at all. One can see that some letters have been removed — I don't contest that — but one cannot say that they were *P.B.* any more than one can say they were any other letters.

Then there is the question of the detachable cuffs — not a very clear story. Police Officer Casanova came to the stand and I asked him: "Monsieur, under seal number forty-four we find the shirt said to be that of Dr. Braunberger. You say that you also found a pair of cuffs? Why didn't you keep them?" He replied: "Because they were a keepsake for Madame Braunberger. I did not think I could take them from her." I asked him: "Were they the same color and made of the same material as the shirt?" and he said, "Yes." Well, that isn't true. Madame Braunberger came to the stand as well. She had the missing pair of cuffs with her. They were not the same, and she herself admitted it.

And then, gentlemen, there is another question. Couldn't they have made a verification? When I think of Estébétéguy, whom Petiot admits having killed . . . They went to the shirtmaker Sulka four times with Estébétéguy's shirts, asking: "Are you sure? Are they really Estébétéguy's?" Well, they never went to show this shirt to David.

And the hat! Ah! the hat, gentlemen, is something truly unbelievable. Madame Braunberger was questioned before the hat was discovered. She said, "My husband had a hat from Gélot." They look at the hat. Not a chance: it is marked "Berteil, rue du 4-Septembre." Then Madame Braunberger says — you must pay close attention to follow the meanderings of her thought — "It's a Berteil hat? That proves nothing. My husband bought it from Gélot, but since Gélot was closed in 1942, he took it to Berteil for repairs. That is why the label on the inside says 'Berteil, 4-Septembre.' "

So it is a Gélot hat, but it is marked "Berteil, 4-Septembre" because it had been repaired there. This is a completely unsatisfactory explanation for all sorts of reasons. The first of them is that Gélot hats have the name marked in the crown. Consequently, simply changing the sweatband would not remove the name Gélot from the hat. Secondly, the Maison Gélot is the only hatter in Paris that makes nothing but custom hats. When a customer goes to Gélot, they take the form of his head, just as a bootmaker makes a mold of the foot and keeps the mold for future reference.

Since I happened to know this detail, I asked Monsieur Gélot if he could not manage to find the form he had made of Dr. Braunberger's head. Madame Braunberger had said, after all, that her husband was one of Gélot's customers. Monsieur Gélot sent me this mold by return post. It represents the exact dimensions of the head, with marks showing the location of the forehead and the back of the head, and bears the written inscription: "Doctor Braunberger, 207 Faubourg Saint-Denis, March 18, 1937."

So I performed a little experiment. I invite you to repeat it while deliberating in your chambers. I compared the shape of the hat marked *P.B.* with this mold. A disaster! It is much too wide and much too short; that is to say, this hat is the hat of a gentleman with, as Dr. Piédelièvre would say, a wide and short head, while, on the contrary, Dr. Braunberger's head would be elongated. I wanted to be sure, so I took a ruler and measured. There was exactly two-and-a-half centimeters difference. For a man who wore nothing but custom-made clothes, two-and-a-half centimeters is really quite a lot. Try taking a hat which is two-and-a-half centimeters too big or two-and-a-half centimeters too small. In the former case, it would sit on your ears, and in the latter it would perch on the top of your head. You would look ridiculous either way!

But I went even further, because I wanted to have a clear conscience. I asked Monsieur Gélot, "Were you closed in 1942?" and he replied: "Not at all. We have never been closed since September 1940." Thus, when you are told that in 1942 Dr. Braunberger did not go to Gélot to have his hat repaired because Gélot was closed, it is not true. Gélot was open. I have his letter right here: "I state, as per request, that from October 21, 1940, the Maison Gélot has always been open."

Next, I tried to find out whether one could have had a hat repaired at Berteil, Quatre-Septembre, in 1942. There was only one problem: Berteil, Quatre-Septembre, closed its doors in 1939. I went to the main offices of the Maison Berteil, and the junior Monsieur Berteil told me it was not possible that anyone had had a hat repaired at the rue du Quatre-Septembre branch in 1942, because that branch had been closed in 1939, eight days after the declaration of war. It had not opened since, and will never reopen, since the site is presently occupied by a rubber manufacturer.

Thus you will remember that, earlier in the trial, I said to Madame Braunberger: "Gélot was open. Berteil, rue du Quatre-Septembre was closed. Thus you went to the store that was closed, and you did not go to the store that was open. You say that you bought a hat at

Gélot, and you say that this is the hat. But it isn't, because the shape is completely wrong. And when you want to have it repaired, you do not take it to Gélot, who sold it to you and would fix it for nothing, because, you say, Gélot was closed, though in fact it was open, and instead you went to Berteil, rue du Quatre-Septembre, because it was open, though we know that it was closed." Madame Braunberger replied: "I can explain. I went to Berteil, place Saint-Augustin."

Maître Perlès did not insist on the point yesterday, but he pointed out something which I should have guessed all along. The Maison Berteil, rue du Quatre-Septembre, must still have had a number of sweatbands with its stamp on them when it closed, and these sweatbands could have been passed on for use by the main store or by other branches. Well, of course, I had to investigate this. And, unfortunately, it is not so. You only need look, first at this certificate, gentlemen, and then at this leather sweatband. You will easily be able to perceive that the name "Berteil, 4-Septembre" and the initials P.B. were imprinted on the same day and by the same machine. The machine is set up to make both impressions at the same time.

I asked for details on this point. I was told: "It's very simple. Many hatters have a machine (I do not know how it works) which makes either perforations or indentations. One puts the sweatband into this machine, and by using a sort of typesetting arrangement, one can simultaneously imprint the name of the store and any initials one cares to add."

I wanted to check one final point, so I asked the court clerk: "When a customer brings a hat in for repairs, the repairs are not made the same day. Consequently, the books would contain records of the date when the hat was to be delivered. Would you be so kind as to check with the Maison Berteil — the branch which is open and which has the records of the Quatre-Septembre store — and see whether Dr. Braunberger ever had a hat repaired there?"

Well, no — there was no entry in that name. I have a notarized certificate here, and will enter it with the rest of the evidence.

Now let me resume the story and remind you of Petiot's statements: "Braunberger, I haven't seen him for thirteen years. I couldn't even recognize him because I met him only once, thirteen years ago.

And I had no reason to take Braunberger. Perhaps, you might say, I would have had some reason to take suitcases, and to take his wife, and with her, all of their most valuable possessions." The only problem is that no one ever came for the suitcases, despite the letters Braunberger sent, and no one tried to help Madame Braunberger escape, despite her husband's request.

There is one explanation (and I don't have to give you any explanations; that is not part of my task here). Think about it for three minutes. Can you see that Dr. Braunberger, either lured into a trap near the Etoile or asked to come there to treat a patient as he was told — we have no way of knowing — may have been stopped by the German police? This hypothesis seems particularly likely since Madame Braunberger has stated (and her statement is in the record) that four days [it was really thirteen days] after her husband disappeared, the Germans came to ask whether, in fact, a doctor who had served in the army medical corps during the last war lived in her building.

Can you imagine that Dr. Braunberger may have managed to escape amidst the crowd in the métro? He was frightened. He wrote a first letter to his wife, telling her (and this is essentially what he wrote): "Don't worry, I will try to escape. Don't worry, I will let you know when you can join me." He wrote a second letter, a third. He crossed the demarcation line. The man who passed him returned, having been paid very poorly for his risks. Dr. Braunberger had left home without money. He was perhaps very nervous and in a deficient mental state (I am not trying to slur his character; this is all in the dossier). He almost betrayed himself and the man who passed him was nearly caught at the border. The latter didn't want to have anything more to do with the family. But he had a letter, and he telephoned to the maid and said: "I have passed the doctor, but I will not pass his wife and I will not come to see her. I was too badly paid." The maid said, "Come, and we will pay you." "No, I'm not interested anymore. I don't want to be arrested. I have a letter for you asking you to follow me, but I won't bring it to you, I'll mail it." And he did mail it.

Couldn't Dr. Braunberger have been arrested by the Germans between 1942 and 1944? Couldn't he have disappeared? What reason do you have [asks Petiot] for saying that simply because I met Dr. Braunberger thirteen years ago, I am guilty? You cannot show any reason why I should have any interest in him, since he had no money, and you know that no one tried to collect any suitcases or to take his wife. What possible reason could I have?

And then you refuse to consider the whole Allard story. You must admit that, whichever way you take it, there are three false witnesses: either Dr. Braunberger, Madame Braunberger, and their maid, Madame Bonnet-Archères; or Roger Allard and his wife and mother. Take your pick!

I don't know anything about it. What is certain, is that there is no way the declarations of these people, who are my adversaries here today, can be reconciled with the thesis you are trying to present.

You have but one thing. Maître Perlès pointed this out, and he was quite right. You have the shirt and the hat. Oh, I forgot one detail. This hat — which is not a Gélot hat, which is not Dr. Braunberger's hat, and which was never repaired at any branch of the Maison Berteil in 1942 — was described yesterday as being "patterned." At least, Maître Perlès read a letter he had received from the Maison Gélot saying that Braunberger had purchased a patterned hat. Fabrics are not my speciality, but I had the impression that patterned was the opposite of solid. I telephoned Gélot and asked him, "What was the hat like that you made for Dr. Braunberger in 1937 — the one which was allegedly repaired in 1942?" He replied, "It was patterned. I even gave a sample of the material to your confrere."

A sample? But he never told us that! Monsieur Gélot said he would give me another sample. I have it here.

PERLÈS   I have one, too.

FLORIOT   Gentlemen of the jury, you may compare this sample with this hat. You can see that they resemble one another as night and day.

Having finished with the eight victims Petiot denied, Floriot turned to the nineteen he admitted having killed. Armed with the dossier, police reports, and criminal records, he took each case in turn and showed that the victim in question had strong ties with the Germans. The pimps and prostitutes were not difficult.

Dreyfus had signed two agreements with the Gestapo. The German Jews were harder, but not impossible. The Basch relatives had shared a hotel in Nice with the Italian Gestapo, and though they pretended to be in deathly fear and to need help moving about without being seen, when they wanted to cross the demarcation line into Paris, they went to a travel agent and booked berths in a wagon-lit. As for the Wolffs, they had their passports, and so on. The audience listened in awe. Everyone, even the prosecution, conceded that Floriot had presented a fine case. So fine, they said, that if Floriot had been defending twenty-seven individual cases rather than twenty-seven all at once, he may easily have won them all.

FLORIOT   Gentlemen of the jury, I have finished. I have gone back over each case, one by one, and examined it without tricks or deceits. I have demonstrated that, in some of these cases, Petiot had the right to execute people who were working against France in time of war. For the others, one by one, I have demolished the accusations brought against him.

Petiot is not a murderer. Ah! he is not an ordinary man, I admit it readily. He did not content himself with just "getting by," as so many did. He brought down his enemies, our enemies. No, this is not a normal man with ordinary qualities and faults. But do not say that he is an assassin . . . do not say that he is a greedy man. His entire life, and every aspect of his behavior prove the contrary. I place Petiot between your hands with full confidence. I know that you will acquit him.

When Floriot sat down at 9:30 P.M., the court gave him a standing ovation.

LESER   Petiot, have you anything to add to your defense?
PETIOT   I would have liked to, but I cannot. I am a Frenchman. You know that I killed members of the Gestapo. You know what you have to do.

A guard took Petiot into another room, and Floriot sent his three chief assistants to keep him company and bolster his spirits during the wait. The assistants, it turned out, were more nervous than he, and Petiot whiled away the time lecturing them on how to recognize fine Oriental carpets and how to buy wisely at auction.

Leser, the two other magistrates, and the seven jurors filed out to deliberate. Locked in the chamber with them were the thirty-kilogram dossier with its reams of testimony; bits and pieces of evidence such as the hat and hatter's mold Floriot wished them to compare; and a list of 135 questions. For each of the twenty-seven victims, the jurors and magistrates had to weigh the evidence and vote on five separate charges. For Madame Khaït, for example:

No. 11 — The above-mentioned Petiot, Marcel André Henri, is he guilty of having fraudulently appropriated clothing, valuables or other personal items from Fortin, Marthe, married name Khaït, in Paris or the department of the Seine on March 25, 1942?

No. 12 — The above-mentioned Petiot, Marcel André Henri, is he guilty of having willfully put to death, in Paris or in any other part of France, Fortin, Marthe, married name Khaït, born at Clichy on September 22, 1888?

No. 13 — Was the voluntary homicide specified above in question No. 12 committed with malice aforethought?

No. 14 — Was the voluntary homicide specified above in question No. 12 committed with premeditation?

No. 15 — Was the voluntary homicide specified above in question No. 12 committed with the aim of preparing, facilitating or effecting the fraudulent appropriation specified in question No. 11?

For each question a vote was taken, and if six or more people were in favor of condemnation, the verdict of guilty was marked down. It was expected to be a long deliberation, but the journalists and spectators left packed in the sweltering courtroom did not dare move for fear of losing their places to members of the crowd at the door who still fought for admission. Everyone discussed Floriot's summation and speculated on the verdict.

No one had much doubt about the outcome, but of how many murders would Petiot be found guilty? And then, too, even when there is no reasonable doubt, one can always find some last lingering uncertainty to furnish the pleasure of suspense.

It was almost impossible to believe that Dreyfus, the Wolffs, and the Basches were collaborators, but high probability is not proof. Petiot almost certainly had not known that Adrien le Basque, Jo le Boxeur, and their friends were collaborators, yet there was indisputable proof that they had worked for the Gestapo. No trace had been found of Guschinov and the Knellers, but as Petiot had said, South America is a big place, and it was obvious to everyone that the prosecution had erred in not making inquiries. There was little evidence to convict Petiot of killing Dr. Braunberger or Denise Hotin. "Presumption of guilt" necessarily relies on a strong web of circumstance, and Dupin never wove it. He forgot some facts, ignored others, and presented the few he retained in such a thin and erratic way that it was difficult to piece them into a whole as Floriot had done. Dupin, spectators muttered, had only one thing on his side; twenty-seven murders are a lot, and only one was needed to have Petiot's head.

The jury had no time for idle literary criticism of the trial, and though they had been well entertained for three weeks, this, in the end, did not blind them. There were doubts about some of the victims and obscure points throughout the story that Floriot had skillfully turned to his advantage. But counteracting these doubts, Petiot himself had sat before them for sixteen days, making jokes, hurling insults, mocking judicial procedure, drawing pictures, and dozing — occasionally bursting into silent tears, but always at moments just a bit too convenient to be believed. Somehow he did not fit the image Floriot wished to paint of a devoted physician and self-sacrificing patriot. He did, on the other hand, look right at home in the role the prosecution tried to depict, and it was the dispassionate, clockwork perfection of his method that weighed most heavily against him. The vision of his crimes was dreadful. It was wartime, so few questions had been asked about those who disappeared. His arrangement had the added advantage that the victims prepared themselves for the slaughter and, in advance, helped cover up the traces of the crime whose victims they would be. They announced to friends that they would vanish, they bundled their money and valuables into tidy parcels, they walked willingly into places that in ordinary times would excite anyone's suspicion, and they even helped their murderer avoid being seen in their company. Perhaps they rolled up their own sleeves to receive a fatal injection. Some of them even paid Petiot and thanked him for what they thought he would do.

Looking back, the jurors could apparently see all this in the man who had smirked with self-satisfaction throughout the trial. Murdering several dozen people is horrifying in itself, but what was truly terrifying about Petiot was that he had organized murder like any other routine business operation. He had shown no emotion when he killed, and had shown no remorse afterward, either then or now. Quite the contrary. He was rather pleased with himself, and while the parents, wives, and children of the victims wept in the courtroom, he seemed intent only on having a good time.

It was 12:35 A.M. when the jury and magistrates returned, much sooner than anyone had expected. They had been out for three hours, and even disregarding the fact that the mechanical task of reading out each question and polling the votes 135 times must have taken the best part of an hour, it meant they had spent an average of only eighty seconds on each question.

The clerk of the court read out the questions, one by one, followed by the verdict. Of 135 counts, Petiot was found guilty of 126. He was innocent of all charges concerning Denise Hotin, and of robbing and of murdering for the purpose of robbing Van Bever and Madame Khaït (numbers 11 and 15, in her case).

Everyone knew the sentence this outcome implied, but the silence had never been so profound as when the audience awaited those final words. Leser spoke; if he had shown himself weak and confused before, his dignity now transfixed the audience. Petiot, Marcel André Henri Félix, medical doctor, age forty-nine, was guilty of twenty-six counts of first-degree murder and was sentenced to die on the guillotine.

The photographers' flashguns illuminated the hollow, exhausted eyes of the spectators, who stared with curiosity and horror at the man whose life was now forfeit. A single person in the courtroom seemed neither stunned by the sentence nor perturbed at the thought of a human being's death, and that was Dr. Marcel Petiot himself. As he had predicted, it had been a good trial, a memorable trial, and he had made people laugh. Beyond that, it seemed, he didn't really give a damn.

As Petiot was led out of the courtroom he turned and shouted, with an unexpected show of passion, "I must be avenged!" Some observers thought he spoke to his wife, some to his brother Maurice, and yet others that it was a call to arms addressed to incognito members of Fly-Tox present during the trial. Even more people assumed this was simply the last contrived enigma in the dramatic role Petiot had written for himself.

The trial was over, and the civil-suit attorneys swarmed around the three magistrates who, alone, would determine the damages to be paid to families of the victims — amounts intended to compensate the survivors for the loss of their parents, brothers, sisters, or children, and based on the deceased person's estimated worth. This came to F880,000 for Dreyfus, F700,000 for Dr. Braunberger, F100,000 each for Guschinov and Paulette Grippay, F80,000 for the Anspachs, F50,000 each for Gisèle Rossmy and Madame Khaït, and F10,000 for Piereschi. Curiously, though the relatives of the Wolffs and Knellers asked for compensation, they received nothing. This made a grand total of F1,970,000, or about 1 percent of the amount Petiot was believed to have taken from his victims after murdering them. There was also an assessment of F312,611.50 in court costs. In time, Georgette Petiot paid about half of this amount, and justice, presumably, was done.

15

MONSIEUR DE PARIS

FLORIOT APPEALED THE CASE on three technicalities: a complaint of false testimony by Madame Braunberger, a similar objection regarding her maid, and another pertaining to the jurors who had been quoted in the *Herald Tribune*. The complaints were lodged on May 13, and were rejected on the twenty-third. He had a meeting with the president of the Republic, the reasons for which were obscure. Neither Floriot nor Petiot had requested a presidential pardon, and none was given.

During a routine daily search of Petiot's cell on May 22, an ampoule was discovered in the hem of the prisoner's uniform. An investigation was opened to see how the vial had been smuggled in; police suspected it was cyanide, and that Petiot hoped to commit suicide before his execution, as Pierre Laval had attempted the previous year.* Petiot's vial turned out to contain

---

* Dr. Paul had been summoned to revive Laval, but had refused on grounds that it was inhumane. Laval had been tied to a stake and shot in a semicomatose state.

a mild sedative that he had somehow managed to conceal when he arrived at the Santé. No one knew why he wanted it. He was perfectly calm, and spent his days smoking and writing poetry, which he gave to the two guards constantly posted outside the door of his cell. He was allowed visits only from his lawyer, from the prison doctor, and from the chaplain or a magistrate, for religious or juridic confessions — but he had no need for confessors and preferred to "take his baggage with him." Each day he asked, "When are they going to assassinate me?"

The man who would guillotine Petiot was a large, small-featured, quiet, white-haired man of sixty-nine years named Henri Desfourneaux, or, as the executioner is known in France, "Monsieur de Paris." The post of headsman is hereditary, passed down to a son or nephew or, if there are no willing male descendants in the family, to a descendant of one of the other great executioner families that had flourished in the days when there was more beheading to be done. Until a century ago, there were executioners for almost all of the large cities in France and, considering the hereditary nature of the business, it is not surprising that the same family often held office in various cities. Ten years before the French Revolution, seven brothers from the notorious Sanson family were executioners in seven different cities, and to distinguish themselves they each assumed the name of the town where they plied their trade: Monsieur de Rennes, Monsieur de Blois, and so on. In the late nineteenth century, all but one of these positions were abolished, and Monsieur de Paris became the sole executioner for all of France.

The guillotine is the private property and responsibility of the executioner and is handed down with the position. Anatole Deibler, Desfourneaux's predecessor, owned two of them — a large one for use in Paris, and a smaller one that could be loaded onto a railroad flatcar and used for executions elsewhere in the country. Deibler was clever with his hands and had made a number of improvements on the machines, such as mounting the weighted blade on wheels so that it would drop more smoothly than it had in soaped tracks.

Deibler died of a heart attack in February 1939 while on his way to his 301st execution. Commonly, the post goes to one of the three valets who help Monsieur de Paris, and generally these men are all from executioner families, since the population shuns them and it is difficult to leave the profession or marry outside the clan. The first valet, André Obrecht, was not of an executioner family, however, and could not be appointed. The second, Desfourneaux's uncle, was too old. So third valet Henri Desfourneaux, who had worked in a factory when not helping with executions, became the new Monsieur de Paris.

His first important job did not go well. It was the last public execution in France, that of mass murderer Eugen Weidmann in June 1939 at Versailles. The executioner's tilting table, to which the prisoner is strapped while standing, should be aligned so that when it is flipped into place the condemned person's neck fits in the semicircular notch called the *lunette*. Weidmann's did not, and the valets had to tug at his hair and ears to drag him into the proper position. When his head dropped, the assembled crowd burst through the police lines and women eagerly dipped their handkerchiefs in the pool of blood on the pavement. The spectacle was so appalling that soon afterward the law was changed and executions henceforth were made private.

There were repeated delays in the scheduling of Petiot's execution. Desfourneaux went on strike for higher wages, and claimed that his guillotine had been damaged by Allied bombing raids and would not work. Simultaneously, there was some debate as to whether Desfourneaux should not be replaced as Monsieur de Paris by his valet Obrecht, since during the war Obrecht had fought for the Resistance, while Desfourneaux had guillotined a number of Frenchmen under German pressure. Some people asked whether Petiot could not be shot to avoid all these problems, but this was impossible, as the firing squad was reserved for traitors. Petiot threatened to die laughing if they couldn't hurry and make up their minds to kill him another way.

Finally the problems were resolved. Article 327 of the penal code absolved the executioner of all responsibility for the people he killed: he was simply doing his job. Desfourneaux was made to understand that he should be happy with his yearly salary of F65,000 for part-time work plus the annual stipend of F10,000 for upkeep of the guillotine. He suddenly remembered that his traveling guillotine — the one used for executions in the provinces — was in good shape and could be set up rapidly.

Petiot had made Floriot promise to tell him when the execution would take place. This was forbidden by French law, and the announcement of the date was customarily made after 6:00 on the evening before the execution. The gates of the Santé were locked at that hour, and thus no one could enter and speak to the condemned. But there were always ways of finding out earlier. On the afternoon of May 23, Floriot learned that the execution had been scheduled for the following morning. He was in court, and so asked his assistant Paul Cousin to inform Petiot. Cousin was terrified. He walked around the Santé for two hours, unable to summon the courage to tell a man he was about to die. When it was almost 6:00 P.M., he forced himself to enter.

"When are they going to assassinate me?" asked Petiot.

"I think," Cousin muttered, trembling, "that it could well be tomorrow morning."

"There, there," said Petiot, laying his hand on the lawyer's shoulder, "don't let it affect you so much. Let's talk about something else."

The execution did not take place the next day. Desfourneaux was having real problems with the guillotine, and it was postponed until the twenty-fifth.

At 2:00 on the morning of May 25, hundreds of policemen

barricaded the streets within a radius of 250 yards around the
Santé prison. At 3:30, Monsieur de Paris arrived at the prison
gates with his three blue-clad valets and a horsecart carrying
the guillotine. The mechanism is so precisely constructed that
not a single hammer blow is required during its assembly; there
were only faint sounds of wood knocking together in the dark
courtyard as the heavy, fifteen-foot-high grooved uprights were
fastened to the supporting base. There was a faint glimmer of
light when Desfourneaux removed the seven-kilogram triangular
steel *couperet* from its leather sheath and mounted it on the
forty-five-kilogram weight that would send it plunging home.
At 4:10 A.M., the streetlights around the prison were extinguished, and the basket, the size of a small office wastepaper
can, was placed beneath the guillotine.

Ten minutes later, four cars drew up in front of the prison
gates, bringing Floriot, his assistant Ayache, Dupin, Goletty, Dr.
Paul, and a dozen other police and court officials. Eight minutes
later, just after dawn, Dupin, Goletty, Floriot, and Ayache entered cell number 7 and awakened Petiot, who was sleeping
peacefully.

Dupin spoke the traditional words: "Petiot, have courage. The
time has come."

Petiot made an obscene reply.

The chains were removed from Petiot's hands and feet, and
he changed from the black prison uniform into the suit he had
worn during the trial. He asked for paper and ink, and for
twenty minutes calmly wrote letters to his wife and son, then
gave them to Floriot. Goletty appeared to be feeling faint.
Petiot jokingly pointed out that he was a doctor and could give
him an injection if he liked. Floriot asked Ayache to take Dupin's
arm, since the avocat général, too, was pale and weak when
faced with the carrying-out of the sentence he had demanded.

"Maître, my friend," Petiot said to Floriot, "if anyone publishes something on my case after my death, ask them to include

photographs of the people I have been accused of killing. Then, perhaps, one day they will be found, and my innocence can be proved." He turned to Dupin and Goletty. "Gentlemen, I am at your disposal."

As Petiot was led into the corridor, prisoners in the neighboring cells pounded infernally on the doors and bid him farewell. He was offered the traditional cigarette and glass of rum. He refused the rum and was smoking peacefully when the prison chaplain asked if he had a confession to make or would like to hear mass.

"I am not a religious man, and my conscience is clean," Petiot said. "But I will talk to you as a man."

"Your wife wanted you to hear mass."

"If it will help my wife, please go ahead."

He was led past the door that opened on the courtyard; paper had been taped over its windows to hide the guillotine only two feet away. In the clerk's office, he signed the register, his hands were tied behind his back, the nape of his neck was shaved, and his shirt collar was cut off.

Two valets led Petiot out the door and down three steps to the courtyard. Dr. Paul, after fifty years and hundreds of executions, later said:

For the first time in my life I saw a man leaving death row, if not dancing, at least showing perfect calm. Most people about to be executed do their best to be courageous, but one senses that it is a stiff and forced courage. Petiot moved with ease, as though he were walking into his office for a routine appointment.

Petiot smiled sardonically at Desfourneaux, and before the executioner lashed his feet together and strapped him to the tilting table, the prisoner turned to Floriot and the assembled witnesses. "Gentlemen," Petiot said, "I ask you not to look. This will not be very pretty."

The blade fell at 5:05 A.M. It is rumored that one court official had concealed a camera beneath his robes and took a photograph at the instant Petiot's head left his shoulders.

Petiot was smiling.

SELECTED LIST OF CHARACTERS

ADRIEN LE BASQUE — *See* Estébétéguy, Adrien.

ALBERTINI, FRANÇOIS (aka François le Corse) — Pimp who, along with his mistress Annette Basset, was among Petiot's presumed victims.

ALICOT, HENRI-CASIMIR — Owner of the Hôtel Alicot at 207 bis rue de Bercy, where Maurice Petiot and Albert Neuhausen stayed when in Paris, and where Georgette Petiot spent the day before fleeing to Auxerre after the rue Le Sueur discovery.

ALLARD, ROGER and ANDRÉE — Neighbors and patients of Dr. Braunberger; Roger and Andrée, his mother, told the police confusing stories about Braunberger's disappearance.

ANNETTE LA POUTE — *See* Basset, Annette.

ANSPACH — *See* Arnsberg, Ludwig and Ludwika.

ARCHÊVEQUE, MAÎTRE JACQUES — Civil-suit attorney representing Renée Guschinov at the trial.

ARNOUX, LÉONE — Former maid and mistress of Georgette Petiot's father, and close friend of Maurice Petiot's family; arrested for receiving stolen goods.

ARNSBERG, LUDWIG and LUDWIKA (aka Anspach, Hollander, Schepers) — Went from Nice to Paris to join their relatives the Basches; presumed victims of Petiot.

AYACHE, MAÎTRE EUGÈNE — Assistant to Floriot during the Petiot murder case.

BARRÉ, GERMAINE — Resistant who was being interrogated by the Gestapo when they released Petiot, and who appeared as a voluntary defense witness at the trial.

BARTHOLOMEUS — See Hotin, Denise.

BASCH, GILBERT and MARIE-ANNE (aka Baston, Hollander, Schonker) — Friends of the Wolffs and presumed victims of Petiot.

BASSET, ANNETTE (aka Petit; Annette la Poute) — Prostitute, mistress of François Albertini, and presumed victim of Petiot.

BASTON — See Basch, Gilbert and Marie-Anne.

BATUT, CHIEF INSPECTOR MARIUS — Police Judiciaire detective who handled much of the early murder investigation under Massu.

BAUDET, RAYMONDE — Daughter of Madame Khaït; her drug habit brought her and her mother in contact with Petiot.

BERETTA, CHARLES — Collaborated with Friedrich Berger, head of the rue de la Pompe Gestapo office; by pretending to be a candidate for escape, he precipitated the Germans' arrest of Petiot, Fourrier, Pintard, and Nézondet.

BERGER, FRIEDRICH — Head of rue de la Pompe Gestapo office, in charge of security in the occupied territory; he arrested Petiot, Fourrier, Pintard, and Nézondet before discovering that he had ruined Jodkum's plans to trace Petiot's "escape network."

BERNAYS, MAÎTRE JACQUES — Civil-suit attorney representing the Wolff family at the trial.

BERRY, GEORGES — *Juge d'instruction* who handled the Petiot murder case from the time of the rue Le Sueur discovery until shortly after the Liberation of Paris.

BORIS, CAPTAIN HENRI — Soldier and friend of Yvan Dreyfus who testified for the prosecution.

BOUYGUES, INSPECTOR RENÉ — Policeman whom Roland Porchon supposedly told about Petiot's crimes in the summer of 1943.

BRAUNBERGER, MARGUERITE — Dr. Braunberger's wife; Floriot attacked her identification of her husband's hat and shirt at the trial.

BRAUNBERGER, DR. PAUL-LÉON — Disappeared after a telephone call from an anonymous "patient," then sent several letters to his wife announcing his intention of fleeing to the free zone.

BROSSOLETTE, PIERRE — Resistance hero (killed in March 1944) for whom Petiot claimed to have worked.

BROUARD, LIEUTENANT ALBERT — Member of the DGER (Military Security) who, with Ibarne (Yonnet), investigated Petiot's alleged Resistance activities.

CABELGUENNE, VICTOR — Civilian who may have committed crimes with Duchesne and Salvage, officers from the Caserne de Reuilly.

CADORET DE L'EPINGUEN, MICHEL and MARIE — Couple who wished to escape and contacted Petiot through Malfet and Kahan; both Petiot and the Cadorets changed their minds, and the couple successfully left France by another route.

CASANOVA, INSPECTOR — Police Judiciaire detective who worked on the Petiot murder case.

CEILLIER, DR. — Psychiatrist who examined Petiot after his 1936 arrest for shoplifting and recommended his hospitalization.

CHAMBERLIN, HENRI — See Lafont, Henri.

CHAMOUX, CLAUDIA (aka Lulu) — Prostitute, mistress of Joseph Réocreux, and presumed victim of Petiot.

CHANTIN, MARCEL — Banker who told Guélin about Fourrier, Pintard, and the escape organization.

CHARBONNEAUX, JEAN-MARIE — Under the name Cumulo, a member of the Resistance group Rainbow who was killed in 1943; Petiot claimed to have worked with him.

CLAUDE, DR. — One of three psychiatrists who together recommended Petiot's release from a mental hospital in 1937.

COLLOREDO DE MANSFELD, PRINCESS MARIA — The owner of the building at 21 rue Le Sueur before Petiot.

COURTOT, ROGER — A Resistant who shared a cell with Petiot at Fresnes and testified on his behalf at his murder trial.

COUSIN, MAÎTRE PAUL — Assistant to Floriot on the Petiot case; he informed Petiot of the execution date.

CUMULO — *See* Charbonneaux, Jean-Marie.

DEBAUVE, HENRIETTE and ARMAND — Directors of the Villeneuve-sur-Yonne dairy cooperative. In March 1930 Armand found Henriette, his wife, bludgeoned to death in their burning home, and rumor implicated Petiot.

DELAVEAU, LOUISE (aka Louisette) — Petiot's young maid and mistress at Villeneuve-sur-Yonne; she disappeared under mysterious circumstances in 1926.

DEQUEKER — Codirector with Guélin at the Théâtre des Nouveautés and his associate in the scheme for Yvan Dreyfus's release.

DÉROBERT, DR. LÉON — Forensic specialist who helped study the rue Le Sueur remains.

DESFOURNEAUX, HENRI — Monsieur de Paris, Petiot's executioner.

DOULET, COMMISSAIRE LUCIEN — Policeman whom Roland Porchon apparently told about Petiot's murders.

DREYFUS, PAULETTE — Wife of Yvan Dreyfus; she paid Guélin more than four million francs for her husband's release.

DREYFUS, YVAN — Radio distributor and Resistant who was forced by Guélin into helping with Petiot's arrest by the Gestapo; he presumably ended up among Petiot's victims.

DUCHESNE, LIEUTENANT JEAN — French Forces of the Interior officer at the Caserne de Reuilly who may have committed crimes for Petiot and played a part in his arrest.

DUNANT, MAÎTRE ANDRÉ — Civil-suit attorney representing the family of Gisèle Rossmy at the murder trial.

DUPIN, MAÎTRE PIERRE — Avocat général who prosecuted Petiot for murder.

DURAN, DR. EUGÈNE — Villeneuve-sur-Yonne physician who defeated Petiot in his second mayoral campaign.

EEMANS — *See* Schonker, Chaïma and Franziska.

EHRENREICH — *See* Schonker, Chaïma and Franziska.

ELISSALDE, AVOCAT GÉNÉRAL — Representative of the procureur général who drew up the Petiot murder indictment and who tried to help Dupin during the trial.

ESTÉBÉTÉGUY, ADRIEN (aka Adrien le Basque) — Criminal and collaborator who, along with his mistress Gisèle Rossmy, was among Petiot's presumed victims.

EUGÈNE, DR. — Alias used by Petiot before his arrest by the Germans in 1943.

EUSTACHE, JEAN — Trucker from Auxerre who transported the rue Le Sueur suitcases and lime for Maurice Petiot.

FILLION, EMILE — One of the policemen who discovered the bodies at 21 rue Le Sueur.

FLORIOT, MAÎTRE RENÉ — Lawyer who represented Petiot in the Gaul–Van Bever and Baudet-Khaït narcotics cases, and who defended him at his murder trial.

FORTIN — *See* Khaït, Marthe.

FOURRIER, RAOUL — Barber who helped recruit "escapees" for Petiot; many of them left from his rue des Mathurins shop.

FRANCINET — *See* Pintard, Edmond.

FRANÇOIS LE CORSE — *See* Albertini, François.

GACHKEL, MAÎTRE — Civil-suit attorney representing the Basch and Arnsberg families at the murder trial.

GANG, ILSE — Friend of the Wolffs and Basches who wrote an anonymous letter to Massu concerning their disappearance.

GAUL, JEANNETTE — Drug addict and prostitute who lived with Van Bever and was arrested for procuring narcotics from Petiot.

GÉNIL-PERRIN, DR. — Psychiatrist who examined Petiot before his release from a hospital in 1937 and again before his 1946 murder trial.

GÉRARD, DR. HENRI — Doctor who unsuspectingly referred Petiot to Dr. Wetterwald.

GIGNOUX, INSPECTOR ROGER — Police detective assigned to the Van Bever and Khaït disappearances in early 1942; he suspected Petiot was involved.

GOLETTY, FERDINAND — *Juge d'instruction* who handled the Petiot murder case from shortly after his arrest until he was sent to trial.

GOUEDO, JEAN — Rue Caumartin furrier who reported his partner Joachim Guschinov missing.

GOURIOU, DR. — One of three psychiatrists who examined Petiot before his murder trial.

GRIFFON, PROFESSOR HENRI — Director of the police toxicology lab who examined the rue Le Sueur bodies for traces of poison.

GRIPPAY, JOSÉPHINE-AIMÉE (aka Paulette la Chinoise) — Prostitute, Piereschi's mistress, and a presumed victim of Petiot.

GUÉLIN, JEAN — Former lawyer, codirector with Dequeker of the Théâtre des Nouveautés; he collaborated with Jodkum to expose Petiot's "escape route" by using Yvan Dreyfus.

GUINTRAND, HENRI (aka Henri le Marseillais; Robert) — Petty criminal who introduced Kahan to Pintard.

GUSCHINOV, JOACHIM — Rue Caumartin furrier presumed to have been Petiot's first Paris victim.

GUSCHINOV, RENÉE — Joachim Guschinov's wife, who neglected to report him missing.

GUTTIN, MAÎTRE HENRI — Petiot's most ardent political opponent at Villeneuve-sur-Yonne.

HANSS, RAYMONDE — Patient of Petiot's who died under mysterious circumstances in 1934.

HENRI LE MARSEILLAIS — *See* Guintrand, Henri.

HENRY, MAÎTRE CHARLES — Civil-suit attorney representing the Grippay family at the murder trial.

HEUYER, DR. GEORGES — One of three psychiatrists who examined Petiot before his murder trial.

HOLLANDER — *See* Arnsberg, Ludwig and Ludwika; Basch, Gilbert and Marie-Anne.

HOTIN, DENISE (née Bartholomeus) — Young woman who disappeared after an alleged abortion and was counted among Petiot's victims.

HOTIN, JEAN — Denise Hotin's husband, who made little effort to find her.

IBARNE, LIEUTENANT JACQUES (aka Jacques Yonnet) — As a journalist, he published Rolland's deposition in *Résistance* and wrote articles on the Petiot case; as a member of Military Security, he investigated Petiot's alleged Resistance activity with Brouard.

JACQUET, MAÎTRE PIERRE — Assistant to Floriot on the Petiot murder case.

JODKUM, ROBERT — Highly placed civilian employee in the Jewish Affairs sector of the rue des Saussaies Gestapo office; he made plans with Guélin to trace Petiot's "escape network," and later furnished information to Massu.

JO LE BOXEUR — *See* Réocreux, Joseph.

JOSIAN — Mysterious, unidentified person the Allards claimed had helped Dr. Braunberger escape.

KAHAN, RUDOLPHINE (aka Eryane Kahan) — Woman who sent the Wolffs, Basches, Schonkers, Arnsbergs, and Cadoret de l'Epinguens to Petiot; she went into hiding after the rue Le Sueur discovery.

KHAÏT, DAVID — Marthe Khaït's husband at the time of her disappearance.

KHAÏT, MARTHE (née Fortin) — Mother of Fernand Lavie and Raymonde Baudet; she vanished shortly before her daughter's narcotics trial and was presumed to be a victim of Petiot.

KNELLER, KURT, MARGERET (aka Greta, née Lent), and RENÉ — Family of naturalized French Jews of German origin; almost caught in a Gestapo raid, they sought to escape through Petiot but presumably were murdered.

LABLAIS, MONSIEUR — Father of Georgette Petiot.

LAFONT, HENRI (aka Henri Chamberlin) — Head of the French

Gestapo on the rue Lauriston, for whom Estébétéguy and several other victims of Petiot had worked; defended by Floriot, he was executed in December 1944.

LAIGNEL-LAVASTINE, DR. MAXIME — Psychiatrist who joined two others in recommending Petiot's release from a hospital in 1937.

LATEULADE, ROBERT — Resistant imprisoned at Fresnes with Petiot who may have been the source of some of his information about the Resistance.

LAVIE, FERNAND — Marthe Khaït's son by her first marriage.

LÉON-LÉVY, MAÎTRE — Civil-suit attorney representing the Kneller family at the murder trial.

LESAGE, AIMÉE — Nurse who lived with Nézondet as his mistress.

LESER, MICHEL — President of the tribunal at Petiot's murder trial.

LHÉRITIER, LIEUTENANT RICHARD — Paratrooper who shared a cell at Fresnes with Petiot and was a star defense witness at the murder trial.

LOUISETTE — *See* Delaveau, Louise.

LULU — *See* Chamoux, Claudia.

MALFET, ROBERT — Man who helped the Arnsbergs and Schonkers go from Nice to Paris and who introduced the Cadoret de l'Epinguens to Kahan.

MALLARD, MADAME — Parisian midwife from whom Denise Hotin allegedly sought an abortion.

MARÇAIS, JACQUES and ANDRÉE — Couple who lived on the fifth floor of 22 rue Le Sueur; disturbed by smoke on March 11, 1944, they summoned the police.

MARIE, RENÉ and MARCELLE — Couple Porchon sent to Petiot but who did not trust the doctor and gave up their escape plans.

MARTINETTI, ROBERT — Presumably fictitious Resistant who Petiot claimed was the real head of the supposed escape organization Fly-Tox.

MASSU, COMMISSAIRE GEORGES-VICTOR — Head of the Police

Judiciaire Criminal Brigade who was in charge of the murder investigation until shortly before Petiot's capture.

MAXIME, ROBERT — Maurice Petiot's shop employee in Auxerre.

MOURON, GILBERTE — Daughter of the deceased Madame Mallard; she testified that Denise Hotin had gone to see Petiot.

NEUHAUSEN, ALBERT and SIMONE — Couple at Courson-les-Carrières who stored the suitcases Maurice Petiot removed from the rue Le Sueur; both were arrested for receiving stolen goods.

NÉZONDET, RENÉ-GUSTAVE — Friend of Petiot's in Villeneuve-sur-Yonne and Paris who was arrested with him by the Germans in 1943; he later claimed Maurice Petiot had told him about the bodies at the rue Le Sueur and was arrested for concealing a crime.

NOÉ, CLARA — The friend and neighbor at whose home the Knellers hid before departing with Petiot.

OLMI, ACHILLE — *Juge d'instruction* who handled the Gaul–Van Bever and Baudet narcotics cases, and who showed little concern about finding Van Bever and Madame Khaït when they vanished.

PAPINI, UGO — Van Bever's business associate and sole friend, who reported him missing.

PASCAUD, INSPECTOR — Police Judiciaire detective active in the murder investigation.

PAUL, DR. ALBERT — Chief coroner in charge of examining the rue Le Sueur bodies.

PAULETTE LA CHINOISE — *See* Grippay, Joséphine-Aimée.

PÉHU, PIERRE — Former policeman who worked for Guélin and served as an intermediary in the negotiations to release Yvan Dreyfus from prison.

PERLÈS, MAÎTRE CLAUDE — Civil-suit attorney representing Madame Braunberger at the murder trial.

PETIOT, FÉLIX IRÉNÉ MUSTIOLE and MARTHE MARIE CONSTANCE

JOSÉPHINE (née Bourdon) — Parents of Marcel and Maurice Petiot.

PETIOT, GEORGETTE VALENTINE (née Lablais) — Dr. Petiot's wife; she was arrested for receiving stolen goods.

PETIOT, GERHARDT GEORGES CLAUDE FÉLIX (called Gérard) — Petiot's son, born at Villeneuve-sur-Yonne on April 19, 1928.

PETIOT, MAURICE — Petiot's younger brother from Auxerre who implicated himself by transporting the rue Le Sueur lime and suitcases.

PETIOT, MONIQUE — Maurice Petiot's wife; Marcel's sister-in-law.

PIÉDELIÈVRE, DR. RENÉ — Forensic expert who studied the rue Le Sueur remains.

PIERESCHI, JOSEPH DIDIONI SIDISSÉ (aka Dionisi; Zé) — Thief and pimp who, along with his mistress Paulette Grippay, was among Petiot's presumed victims.

PINAULT, COMMISSAIRE LUCIEN — Police Judiciaire detective who worked on the murder investigation and took over Massu's position when the latter was suspended.

PINTARD, EDMOND (aka Francinet) — Makeup artist and former vaudeville song-and-dance man who collected prospective refugees and passed them to Fourrier.

POIRIER, INSPECTOR — Detective who worked on the murder investigation.

PORCHON, ROLAND ALBERT — Used-furniture dealer who claimed Nézondet had told him about the bodies at the rue Le Sueur in 1943; he also sent the Marie couple to Petiot.

REDOUTÉ, GEORGES — Housepainter who harbored Petiot in his rue du Faubourg Saint-Denis apartment after the rue Le Sueur discovery.

RÉOCREUX, JOSEPH (aka Jo le Boxeur; Iron Arm Joe) — Pimp, thief, and collaborator who, along with his mistress Claudia Chamoux, was among Petiot's presumed victims.

ROART, CHRISTIANE — Neighbor of the Knellers and René Kneller's godmother; she told police about the family's departure.

ROGUES DE FURSAC, DR. — Psychiatrist who examined Petiot in 1936 and recommended his release from a hospital.

ROLLAND, CHARLES — Possibly fictitious informant whose supposed interrogation by Massu concerning Petiot's alleged Gestapo activities was transcribed in the newspaper *Résistance.*

ROMIER, LUCIEN — Vichy minister of state who Petiot claimed had helped his escape organization procure false identity papers.

ROSSMY, GISÈLE — Mistress of Estébétéguy and a presumed victim of Petiot.

ROUGEMONT, EDOUARD DE — Graphologist who testified about the letters supposedly written by Marthe Khaït, Dr. Braunberger, Denise Hotin, and Van Bever.

SAINT-PIERRE, DR. LOUIS-THÉOPHILE — Through his patient Guintrand, he introduced Kahan to Petiot.

SALVAGE, CORPORAL JEAN — French Forces of the Interior officer at the Caserne de Reuilly who loaned Petiot an apartment and who may have committed crimes for him and played a part in his arrest.

SANNIÉ, PROFESSOR CHARLES — Director of the police identification lab who examined 21 rue Le Sueur, the remains, and the victims' personal effects.

SCARELLA, JOSEPH — Chef who ultimately refused Petiot's offer to send him to Argentina.

SCHEPERS — *See* Arnsberg, Ludwig and Ludwika.

SCHONKER, CHAÏMA and FRANZISKA (aka Stevens; Ehrenreich; Eemans) — Parents of Marie-Anne Basch and Ludwika Arnsberg; presumed victims of Petiot.

SIMONIN — *See* Soutif.

SOUTIF — French Forces of the Interior captain (under the name Simonin) and an undercover collaborator; he arrested Petiot on October 31, 1944.

STÉFANAGGI, MAÎTRE DOMINIQUE — Civil-suit attorney representing Piereschi's family at the murder trial.

STEVENS — *See* Schonker, Chaïma and Franziska.

TEYSSIER, JOSEPH — One of the policemen who discovered the bodies at 21 rue Le Sueur.

TURPAULT, MARIE — A friend of Nézondet's mistress to whom he told the story about rue Le Sueur he claimed to have heard from Maurice Petiot.

VALÉRI, CAPTAIN HENRI — Alias used by Petiot at the Caserne de Reuilly; he took the name from a plaque identifying the previous occupant of his apartment at 66 rue Caumartin.

VALLÉE, RAYMOND — Friend of Madame Braunberger's at whose house Dr. Braunberger and Petiot first met, and through whom Madame Braunberger received the first letter from her husband after his disappearance; Vallée's wife was Georgette Petiot's cousin.

VAN BEVER, JEAN-MARC — Arrested in 1942 with his lover Jeannette Gaul for narcotics abuse, he disappeared one month later, presumably at Petiot's hands.

VÉRON, MAÎTRE PIERRE — Civil-suit attorney hired to defend Madame Khaït's daughter on a narcotics case involving Petiot; he later represented the Khaït relatives at the murder trial and was, coincidentally, hired to represent the family of Yvan Dreyfus.

WETTERWALD, DR. FRANÇOIS — Imprisoned Resistant whose papers Petiot stole in order to enlist in the French Forces of the Interior.

WOLFF, MAURICE, LINA, and RACHEL — Refugees who tried to leave France and who presumably ended up victims of Petiot.

YONNET, JACQUES — See Ibarne, Lieutenant Jacques.

BIBLIOGRAPHY

Barret, Claude. *L'Affaire Petiot.* "Le Crime ne paie pas" collection. Paris: Librairie Gallimard, 1958.

Bertin, Claude, ed. *Les Assassins hors-série: Gilles de Rais. Petiot.* Vol. 10. Les Grands procès de l'histoire de France. Paris: Editions de Saint-Clair, 1967.

Gordeaux, Paul. *Le Docteur Petiot.* Paris: Editions J'ai lu, 1970.

Manière, Pierre. *Marcel Petiot, ou l'échec d'une ambition politique.* Privately printed by the author, n.d.

Massu, Georges-Victor. *L'Enquête Petiot — la plus grande affaire criminelle du siècle.* Paris: Librairie Arthème Fayard, 1959.

Nézondet, René. *Petiot le possédé.* Paris: Nézondet (copyright), 1950.

Perry, Jacques, and Chabert, Jane. *L'Affaire Petiot.* "L'Air du temps" collection. Paris: Librairie Gallimard, 1957.

Petiot, Dr. Marcel. *Le Hasard vaincu . . . les lois des Martingales.* Paris: privately printed by the author, 1946.

Planel, Alomée. *Docteur Satan ou l'Affaire Petiot.* Paris: Editions Robert Laffont, 1978.

Seth, Ronald. *Petiot, Victim of Chance.* London: Hutchinson & Co., 1963.

Tavernier, René. *Alors rôdait dans l'ombre le docteur Petiot.* Paris: Presses de la Cité, 1974.

Varaut, Jean-Marc. *L'Abominable Dr. Petiot.* Paris: Balland, 1974.

Information was also drawn from the following newspapers:

L'Aurore, Combat, Le Figaro, France-Soir, Franc-Tireur, Libération-Soir, Le Matin, Le Monde, The New York Herald Tribune (international edition), *L'Oeuvre, Le Parisien Libéré, Paris-Soir, Le Petit Parisien,* and *Résistance.*

A NOTE ON THE AUTHOR

Thomas Maeder grew up in Philadelphia and studied physiological psychology and developmental neurobiology at Co-
lumbia University and the University of Pennsylvania. He
has worked in industrial design and exhibit design related
to medicine and science, as a magazine science writer, and
as senior adviser for scientific strategies at the Georgetown
University Medical Center. He is now executive director of
the educational arm of the Advanced Medical Technology
Association. He lives in Narbeth, Pennsylvania.